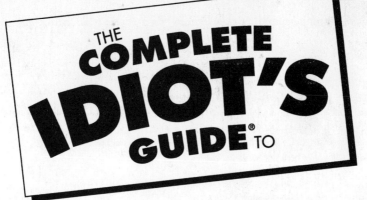

THE **COMPLETE IDIOT'S GUIDE**® TO

Day Trading Like a Pro

Second Edition

by Peter J. Sander

ALPHA

A member of Penguin Group (USA) Inc.

This book is dedicated to all who have seen the light to "do-it-yourself" investing, and now wish to take it a step further.

ALPHA BOOKS

Published by the Penguin Group

Penguin Group (USA) Inc., 375 Hudson Street, New York, New York 10014, U.S.A.

Penguin Group (Canada), 10 Alcorn Avenue, Toronto, Ontario, Canada M4V 3B2 (a division of Pearson Penguin Canada Inc.)

Penguin Books Ltd, 80 Strand, London WC2R 0RL, England

Penguin Ireland, 25 St Stephen's Green, Dublin 2, Ireland (a division of Penguin Books Ltd)

Penguin Group (Australia), 250 Camberwell Road, Camberwell, Victoria 3124, Australia (a division of Pearson Australia Group Pty Ltd)

Penguin Books India Pvt Ltd, 11 Community Centre, Panchsheel Park, New Delhi—110 017, India

Penguin Group (NZ), cnr Airborne and Rosedale Roads, Albany, Auckland 1310, New Zealand (a division of Pearson New Zealand Ltd)

Penguin Books (South Africa) (Pty) Ltd, 24 Sturdee Avenue, Rosebank, Johannesburg 2196, South Africa

Penguin Books Ltd, Registered Offices: 80 Strand, London WC2R 0RL, England

International Standard Book Number: 1-59257-432-7
Library of Congress Catalog Card Number: 2005929454

07   06   05   8   7   6   5   4   3   2   1

Interpretation of the printing code: The rightmost number of the first series of numbers is the year of the book's printing; the rightmost number of the second series of numbers is the number of the book's printing. For example, a printing code of 05-1 shows that the first printing occurred in 2005.

Printed in the United States of America

Note: This publication contains the opinions and ideas of its author. It is intended to provide helpful and informative material on the subject matter covered. It is sold with the understanding that the author and publisher are not engaged in rendering professional services in the book. If the reader requires personal assistance or advice, a competent professional should be consulted.

The author and publisher specifically disclaim any responsibility for any liability, loss, or risk, personal or otherwise, which is incurred as a consequence, directly or indirectly, of the use and application of any of the contents of this book.

Most Alpha books are available at special quantity discounts for bulk purchases for sales promotions, premiums, fund-raising, or educational use. Special books, or book excerpts, can also be created to fit specific needs.

For details, write: Special Markets, Alpha Books, 375 Hudson Street, New York, NY 10014.

Publisher: *Marie Butler-Knight*
Editorial Director: *Mike Sanders*
Senior Managing Editor: *Jennifer Bowles*
Senior Acquisitions Editor: *Paul Dinas*
Development Editor: *Jennifer Moore*
Copy Editor: *Amy Borrelli*

Cartoonist: *Shannon Wheeler*
Cover/Book Designer: *Trina Wurst*
Indexer: *Tonya Heard*
Layout: *Ayanna Lacey*
Proofreading: *Donna Martin*

Contents at a Glance

Contents

Foreword

You can make a lot of money day trading.

You can lose a lot of money day trading.

Where you fall between these two bookends of reality depends on many factors. Luck isn't one of them. Day trading is not an easy way to make money and it is not something everyone can do. However, if you are interested in learning about this exciting profession, you have the right book in your hands.

The Complete Idiot's Guide to Day Trading Like a Pro, Second Edition, isn't about "selling" you on day trading. It is an insider's look at what day trading is really about, how it works, and what it takes to succeed. Day trading is a practiced, disciplined approach to making money in the stock market. It requires skill, knowledge, and strategy. This book is about the real world of day trading, which is fast-paced, exciting, and unforgiving of the unprepared.

Starting with the basics, the author takes you through the markets, examines different securities, and dives into the day trader's world. The book is very readable with numerous illustrations and jargon-busting definitions to help you along the way.

The markets are more dynamic than ever, which creates new challenges and opportunities for those clever enough to know how and where to participate. Follow the lessons in this book and you'll have an idea where those opportunities are.

Is there luck involved? Even some successful day traders will say there is an element of luck to their success. I would disagree. My experience is that people who seem to have consistent good luck are the same people who work the hardest. Everyone gets a break now and then; however, you will not succeed at many things in life—and certainly not day trading—if you count on luck.

The author paints a clear picture of the challenges and opportunities facing day traders. He addresses head on the difficulties you'll have to overcome as well as the unlimited opportunities available to skilled day traders. Yes, you can make a lot of money day trading, but you'll earn it.

When you finish this book, you'll have a good idea if day trading is for you. If you decide that you want to pursue a career in day trading, you are off to a great start. This book is a solid base to build on. On the other hand, if you decide day trading is not for you, my guess is you learned some things about the market and trading that you didn't know before, and that information alone is worth the cover price. Either way, you're ahead of the game.

—Ken Little

Ken Little is a veteran financial writer and editor. He is the author of seven books on investing and personal finance. Little is also the editor and writer for the stocks website for About.com (www.stocks.about.com). He has day traded with modest success in the past and wishes this book had been available.

Introduction

Five years ago, day trading could be best described as a phenomenon. As euphorically reported in the first edition of this book, everyone was talking about it. Newfangled technology, particularly the Internet, had made it all possible. It seemed like almost everyone was doing it, from retired uncles to the room-service waiter who just delivered your breakfast. Rumors abounded about people quitting their jobs, trading for a couple of hours in the morning, and then heading for the golf course or day spa.

Like most gold rushes, it was a frenzy. Some made money—and a lot of it—very quickly by trading. Others got rich selling the tools, training, and services needed to work the "mines." People who never witnessed the Depression or even a bear market (because there hadn't really been one since 1982) put their savings, their homes, and their careers on the line to dig for the gold. Trading, and what people were buying and selling, had become the cocktail party topic *du jour*.

But like all parties—and gold rushes—it was destined to end. The once-friendly stock market became fickle and negative. In what is now known as the bursting of the bubble, excessive valuations, bid up in part by traders, washed out. Traders lost, and they lost big. Markets shifted to decimal trading, meaning traders had to sit and watch—and try to profit from—tiny penny fluctuations in stock prices. Professional traders got wise to the existence of day traders, viewed them as competition, and did what they could to shake them out. Trading got less profitable and, at the same time, harder to do.

Still, many market players are coming to realize that simple buy-and-hold strategies and managed investments may not, by themselves, achieve investing objectives. Investors are realizing that nobody has more of a vested interest in their wealth than they do, and that they can't always trust corporations and professional investment advisers. More and more people are taking the wheel themselves, at least for part of their portfolio.

Trading plays a role in making markets perform better. Traders increase liquidity and prevent special interests from controlling markets. Good traders can profit by helping to redistribute securities to where they are needed, as any dealer in real estate, antiques, or livestock will do in their markets. Traders are here to stay.

New trading tools more suited to the individual traders have made it easier than ever to do day and short-term trading. While these tools, and more rational markets, have brought many traders back to the markets, today's trader is also more knowledgeable and sophisticated than before. The bursting of the "bubble" brought a new sobriety and diligence to trading. Trading certainly isn't any easier than it used to be; in fact, it is harder. Further, most traders—as many as 70 percent by some estimates—*lose*. But for those willing to invest in developing the necessary skills and to work hard daily for the rewards, it works.

This book is tailored to the new trader who wishes to make those investments to adopt today's more sober, balanced trading style.

The Place to Start

The Complete Idiot's Guide to Day Trading Like a Pro, Second Edition, provides a complete introduction to today's trading world. It talks about markets and how they work, and trading tools, strategies, and techniques. It also talks about the habits and character of the successful trader.

Good traders never stop learning. This book, by itself, won't provide all of the knowledge and technique, let alone experience, required to become a good trader. New traders should plan to read a wide variety of materials on trading and perhaps even take a training course before going it alone.

After reading this book, you may well decide that this nerve-wracking business of day trading isn't for you. It isn't easy, and some people just aren't cut out for it. Even so, you'll come away with a better idea of how today's markets and investing tools work. Such knowledge will make you a better investor, regardless of your style and objectives.

How to Use This Book

This book is divided into five parts.

Part 1, "A Day at a Time," introduces you to day trading: what it is, how it started, the latest trends, and what it takes to be trader.

Part 2, "A Trip to the Markets," explores the different markets, what traders trade, and why they trade it.

Part 3, "Tools of the Trade," examines the broad assortment of information and trading tools available, including news feeds, quote fees, and various types of trading platforms.

Part 4, "Reading Market Action," gets down to the brass tacks of figuring out how markets and individual securities behave. You'll learn some basic ways to analyze trading activity and patterns, including the Level II quote window and basic technical analysis and charting.

Finally, **Part 5, "Developing Your Own Trading Style,"** will help you build your own day trading game plan. We'll lay out the basic trading styles and strategies and follow up with a discussion of the trading, risk, and money management habits required to make it all work.

Extras

Although they aren't required reading, we think you'll find the following sidebars helpful as you read through this book. Keep an eye out for these:

Trade Secrets _____

Tips and advice for improving your trading skills.

Alert! _____

Issues and pitfalls to avoid.

Behind the Screen

A peek behind the computer screen for an inside look at the trading world.

Trading Terms _____

Words and terms you will need to know: the vocabulary of the day trader.

Acknowledgments

All writers sit before the keyboard with a hidden host of helpers behind them. Friends, family, and colleagues—no one really writes a book alone. I'd like to recognize a few especially helpful contributors to the project:

Commodities traders and fellow Ultimate Frisbee players Ken Pomaranski and Andy Barr, who not only made Chapter 8 possible, but also, along with others, provide the exercise to keep body, mind, and spirit in shape to trade, to invest, and to write.

Paul Dinas of Penguin Group (USA) Inc. for guidance and Jennifer Moore of U.P. Edit for excellent developmental edits throughout the project.

Special Thanks to the Technical Reviewer

The Complete Idiot's Guide to Day Trading Like a Pro, Second Edition, was reviewed by an expert who double-checked the accuracy of what you'll learn here, to help us ensure that this book gives you everything you need to know about trading. Special thanks are extended to Ken Little. For more traditional investing tips, take a look at his website: www.stocks.about.com.

Trademarks

All terms mentioned in this book that are known to be or are suspected of being trademarks or service marks have been appropriately capitalized. Alpha Books and Penguin Group (USA) Inc. cannot attest to the accuracy of this information. Use of a term in this book should not be regarded as affecting the validity of any trademark or service mark.

Part 1

A Day at a Time

Exactly what is day trading, and what do day traders trade? In this part you'll not only find out what day trading is, but why it's so popular. In addition, you'll learn about the various styles traders employ, and what kinds of securities traders typically trade.

We also answer the questions on the minds of many new traders: What does it take to be a trader? Are you cut out for it? Read on to find out.

Chapter 1

What Is Day Trading?

In This Chapter

- Key terms every day trader must know
- A day in the life of a day trader
- What makes day trading possible
- Trading as part of an overall investing strategy
- Deciding if trading is for you

Presumably you bought this book for a reason. You're interested in learning more about trading. You may want to trade for a living, to enhance investment portfolio returns, or just for the sheer thrill of playing directly in the markets. Thousands of individuals rub shoulders with professionals to deal in securities every day. What follows will cover the many types of traders, trading strategies, and tools, including pure "day" trading. It will help you sort out just exactly what trading is and what a trader does.

Few areas give as much public access to a professional space as trading. You can't practice medicine if you're not a doctor, and you can't fly a plane if you're not a pilot, but you can trade stocks and other securities—as much or as little as you want—using the tools and techniques of the pros.

Day trading for the average individual is a child of the 1990s, but the practice continues to develop and grow. The late-1990s bull market attracted a lot of slop—countless green traders made money despite not knowing what they were doing. Generally, today's trader must bring more knowledge and skill to the market to succeed.

A bit of a disclaimer: this book is designed to provide a knowledge foundation needed to move forward in trading, but won't teach you by itself to be a successful trader. The burden to learn and grow is yours. This chapter defines and outlines what trading *is* and sets the stage for the rest of the book.

Starting at the Beginning: A Few Definitions

Trading jargon and terminology are thrown around rather freely by the media, Wall Street, and the financial community. But be careful: one person's "trading" may be another person's "investing." People have different investment objectives and time horizons for different parts of their portfolio. It's easy to get confused.

So, to begin, let's get a clear working definition of trading.

> **Trading Terms**
>
> **Trading** is participating actively in a securities market with the intent to capture short-term price fluctuations. **Day trading** is buying and selling securities throughout the course of a day (sometimes called "intraday") without holding any positions overnight.

Definition: Trading

Trading is the act of buying and selling securities (stocks, futures contracts, options) with the intent to capture short-term price movements. Traders place more emphasis on short-term dynamics in the marketplace than on the long-term value or performance of the company or commodity being traded.

Definition: Day Trading

Strictly speaking, *day trading* means entering a securities position and closing it out during the same trading day. No positions are held overnight—the account is converted to 100 percent cash at the end of each trading day. You buy or sell, then reverse or "close" the position before quitting time. For the pure day trader, there are no exceptions to this rule. In fact, day traders quip that "long-term investments" are simply day trades that didn't work!

True day trading means participating directly with the same objectives and tools as professional traders—dealers—already in the marketplace.

Definition: Active Trading

Active traders try to capture short-term price fluctuations with no specific time horizon. They are active in the sense that they buy and sell securities fairly often. Most brokers today define the active trader as one who places more than 10 trades, or buy or sell orders, in a month. Some trades may be "day" trades but most are not. Some trades may be *position* or *swing* trades, where the goal is to capture a short-term gain in a time period ranging from a few days to a few weeks.

Many "active" traders have something else to do—a job, a profession, an active retirement—but stay close to the markets and capitalize on opportunities where they spot them. For these investors, trading is far from a full-time occupation.

As will be explored later in this chapter and book, many traders apply a mix of pure "day" trading and other short-term swing and position trading activities.

> **Trade Secrets**
>
> Why do pure day traders close out all positions before the end of the trading day? First, it helps them maintain discipline by not holding bad positions overnight. Closing out positions also avoids news risk—the chance of unexpected geopolitical or economic events—occurring overnight. It also minimizes or avoids margin, or loan interest paid on funds borrowed from brokers. Such interest is normally assessed only on loan balances held overnight (see Chapter 11 for more on margin).

What a Day Trader Really Does

Boiling it all down, a trader is really a dealer in the market. As a dealer, the trader is buying and selling alongside the "professional" dealers. These dealers range from other traders to trading specialists, known as market makers, from the leading investment banks and trading firms in the world. All together, these dealers collectively roll up their sleeves, trade their wares, and in so doing, create a market for a security.

At Work in the Open Marketplace

Consider, for example, an open market set up to buy and sell poultry. There will be various kinds of buyers of chickens—individuals with families to feed; "institutional" buyers buying chickens to resell to others, serve in restaurants, process into frozen chicken fingers; and so forth. There will be sellers of chickens—dealers who bought chickens from farmers or from other dealers to bring to market. Collectively these dealers form the market. They post prices to buy and sell chickens (bid and ask, or offer, prices). Or there may be an auctioneer, matching all available chickens to buyers according to the prices they're willing to pay.

An individual long-term investor is analogous to the individual who wants to buy a chicken to feed his family. This person enters the market to buy a chicken or two at the market price. He wants a good price, but doesn't care so much about the price to the nearest penny as to wait in the market for hours. He doesn't have the time, the knowledge, or the buying power to influence the price anyway. So he buys and moves on.

Similarly, institutional investors buying for pension funds, foundations, and the like will come into the market occasionally and haggle for price. Dealers will work hard to satisfy their needs, knowing they have other things to do and knowing they aren't likely to turn around and resell their chickens the next stall over for a profit. They are analogous to the food processors mentioned in the example.

Finally, there are the dealers. Dealers make their living by buying and selling chickens. They try to buy low and sell high (or sell high and buy low, also called selling short) to capture small profits through the day. Big dealers make profits by trading and by selling to large buyers. Small dealers make profits by selling to individuals and other dealers in need. Either way, they are dealers.

Behind the Screen

Today's securities markets are far more complex than our chicken analogy. There may be auctioneers working side by side with individual dealers. Individual buyers and sellers might meet each other out in the parking lot and work out deals without even entering the marketplace. Moving forward, this book will cover the auctioneer market (analogous to the New York Stock Exchange, or NYSE), the dealer market (NASDAQ), and the parking lot (electronic communications networks, or ECNs).

The Role of the Day Trader

Day traders can be counted among the dealers. They buy and sell to capture small gains in the market driven by small changes in supply and demand. Good dealers study factors that drive supply and demand and follow the trading patterns in the market. They stay on top of news that might affect demand and supply and to market patterns that might signal short-term price fluctuations. That's how they make their money—whether selling chickens, stocks, or other securities.

What Makes It All Possible

Day trading is a product of today's technology—specifically, the immense capability to move information almost anywhere at the speed of light, cheaply and reliably. Day trading, the way it is done today, was almost impossible 10 to 15 years ago. The information age, and especially today's high-speed networks, have made it possible for individuals to see the whole market and work side by side with other dealers in the marketplace from almost anywhere.

What does that mean? Simply, with a $1,000 personal computer and a phone line, you can trade. Perhaps not as well as others who might have more reliable real-time access to more information, but you can bring your virtual chickens to the market and buy and sell with the pros.

> ### Behind the Screen
>
> If you haven't experienced today's trading tools and platforms firsthand, you'll be amazed—and maybe bewildered at first. That said, they bring a much better understanding of markets and how they work.

Data Becomes Information

Equally important are the tools that convert that data into information, showing us the inner dynamics of the market—trends, patterns, news, information from multiple markets, and so forth—needed to be a dealer on the cutting edge. These tools come in the form of software, and there are exceptional software tools available, many at relatively low cost, to make sense of all that data.

Trade Secrets

Sophisticated software packages use advanced statistics and quantitative "data mining" tools to ferret out complex trading patterns virtually invisible to the human eye. Still further advances are being made using artificial intelligence—the ability to automate complex decisions based on analytics and trading experience. The speed, pace, and sophistication of today's securities markets makes such advanced tools compelling, though not necessary for most day traders.

Direct Access

Software and hardware combine to give traders real-time access to the markets as well. Even a conventional Internet access can give two-second executions on simple trades—not bad. More sophisticated "direct access" order placement and routing technology gives traders the ability to specify order routing into the markets in real time. They can single out individual dealers and trade directly with them, instead of "shouting" their order to the whole world.

Is Day Trading a Good Thing?

Day trading has certainly received a lot of press during the last few years. Most of that attention has been negative; some pundits blame it directly for the boom-and-bust cycle of the late 1990s and the difficult 2000 through 2003 period.

Like a lot of powerful tools and gizmos available today, day trading and its tools can be a bad thing if misused. Like a fool with a high-powered rifle or a 500 hp engine in a Honda Civic, it is easy to make a mistake, and the results can be spectacular. Just as prices and markets can change quickly for the better, so they can for the worse. People who don't handle it right are likely to get burned without even knowing why. Chapter 3 discusses what is required—both in skills and personal character—to be successful.

Is Day Trading Gambling?

When day traders hold securities positions for only two to three minutes, they are hardly betting on a company's fortunes, or on the fortunes of some part of the economy. But are they simply gambling on small price movements that have no real supporting basis or underlying cause? Can this in any way be called investing, or is it just gambling?

Although some traders may be gambling, most are trying to eke out an honest living—or supplement their income—by dealing directly in the market. Day trading is only gambling—and this is only a gambling book—if you're a gambler.

The Role of Traders

So why should traders make a living trading securities? Aren't they just collecting crumbs falling off the huge cake of capitalistic finance? What have they contributed to the world economy? To society?

Turns out, in fact, that traders perform an important function. Just like the dealers in the chicken market, they provide more choices from whom to buy and to whom to sell. They keep market makers and other industry insiders honest by providing visibility and introducing viable competition to make prices more truly reflect supply and demand. Or, putting it another way, they provide *liquidity* and transparency to the markets.

> **Trading Terms**
>
> **Liquidity** refers to the availability of enough buyers and sellers to quickly and easily execute transactions in a market. The effects of liquidity are fast, reliable executions and predictable prices.

More About Liquidity

Suppose you want to buy a chicken for dinner tonight. Imagine that only one poultry dealer had all the chickens available. What if all your neighbors wanted a chicken the same day? What if the dealer's supply chain were interrupted? Do you think you would get the best price? Do you think buying the chicken would be easy and free of uncertainty? Probably not. You might not get the chicken, and even if you do, it probably won't be at the price you had in mind.

Competition among many dealers reduces this risk. More "liquidity" brings more choices and fairer pricing. It helps to democratize the markets, that is, avoid having prices controlled by a few powerful interests. Such control still happens, but the effects are reduced by having large numbers of market players—*traders*.

Who Wins and Why?

"Isn't this a zero-sum game?" you ask. If someone wins, then someone has to lose, right? You pick up five cents on a trade, someone else loses that nickel.

That's a true statement in the strictest sense. If you buy low and sell high, the person who bought from you buys at the higher price and "loses" the difference between that high and the previous low. But that person wasn't in the market when you bought at the low. They may not really care about that nickel or dime—for them it might be a long-term investment.

If you buy a stock as a trader, you aren't necessarily buying it from another day trader who loses. Often you are buying and selling between other longer-term holders who just didn't reach the market at the same time. You're being paid for holding the securities for the time involved—however short—and for providing liquidity to the market.

Likewise, if you lose, you can't really blame other traders. In the day trading game, winning and losing isn't about beating or getting beat by others. It's about participating in the market as a dealer and making correct judgments about that market. If you see more, judge better, act faster, and stick to your plan, you'll win. The other side of the trade may not have the same objectives, and may not care about the short-term result. They benefit from the fact that you were in the right place at the right time in the market.

Become a Better Investor Through Trading

The material in this book should help *all* investors—short- *and* long-term traders, active and long-term investors alike. Even if you are a "poster child" long-term, value-oriented investor, this book should help you get better market and investing information and to better understand market dynamics. If nothing else, you'll get a better price when you *do* buy and sell. Knowledge and use of trading tools gives investors greater control over their investments. In today's investing world, that's a good thing.

Trading as Part of an Investing Strategy

Trading can be blended effectively with other investing strategies with the simple goal of enhancing investment returns. More investors today are taking charge of their investing portfolios, and strategically segmenting them into components, each managed differently to achieve better overall returns.

Segmenting an Active Portfolio

Investors may segment portfolios in the following ways:

♦ **Foundation portfolio.** The foundation contains long-term growth or income-oriented investments, usually including retirement accounts, real estate, and so on.

♦ **Rotational portfolio.** The rotational portfolio contains investments managed actively but not necessarily traded actively. Investments are rotated among asset classes according to current business conditions.

♦ **Opportunistic portfolio.** The opportunistic portfolio is set up to capture short-term opportunities in the market. Most trading activity occurs in this portfolio, where investors trade actively to capture short-term gains. The objective of this segment is to add current income to the overall portfolio.

Trade Secrets

For more on portfolio segmentation, refer to my *Active Investing: Take Charge of Your Portfolio In Today's Unpredictable Markets* (Adams Media, 2005).

How much money you invest in each portfolio depends on your objectives, risk tolerance, and how much you have to invest in the first place.

To Trade or Not to Trade

Trading might sound easy, almost like a video game—see it, click it, make money. But in reality, trading is probably one of the most demanding ways to earn money out there. It takes concentration, effort, and intensity required by few other professions other than perhaps air traffic control. Numbers go by in rat-a-tat-tat progression. The markets are *fast*—few have any idea how fast until they see it in action. Other players in the market are working against you, trying to fool you, trying to profit from your mistakes. Keeping up with the pulse of markets in real time is, in a word, *exhausting*.

Over time you'll get used to it and learn to focus on just the information needed, but most new traders find the experience stressful. It is a safe bet that most new traders experience headaches the first few times through. At the same time, it can be stimulating and exhilarating. It is by no means for the faint of heart, or really, for the faint of body. Trading is physically, as well as mentally, demanding.

Trading also requires up-front investments in training and technology to make it work, and also a humble tolerance for failure. Few traders win consistently right off the bat; it involves developing a technique and style that suits you.

Those unwilling to invest this time and effort, and those looking for easy money, are unlikely to succeed. Chapter 3 explores the different trading styles and up-front requirements in more detail.

What You Should Already Know

Trading—and this book, for that matter—is no place for beginning investors to start. Before you begin trading, you should have some experience with investing. Although we review the major securities markets and explain how they work, we assume you already know what a stock is and what it represents, how to read basic financial data, and are at least somewhat familiar with other types of securities. We assume you've bought and sold stocks before, at least through a conventional broker. We assume you're pretty good with a computer and the Internet. Further, we assume that you're interested—and have time to learn—the dynamics, inner workings, techniques, and excitement of trading securities.

A Fair Warning

Day trading is not a game for beginners. Do not quit your job, mortgage your house, cash out your children's college fund, or dip into your retirement account in order to become a day trader—at least until you acquire the experience and capability to do it and do it right. Day traders can make money, yes, but they can just as easily lose money and lose it very quickly.

CAUTION

Alert! _____

It should go without saying, but don't hock the family jewels to day trade. Trading can be highly speculative and should not be undertaken with any money you can't comfortably afford to lose.

There are no guarantees that you'll become a good trader by reading this book. In fact, this book should be the first of many you read on the subject, and you should consider using other training tools as well. You will not become a securities analyst, a great stock picker, or securities "professional" just by reading this book.

With these warnings out of the way, read on.

The Least You Need to Know

- Day trading means taking an investment position and closing during the same trading day.

- Effectively, traders and especially day traders function as dealers in the market.

- Trading has been around for a long time, but recent networking and software technology have brought professional tools to the general public.

- Trading helps to improve market liquidity and keep market players honest.

- Few investors commit 100 percent of their investments to trading; most trade a small portion of their portfolio to produce short-term income.

- Trading is hard work and a learned skill. It is very risky if you don't know what you're doing.

Chapter 2

Day Trading Makes a Comeback—Again

In This Chapter

- ◆ The current state of trading
- ◆ How trading has evolved since the 1920s
- ◆ The impact of personal technology on trading
- ◆ The impact of new rules and market tools on trading

One of the best ways to learn about the present and future is to examine the past. Following that principle, this chapter explores the current state of trading and how it became what it is. As you might expect, it's a fast-changing and dynamic story, and may very well have changed again before you read this. Let's begin our history in the present, and move back through time from there.

The State of Trading Today

One might justifiably wonder how trading, and particularly day trading, survived the turbulent years of the late 1990s and early "oughts" (2000–04).

During the late 1990s, thousands of novice traders entered the markets, captured "easy" gains in the exuberance, and lost it all as the "dot-bomb" debacle took hold. New rules emerged, brokers became more demanding of prospective traders, and most of all, a lot of people "burned" by the experience simply went back to their day jobs.

But did individual day traders go away? Did trading revert to the exclusive realm of professional traders? Answer: not really. Traders are still around, but they have become more sophisticated in response to more demanding conditions.

By the Numbers

Today, most forms of trading, including day trading, are alive and well. The two research firms that follow these trends estimate that anywhere from 300,000 to 1 million individuals trade actively. The wide divergence of these numbers suggests that many part-timers and "dabblers" are out there doing some trading, but not as a full-time activity.

Research suggests that perhaps 10 percent of that number is engaged in full-time, true "day" trading. The remaining 90 percent of day trade is conducted on a part-time basis to supplement income or for pure pleasure. Most part-timers are probably active traders, meaning that they trade short term but not necessarily in a single day. These traders usually trade a minimum of 10 times a month and likely a few trades per day. Many of these individuals operate while doing something else, trading from their cubicles and before and after work as time permits. Contrast this to the true full-time trader, who may place 20 to 50 trades per day—some up to 250 or more per day.

Behind the Screen

It is easy to see the impact of traders, professional and individual alike, on the market. Consider, for example, the shares of Sun Microsystems. There are about 3 billion shares outstanding. During 2004, NASDAQ reported a trading volume of over 10 billion for the year. That means that the *average* share changed hands three times during the year, giving an *average* period of ownership of four months. Considering that the majority of shares are held by institutions as well as Sun employees, mainly as long-term investments, that suggests an enormous number of shares changing hands over and over, some even several times a day.

A More Rigorous Endeavor

Like in any gold rush, the easy money was made by those who got there first. The early day traders of the 1995 to 1998 period were able to capitalize on speed and information to "beat" others in the market-place. Many were able to simply buy shares available in the market at low prices and turn them around, or "flip" them, almost immediately to onrushing investors. Repeatedly capturing "spreads" of an eighth, a quarter, or even half a point made these traders quite wealthy. *Market makers* were busy serving institutional clients and didn't really pay that much attention to those early traders—at least at first.

Since then, technology has enabled more traders to enter the market, creating more competition. Market makers have wised up to individual trading practices, and there are more of them in a given (NASDAQ) stock. And the shift to decimal trading—reducing *spreads* (the difference between the *bid* and *ask*, or *offer*, price of a security) from sixteenths (6.25 cents) and eighths (12.5 cents) to pennies—has reduced the opportunity to "scalp" profits in the market. Finally, the lack of direction in today's markets has made trading more difficult, for one can't just buy in and let the overall market trend float their boat. It's easy to make money when everything is going up 20 percent per year.

Trading Terms

A **market maker** makes a market in a security, buying and selling the security on behalf of his or her firm (usually an investment bank or brokerage) and the firm's clients. Think of it this way: a Ford dealer is a market maker for Ford cars, new and used.

Trading Terms

The **bid** price is the price at which the market maker (NASDAQ) or specialist (NYSE) is willing to buy the stock from you. The **ask,** or **offer,** price is the price at which he/she will sell the stock to you. The difference is the **spread.** In a sense, bid is wholesale, ask is retail, and the spread is the profit margin.

Response: Evolved Traders

Darwin would have predicted it: the natural response to more difficult conditions is a stronger, more seasoned species.

Trading professionals and those who provide trading tools recognize a shift in the nature of the people involved. Gone are most of the novice "cowboys" out there shooting wildly at everything that moved. Today's trader has become more skilled and sophisticated, taking a more professional approach to trading, analysis, and risk management. Today's trader is likely to be better trained, more knowledgeable about the markets, and more risk averse.

Many of today's traders have moved beyond the crowded venues of NASDAQ technology stocks to trade a broader range of stocks and to trade other kinds of securities. Commodities trading, perhaps inspired by the active oil and gold markets of 2004, has increased dramatically. Traders have learned to trade index futures, options, exchange traded funds, and other "basket" or derivative securities with skills.

Trading styles have also evolved. Simple "scalping" of spreads has diminished in favor of more momentum or technical trading, that is, where traders identify—and profit from—shifts in supply and demand through a set of complex technical signals and mathematical models.

Consolidated Platforms

One of the biggest changes trading has witnessed in the past few years has been the consolidation of trading platforms (for an explanation of trading platforms, see Chapter 13). Sophisticated trading software, designed for and once available only to professional traders, became available to individuals, but at a high price and without much training and support. There weren't enough qualified traders to keep the high-end providers alive, however. At the same time, many investors were using a variety of Internet-based online brokers to trade, but they found their tools largely inadequate for very short-term trading. Additionally, online brokers saw a profitable market niche in serving the needs of very active traders, and they saw desirable technology in high-end platform tools easier to buy than to build for their own trading platforms.

The predictable result: large brokerage firms catering to individuals started to buy high-end platforms for their customers. Most notably, Charles Schwab & Co., Inc. bought CyberTrader, Inc. and Ameritrade bought Tradecast. Ameritrade's purchase of Datek and its high-end "Watcher" tool signified this trend and another—the overall consolidation of players in the brokerage industry. Some estimate that at its peak in 1999 to 2000, there were more than 200 electronic brokerage platforms; that number has shrunk to about 75 today.

But that doesn't mean that consolidation is complete; there are still 45 to 50 distinct high-end stock-trading platforms out there, and still more aimed at commodity and futures trading.

Hedge Fund Involvement

Hedge funds are another important factor in today's trading—and the markets in general. A hedge fund is a lightly regulated group of private (and sometimes institutional) investors who pool their money under a fund manager for the purpose of trading to beat market returns. These funds are loosely regulated because they don't have many investors and most are hand-selected, thus they avoid SEC investment company requirements. Investors must pass stringent minimum net worth and risk tolerance requirements.

How do these funds beat market returns? Many invest in complex securities like convertible and high-risk bonds, foreign markets, and similar investments. But many do it by—as you might have guessed—actively trading the markets.

In recent years it has been estimated that up to 18 to 20 percent of daily market volume can be accounted for by hedge fund activity. Sharp swings in volume and market direction near the beginning or end of the trading day can often be attributed to hedge funds, though their specific activities cannot be seen because they are not required to report their trading activities.

What it all comes down to is this: a lot of day trading is occurring in today's markets, and today's individual day traders look more and more like the professionals they trade with. How did it all evolve? Read on.

A New Revolution, an Old Idea

Stock trading has probably gone on as long as public stock markets have been around. In the United States that is largely regarded to be the late 1700's with the advent of the New York Stock Exchange at the famous corner of Wall and Broad streets. But such a trading venue, without electronic communications, was hardly available to the masses, so "individual" trading in stocks really took a while to get started. The first notable trading activity by "main street" players probably occurred in the "bucket shops" of the 1920s.

Bucket shops were likely the first real day trading venues. Similar to today's off-track betting parlors, bucket shops provided smoky venues for customers to buy and sell stocks with each other, or with the "house" (like in Las Vegas), and only sometimes through the stock exchanges. Bucket-shop speculators were essentially gaming for every up or down move that came across the (then new) electronic ticker tape. Many were illegal, and dealt in illegal or even nonexistent securities. For many, they provided a source of income, and for most a source of good fun. Even more fun was to be had with margin money: you could have your fun, with up to 90 percent of the money on loan from the house.

The Dark Ages

The disastrous events and new public disfavor regarding stock speculation brought on by the 1929 crash resulted in a host of industry regulations and increased margin-equity requirements. You could no longer borrow 90 percent of the value of your stock; now you had to put up initial "equity" of 50 percent. Licensing rules eliminated the bucket shops and forced a return to a tradition already 136 years old—high, regulated (that is, fixed) commission rates. The concept of day trading had been born, but it would lie dormant for decades. It faded into sort of a "dark ages," suppressed by the regulating commissions and a securities trading and brokerage system that simply didn't support fast, cheap executions.

> **Trade Secrets**
>
> In England, you really can gamble on the stock market. British bookies are famous for their willingness to handle just about any bet. You can bet that the stock-market index will finish higher than predicted, or wager that it will finish lower. You can even buy and sell call and put options on sporting matches.

It wasn't until the early 1970s that several factors came together to improve the climate for trading. Initially, it was rule changes and important modifications in markets and market structure. Later, mainly in the late 1980s and 1990s, the advent of fast, cheap, networked computing led to a quantum leap in individual trading capability.

Trading Stocks the Old-Fashioned Way

Most of us over 40 probably remember the stock-buying olden days, when the process worked like this:

1. You made an appointment to see a stockbroker.

2. You sat down with the broker and told him (yes, pretty much always a "him") what you were interested in buying.

3. The broker checked the stock's current price on the (then highly advanced) Quotron screen.

4. Once you decided what you wanted, the broker would scratch it down on a five-part carbon form about the same size and legibility of a drug prescription.

5. He would then walk it (or in bigger offices, vacuum-tube it) to a clerk in the back, who would teletype or phone it to the firm's agent in New York, who would communicate it to another agent or "floor broker" at the NYSE, then to the "specialist" for execution (everyone a "he," if you're still interested).

The process would be reversed to communicate the results of the transaction back to your broker through the firm's "back office." Your broker might get a confirmation from the back office, and he would call you to inform you of the trade. If your line wasn't busy and you were home to receive the call, you would learn that the trade had gone through. Remember, this was back before the days of voicemail.

Little would happen until five days later when the invoice came to your mailbox. You wrote a check and mailed it. A few weeks later the certificate showed up in a big brown envelope. The commission on your trade might have been $100, perhaps $200, regardless of the broker used. Then, when you sold your stock, you would pay that commission again. Since commissions were based in part on the value of the sale, even more commission might have been paid for the sale.

Imagine trying to trade frequently with such a system!

The Technology Renaissance

Technology brought the prospect of true electronic trading limited only by the physical speed of light. Progress until then had brought electronic quotes and trade reporting, but hadn't automated trading itself beyond the speed of people, pens, and paper.

The Securities and Exchange Commission (SEC), responding to growing popular interest in investing (and ever-fading memories of the Depression), relaxed some of the stifling rules and regulations that had made investing inaccessible and expensive for most individuals.

The Age of the Electronic Market

NASDAQ (which stands for National Association of Securities Dealers Automated Quotations) came into being on February 5, 1971. NASDAQ was the first truly electronic market. Market makers would post their bids and offers and execute orders with the public (and each other) at the speed of light with the right keystrokes. No more unanswered phones, pokey clerks, and stressed-out agents. (For more on NASDAQ, see Chapter 7).

While the New York Stock Exchange still maintains its human-powered "specialist" system to match buy and sell orders (see Chapter 6), the NYSE's mechanisms for consumer-sized order placement have also been automated. Orders move at the speed of light to the trading floor.

The Rise of Personal Technology

Electronic stock markets like NASDAQ and the Quotron-based world of real-time information exchange revolutionized the internal workings of the securities industry. Did this change bring on the day trading phenomenon as we know it today? Not really, unless you were a stockbroker yourself or were working very closely with a brokerage firm. As an individual you still couldn't participate directly in the markets.

But another revolution was around the corner—a revolution in *personal* technology. In the '80s, both the personal computer and the Internet were, for all practical purposes, born. But very few people knew how to use them. For those who did, it was no faster—and considerably less reliable—than picking up the phone and calling your broker (or "telebroker," for those in cyberspace, early '80s style).

By the mid '90s, PCs and modem connections got fast and cheap. Software could pull up quotes and graphics at the click of a mouse. The Internet became "packaged," with usable browsers like Netscape Navigator or Microsoft Internet Explorer. Even more important, Internet-enabling languages such as Java and HTML made it possible for website hosts to create powerful, fast, easy-to-use sites very quickly. These sites became tied together and easily accessible through the structure and standards of the World Wide Web. Through the web and more direct forms of network access, these high-performance sites tied into quote databases and execution systems anywhere in the world—but usually through market players and information providers serving as middlemen.

Faster Connections

Internet connections at 56K transfer rates were pretty good, especially considering the technologies available until that time. But standard Internet connections can vary in speed and be frustratingly unreliable at times. In the late 1990s, broadband access became available to individuals, with more direct connections and speeds to 50 or even 100 times faster than standard modem connections. Initially the technology was tied to the somewhat expensive and cumbersome "ISDN" connection; since 2000 the advent of DSL and cable-driven broadband has become much more widespread and cheaper. For all intents and purposes, it is available to the masses. The result: real-time information and direct access to the markets have become largely available to anyone.

The Information Revolution

Using almost any Internet-based portal (like Yahoo!Finance at finance.yahoo.com), at the click of a mouse, you can get detailed delayed quotes, stats, company research and profiles, analyst expectations, and graphs of a company's stock performance for one day, five years, or anything in between, quickly, and for free. Premier users and subscribers can usually access real-time quotes, and often even free *streaming* quotes and news at some sites.

Internet Trading

Internet trading, combined with electronic trading systems created by the major markets, enables traders to buy and sell almost instanta-neously. It isn't perfect, but it's surprisingly close. Many Internet brokers—E-Trade, Ameritrade, TD Waterhouse, and others—advertise confirmed 10-, 5-, or even 2-second trades or no commission paid. Most "market" orders placed for actively traded stocks through electronic brokers will execute within seconds, and are accompanied by an electronic acknowl-edgement.

> **Trading Terms**
>
> **Streaming** quotes are a continuous data feed that doesn't need to be constantly "refreshed." Streaming news is much the same thing—news stories and information coming to you automatically without any "fetch" process. Most quality trading platforms—and even some of the free Internet portals—have some streaming information and quote features. They also allow users to select, or filter, the information down to the specific stocks and news items desired.

Most Internet-based brokerage services offer a wide assortment of quotes, news, and research information—most or all of it for free. But there is still another big step up in the breadth and depth of information—and the speed of transactions—required by many traders to become true dealers in the market. That step is …

High-Performance Trading Information

In a large part due to technology, and in a large part due to the breadth and speed of business itself, today's markets move at lightning speed. It should come as no surprise that playing as a trader—as a dealer—in these markets requires professional-caliber tools. Learning and using high-performance trading platforms is almost essential—not to gain an edge but just to keep up.

High-performance trading platforms give real-time, streaming access to news, market data, and quotes. The breadth and depth of these platforms is truly amazing. Real-time access to NASDAQ Level II quotes—a big step forward for individual traders—is but one example.

"Level II" quotes are one of the key features of the advanced platforms. Level II gives access to the full computerized set of posted dealer and individual quotes for a NASDAQ stock (and, to a degree, "listed" stocks such as those traded on the NYSE and AMEX). These quotes are both *at* and *away* from the market—that is, at the *best bid* and *ask* prices and prices *away* from the best. With this tool a trader can gauge supply and demand in the entire market, not just at the best prices. The importance of Level II, and tips for reading it, come along in Chapter 15. For now, know that it is a vital tool for a trader playing actively as a dealer in the market.

> **Trading Terms**
>
> **At the market** refers to the best bid and ask quote available in the market. The **best bid** is the highest bid in the market; that is, the most that some other party—dealer or individual—is offering to pay for your stock. The **best ask,** or offer, quote is the lowest offer in the market; that is, the best price offered for you to buy the stock. **Away** from the market refers to quotes (or firm orders) that are lower than the best (bid) or higher than the best (ask, or offer) prices in the market.

High-performance trading platforms give broad and deep trading data and quotes. Beyond that, they give direct trading access to the markets. That is, instead of placing an order that gets represented in the market by your broker or even a middleman, it goes directly to the market and even to a specific market maker. The time savings and reliability of direct-access trading often pays off regardless of trading strategy.

These high-performance trading platforms were originally designed for use by professional traders and market makers. Not surprisingly, they come at a price and with a certain amount of know-how required to use them effectively. Fortunately, due to the brokerage consolidation mentioned earlier, some of the more important features have been integrated into more mainstream trading platforms. How these advanced and "hybrid" platforms work and what they cost will become clearer as this book goes forward.

Trade Secrets _____

Is the Internet good enough for trading purposes? The Web is a great way to distribute information and execute transactions, but for some high-performance trading applications, it may not be reliable enough. Advanced trading platforms feed a lot of data continuously, and those with a 56K modem in particular will experience a lot of interruptions. Most traders will want to invest $40 to $50 a month on DSL or cable broadband service. Really serious traders might spend $300 a month or so on a dedicated "T1" network line. All traders should test their connections and have a backup available. The good news: server and PC hardware and platform software have become much more reliable.

New Rules, New Tools

Beyond the technology-based changes you just read about, there have been other rule and tool changes without which today's trading would be all but impossible. Most of these changes have made trading faster, cheaper, and fairer, and have reduced the "spread," or profit margin, collected by market professionals. A more level playing field has been created, one where individual traders can compete side by side with the pros.

The following sections outline the various rule and tool changes.

Rule Change: Commission Deregulation

The seeds of the day trading revolution were planted in the 1920s and began to germinate with changes brought on by electronic transaction technology. But arguably the opening shots of the revolution were really fired on "May Day," May 1, 1975, when regulated—fixed and costly—brokerage commissions became a thing of the past. New "discount" brokers popped up, reducing the standard industry commission of several hundred dollars to something less than $100. The commission revolution, started by firms like Charles Schwab, has taken on new strength in recent years with the advent of electronic Internet trading, which has driven down the same commissions to less than $20 for most and to $5 or lower under some circumstances.

Doing the math makes the impact of this change clear. A one-day turnaround on 1,000 shares of XYZ, instead of costing $200, might now cost $9.95. Make 10, 15, or 25 trades a day, and the savings really add up. Put another way, your trade only has to be about 5 percent as successful to break even as it would have had to be in 1969.

Trade Secrets

In 1999, online discount brokers were thought to be the first form of e-commerce to really profit from the Internet. Trading volumes were growing exponentially while costs were largely contained to initial investments in Internet tools and customer service. But in 2000 the bottom fell out and "retail" trading volumes dried up. Charles Schwab once employed 26,000; in early 2005 that number had dropped to 13,900, and the firm has had to revert to offering more "full" services to certain customers. They also bought the advanced trading platform CyberTrader Pro® to capture more profitable and stable high-end traders—and to incorporate its technologies into other Schwab products. Discount brokers have profited from the Internet, but the road has been bumpier than expected.

Tool Change: NYSE SuperDot

DOT stands for designated order turnaround system. SuperDot is the NYSE's electronic-order routing system. With SuperDot, orders can be routed electronically to a specialist's "book" (more about this in Chapter 6) without human intervention. SuperDot gives traders almost instant access to the floor and usually provides trade confirmations in 60 seconds or less.

Tool Change: SOES on NASDAQ

If you were around (and trading) on October 19, 1987, you remember an ugly day in the markets. As the market began a 22 percent tumble, investors who tried to unload stock in the panic simply couldn't. Brokers, if available, couldn't find a market maker who would even answer a phone, let alone post a bid to buy or an offer to sell.

NASDAQ had created SOES, or small-order execution system, a few years earlier. SOES automates trading for orders less than 1,000 shares, allowing a customer or broker to automatically transact a stock with a market maker at the posted bid or ask price. With the 1987 crash, the SEC decided to make SOES mandatory for NASDAQ market makers. This means all market makers have to post quotes on both sides of the market (that is, to buy and to sell) that can be executed automatically by someone else in the market. The result: a faster and more liquid market for "retail-size" orders.

Rule Change: Limit Order Protection Rule

In response to criticism from both the public *and* the SEC, the NASDAQ implemented limit order protection in 1997. There are two parts to this rule. One part requires a market maker to post any limit order—a customer order placed with a fixed price—that improves on the existing price. If your order improves the price over the going market, it becomes next in line and will get posted in the market for everyone to see. The market maker can't hide it to preserve a spread and inflate his or her *own* profits.

The other part of the 1997 rule prohibited market makers from displaying better prices in "private" or electronic-network markets than they do to the public through NASDAQ systems. With this change, the playing field was leveled even more.

Rule Change: Decimal Trading

In 1997, both the NASDAQ and the NYSE implemented minimum quotable trading intervals of one-sixteenth (6.25 cents) per share. Previously these had been in eighths. The result was to drive down "spreads" and require a smaller price movement to allow an investor to "cover the spread and move ahead."

In 2000 the major exchanges started decimal trading, where prices move in increments of one cent. Two results: (1) It's harder to trade for the spread, or "scalp" the markets, as the spread is often a penny, and (2) prices appear more nervous—that is, there is more fluctuation up a cent, down two cents, etc. Decimal trading has added a fatigue factor to trading, though it has also brought more pricing precision to the markets.

Toward More Electronic Trading

At the time of this writing there is a continuing push to make more of the markets work electronically and to eliminate the human-intensive NYSE specialist system. The strongest move to date is the recently announced (April 2005) merger of the electronic exchange Archipelago with the NYSE. Surely part of the rationale is to bring the NYSE into the electronic age. The jury is still out on which way this will go. Similar efforts are in progress in commodity and bond markets, but pure electronic trading is still far from a reality in most markets outside of NASDAQ.

The Least You Need to Know

◆ Trading is not a new thing. But individual access to sophisticated trading tools and markets is relatively new.

◆ Today's trading, and today's traders, are more highly "evolved" than during the late 1990s boom.

◆ Broker and trading platform consolidation have made high-end trading tools more accessible to individual traders.

◆ Personal technology advances and Internet-based trading tools were a major leap forward for individual traders.

◆ Direct-access trading platforms give full professional capability to individual traders.

◆ Important rule changes, including commission deregulation, as well as market tool changes, have improved individual access to markets.

3

What It Takes to Be a Trader

In This Chapter

- ◆ What it takes to succeed as a trader
- ◆ A comparison of different trading styles
- ◆ Trading as a part-time activity
- ◆ A skills and character assessment
- ◆ What you'll need to get started

So you're interested in becoming a trader, but aren't sure whether the lifestyle suits you? In this chapter, we examine trading, and more specifically day trading, with your personality in mind.

We start with a broad examination of the character, personality traits, and personal commitment required to be a trader. We then go into the different trading styles employed in the trading world, and match personal character traits to those styles. After a short discussion of whether or not trading is feasible while doing another job, we offer a list of personal attributes and qualifications held to be important by most traders. Finally, we end with a short discussion of the technology requirements and up-front costs.

Because some of this material might not be totally clear until you learn more about actual day trading tools and techniques, you might want to return to this chapter after you finish reading the rest of the book.

What It Takes to Be a Trader

Like any professional activity, trading requires a certain set of skills and personality traits. Whether you should trade and, beyond that, what kind of trading you should engage in, depends to a degree on your ability and willingness to commit time; your degree of skill and experience; your aptitude and comfort with information and decision making; your self-confidence; your self-control; your financial control; and even your mental and physical stamina. That's a lot of ground to cover, so let's take these traits one at a time.

Time Commitment

Make a few trades in the morning, shut down the computer, and hit the golf course. That's the popular image of trading as reported by the press and a few lucky traders, but rest assured we just described the exception, not the rule. Good traders spend hours concentrating on market behavior, analyzing movements, researching, recording results, and learning from those results.

Traders put in a lot of "overtime"—often beginning work before the markets open, remaining glued to the screen during the trading day, staying tuned in to "after hours" trading, and occasionally even watching far into the evening to try to pick up the direction of the next day's activity from news reports, foreign markets, and futures trading. Figure on an 18-hour day with breaks.

Trading Terms

Traders often refer to people who trade while doing another job as **cubicle traders**.

Not ready to commit three quarters of your day to trading? You'll be happy to hear that some trading styles may work for part-time or *cubicle traders*. That discussion follows later in this chapter.

Skill and Experience

Trading is a learned skill, and it is usually learned by doing. Many traders make the mistake of thinking they can read a book or two, take an online course, and hit the ground running. Although it's essential that new traders commit to studying the literature and learning the markets and platforms they use, they must be prepared to continue learning as they go. They should also accept—and prepare for—the likelihood of losing some money as they gain experience.

Judgment

It's obvious that trading involves a lot of independent judgment, but it's the *kind* of judgment that throws off a lot of beginners. It is a numbers-based, pattern-based judgment requiring close tracking of thousands of facts and figures through the day. It can wear out even the most dedicated numbers-geek, and may drive the non-numbers people nuts, especially if they adopt fast, close-to-the-market trading styles.

Self-Confidence

It goes without saying that one must possess a degree of self-confidence to put thousands of dollars on the line each day. But it's a quiet, controlled confidence, not unlike that exhibited by professional golfers. It's self-confidence without ego, perhaps. Egotistical traders tend to get carried away with their wins and angry with their losses, and both behaviors can get in the way of success rather quickly.

Self-Control

Self-control goes hand in hand with self-confidence. Good traders move on when they make a mistake. It is impossible to get revenge on the market, and good traders know this. Too many novice traders let their emotions do the dealing and end up throwing good money after bad. The calm but inwardly intense demeanor of most professional golfers is again a good model to follow.

Financial Control

Traders must always be aware of their financial situation and constantly monitor and control it. They must also have a healthy attitude about money (not "I want to make a million bucks in a month"), and only trade with money that they can afford to lose.

Financial control also involves keeping records for taxes, which can be an onerous chore, especially for very active traders.

An Ability to Tolerate Risk

Risk tolerance draws on the previous three characteristics: self-confidence, self-control, and financial control. Traders do not need the risk tolerance of gamblers or test pilots, but they should have a healthy tolerance for loss and the ability to absorb such a loss if it occurs. The trader who does nothing for fear of losing will ultimately lose. Those who continually fret about the possibility of losing and get upset when it happens are probably not cut out for this kind of work.

An Ability to Concentrate

Trading takes focus. Anyone who thinks they can do trade full-time while also watching two preschoolers at home is, pure and simple, nuts. Things will inevitably "happen" when the trader is least able to focus. Distractions affect the processing of information and can also delay trades. It's possible to trade while doing another job, but it takes the right situation. Without the right situation, which will be described later in this chapter, both the trading and the job will inevitably suffer.

> **Behind the Screen**
>
> I'm a firm believer in the need to "clear one's head" through exercise, a process that refreshes the mind and clears out the junk in one's body. Physical stamina leads to mental stamina and helps in the key areas of self-confidence and concentration. Whether it's a walk, a bike ride, or an intense game of Ultimate Frisbee, exercise is important.

Mental and Physical Stamina

The need for mental stamina will become obvious to any trader who sits in front of a computer screen watching numbers and news items going by rat-a-tat-tat for hours. It takes a certain amount of mental fortitude and toughness, some of which can be acquired on the job as one gets used to it. Expect a headache the first few times through.

Surprisingly, physical stamina is important, too. You'll spend hours sitting in one position focused on a computer screen or two.

Trading Styles

No two day traders are alike. In fact, diversity is a good thing in this business. For if all day traders were alike, day trading wouldn't work! Think about it. Everybody would do the same thing at the same time—buying the same stocks, responding to the same charts and indicators, and following the same trading patterns. In other words, there would be no market.

Different traders trade different things (*what* traders trade is discussed in the next chapter) and employ different styles to achieve their goals. Style choices depend on individual tastes, skill sets, time availability, and risk tolerance.

The purpose of this chapter is not to teach you how to use different trading styles to profit, but instead to help you understand what's involved in each trading style, so you can decide what form, if any, of trading fits your personality and your schedule.

We've identified four major trading styles: the pure dealer, the momentum trader, the range trader, and the pattern trader. Each style has unique characteristics in terms of …

♦ Time horizon.

♦ Personal time commitment.

♦ Required skill sets.

♦ Risk.

Let's look at each style in turn.

The Pure Dealer

The pure dealer is the "chicken dealer" described in Chapter 1. This trader makes money by buying low and selling high several times, perhaps hundreds of times, throughout the day. The slang phrase "scalper" applies to these traders, meaning they "scalp" a penny or two at a time, picking up securities at one "wholesale" price and putting them back onto the market very quickly at a slightly higher "retail" price. Timing is everything, and these traders thrive on action.

Short Term, High Intensity

Pure dealers have the shortest time horizons, often just a few seconds. Obviously, high levels of concentration and the ability to read and judge markets quickly are essential. This is not a style of trading that can be executed while doing something else; it requires full-time commitment.

> **CAUTION**
>
> **Alert!**
>
> Whether a pure dealer can make enough money by only trading a few hours a day is debatable. Some traders (particularly on the West Coast) may engage in dealing before they start work (the market opens at 6:30 A.M. Pacific Time). Others may deal during lunchtime, but be warned that it is a very poor rest break from a normal job.

You Can Log Off After Hours

Pure dealer trading, while requiring a high degree of concentration while connected, requires relatively little outside time. Compared to other styles, it isn't as important to study market or trading patterns, although it can help. What needs to be studied is what is happening on the trading "floor"—in real time. So traders with other night-time commitments might gravitate towards pure dealer trading.

Timing Is Everything

Pure dealer trading requires considerable self-control and risk-management skills. The discipline must be there to get out of a bad trade quickly if the market is misread—otherwise it will take a bunch of good trades to make up the loss. Such risk management decisions must be made quickly and well to succeed. Pure dealer trading is no place for traders who have trouble making decisions.

Pure dealers must also have access to real-time information and direct-access trading tools. Seconds wasted is pennies lost. And those pennies add up quickly.

The Momentum Trader

Momentum traders seek to profit from riding waves in individual securities. They try to spot stocks that are "in play," that is, responding or likely to respond to news or rumor. The hope is to find the right entry and exit points; that is, to enter a trade before most of the move takes place and exit the trade as it starts to reverse. Momentum traders drive their trades off of news events and analysis of certain technical indicators.

Setting the Alarm

Momentum traders are likely to enter positions near the beginning of the trading day. They may watch these positions unfold through the day just like pure dealers do, but it's not as essential. Many momentum traders set some form of alert—an e-mail message, screen beep, cell phone call or page—to notify them when the market reaches a certain price point. Or some may set fixed price limit or stop orders (see Chapter 10) to trigger automatically at the desired price. Either way, momentum trading can usually be done while you're doing something else as long as the trading tool "dogs" are set to bark at the right time.

Before and After Hours

Of the different trading styles, momentum traders invest the most time and effort into selecting the securities they want to trade. These traders are voracious readers of business news and information, and many watch cable news and after-hours action closely to ferret out the next day's big movers. Ditto for early in the morning—momentum traders watch premarket activity and news bulletins closely. This can be a problem for Hawaii traders, where markets open at 3:30 A.M.—they probably rise at 2 or 2:30 in the morning to take the market pulse.

Avoiding Greed

Greed can be dangerous for *all* traders, but it's the worst enemy of the momentum trader. Few forces compare to the one that compels us to hang on to a winner to see if we can eke just a little more out of it. After all, it's a winner, right? The problem is, *reversals* can be swift. So momentum traders must not only be able to spot entry points but also exit points, and must stick to their plan with the utmost of discipline.

> **Trading Terms**
>
> A **reversal** is a change in direction, a "top" or a "bottom" indicated by a change in supply/demand sentiment in the market. Most reversals are followed by increasing momentum in the other direction.

Safety Nets

Momentum traders constantly risk missing key reversals, whether because of greed, inattention, poor planning, or just plain old bad luck. Good momentum traders must have the discipline to set "stops" behind their trades, guaranteeing some locked-in profits. The techniques for doing this can be tricky and will be covered later, but all momentum traders must think in terms of safety nets.

The Range Trader

Range traders trade off the highs and lows of observable trading ranges. In normal markets (meaning markets not affected by some external turbulence), many stocks (and commodities) trade in fairly definable ranges. Why? Because when they reach the bottom of the range, they are perceived to be priced attractively and buyers step in. At the top end of a range, they appear to be overvalued to the market, and selling ensues.

Trade Secrets _____

Trading off the highs and lows of observable trading ranges is also effective for other short-term trading, most particularly the swing trader. Swing traders capitalize on these very "swings" between *support* and *resistance* levels—that is, the apparent bottom and top of the trading range.

With certain risks, range trading works for day trading, for stocks tend to set patterns of intraday highs and lows.

"Hands Off" Trading

Range trading is perhaps the easiest to do without real-time focus and concentration on the markets; hence it works better than most other trading styles for the part-time or cubicle trader. Range traders study charts, often in the evening after a trading day. As the trading day begins, they choose an entry point and an exit point. Then, using fixed price (limit/stop) orders and alerts, they try to get in at the bottom of the range and out at the top. Since these price points are set at the beginning of the day, there isn't much for the trader to do during the day outside of checking the order status and watching alerts.

Range Trading Challenges

Range trading tends to require less commitment than other styles and tends to be the least stressful. The risk is that news or market events can blow a security out of its range while not being watched. Of course, there is also the risk that an attractive "bottom" might fall out. The point is this: it's good to watch closely when possible. In addition, stock (or commodity) selection is very important for range traders—some securities trade in more predictable ranges than others.

Pattern Trader

Going beyond the range trader, the pattern trader looks for patterns in stock activity as might be depicted on a chart. These traders study charts continuously, looking for securities that fit certain repeatable trading patterns. Range trading is really a form of pattern trading, where the pattern is a *channel*, or an observable range. Pattern traders look for shapes in charts and the performance of securities compared to previously established averages. They also track certain mathematical signals known as oscillators which track and measure trading patterns. Some also use cross-market strategies, looking for price and price movement differences between similar securities, with the expectation that similar securities trade in similar patterns. The art and science of analyzing such patterns for predictable behavior is known as technical analysis and is the subject of Chapter 16.

Midnight Oil

Pattern traders look for certain patterns emerging during the day, but most spend many off-market hours looking at charts for patterns and mathematical signals. Pattern trading can usually be done by someone who works during the day, but he or she must be available in the evenings and on weekends to study charts. Intraday pattern trading naturally requires more commitment and concentration during the trading day.

The Cubicle Trader

So, getting back to an important point you're probably interested in: is it possible to day trade while doing a day job? The answer is yes, with major limitations. The obvious limitations are the impact on the job itself and job performance, the ability to concentrate, and the availability of real-time information and trading access.

Very committed and active forms of trading, like the pure dealer style described earlier, are probably not suitable for cubicle traders, unless it is possible for you to set aside a large chunk of time—a couple of hours at least—off the job. But the other styles, most particularly range trading, can be pulled off if done with a degree of discipline. These styles allow the trader to let some of the tools—alerts, fixed price orders, and so forth—do the work.

Behind the Screen

Many professional people travel, and what better way to spend all of that downtime in airports and hotels than to trade? Unfortunately, access to information and markets becomes more challenging—but not impossible. Laptop computers and PDAs coupled with wi-fi wireless services provide the hardware infrastructure to keep in touch. Good mobile streaming information and quote resources (www.esignal.com is an example) are available with charting, alerts, and news features for stocks and other securities. Combined with a basic or advanced Internet broker platform, many trading styles and strategies can be carried out while on the road.

How Much Can a Day Trader Make?

There is no set answer to this question. Sure, some traders rake in $50,000, $100,000, or more in a week, but these cases are truly exceptional. How much a trader makes largely depends on three things:

- Trade frequency
- Trade size (shares or dollars per trade)
- Trade risk, or aggressiveness

Some day traders trade in minimum 1,000-share lots, others stick to 100-, 200-, or 500-share lots, depending on the price of the stock traded and how much capital they want to risk. Obviously, the larger the lot, the more profit (or loss) can be realized from small price changes. An uptick of 10¢ on a stock can earn you $10 with 100 shares or $100 with 1,000 shares. If you trade in 1000-share lots and capture 10¢ 10 times a day and lose 10¢ five times, that's $500 a day, or roughly $10,000 a month.

Sounds easy, but winning two thirds (10 out of 15) of the time requires skill and patience. And don't forget to factor in transaction costs, taxes, and the cost of your trading platform.

Some day traders make 100 or more trades in a day, and may win on 5 or 10 more trades than they lose on. This is a very credible strategy if it can be maintained, but it is a lot of work.

The bottom line is this: it really doesn't take a large number of profitable trades to realize a net of $300 or so a day. Three hundred bucks times about 240 trading days per year yields $72,000 in gross income per year. Not enough to make you rich, but not bad. And many traders have earned considerably more.

The Right Stuff

Now that you have a better sense of the major trading styles, and how they compare, it's time to start thinking about whether you have what it takes to be a trader. Following is a list of attributes most traders hold to be important. Most of these are personal attributes; only a few are possessions. Those who fly airplanes may notice some similarities:

- **Knowledge.** An understanding of the inner workings of the market and securities traded, what makes them move and why.

- **Confidence.** Absolutely critical. Second-guessing will result in missed opportunities, missed gains, and extended losses.

- **Ability to act.** Also critical. You have to be able to pull the trigger, both to get in and get out. No room for the tentative. Also important is the ability to *not* act—see "Patience" below.

- **Willingness to learn.** From your mistakes. When something doesn't work, don't get mad or back away. Figure out *why* it didn't work.

- **Willingness to try.** Nothing ventured, nothing gained. The willingness to try new things opens doors to new information, strategies, and tactics. Also important: what works today may not work tomorrow, as market makers and other traders get familiar with it. Too many people in the market doing the same thing can crowd a trader out. Take measured risks; seek new experiences.

- **Willingness to accept failure and responsibility.** This is huge. The losing day trader who blames someone else or bad luck for his troubles is doomed. Don't dwell on it.

- **Passion.** Like any job, it's best if you love it. If money, lots of numbers, and fast, independent action turn you off, then day trading isn't for you.

- **Patience.** "Willingness to act" and similar adages don't mean shooting from the hip in hopes of hitting a bull's-eye. Pick your targets and aim carefully. If you see a new opportunity, especially on a stock heretofore unheard of, watch it for a while. You probably won't starve in the meantime. It's okay not to have any positions open if the time just isn't right. Sometimes you will have to practice not just patience, but also restraint.

- **Reverse psychology.** A contrarian approach helps. There's a lot of dumb money (and novice day traders) out there. Think—don't always follow the crowd.

- **Facility with numbers.** Only a few forms of trading require advanced math, but nearly all trading requires a comfort level and aptitude for dealing with a lot of numbers and patterns of numbers. This facility isn't easily acquired if you don't have it.

- **Concentration.** Concentration is the "C" word of trading. So much information flies by so fast, especially for the pure dealer trader. It's hard to stay on top of it, avoid distractions, and stay focused.

- **Discipline.** Discipline is the "D" word of trading. In order to trade successfully you must stick to your plans despite the uncertainty and turbulence of the market. Don't hold out for that extra nickel if you know that momentum is slowing on an up move. Get out when you hit your objective. Sell a small loss before it becomes a big loss (which they usually do). Avoid greed, hope, and fear! Keep track of what you do. Write things down. Take a day off when you need to.

- **Skill.** Know your tools and how to use them.

- **Stamina.** Trading is hard work. Watching the numbers go by, interpreting, making decisions, and keeping track of what's going on all require a lot of effort. A good day trader is conditioned for short, intense periods of brain and eye work.

- **Goals.** Sit down and think about what you're trying to achieve. $200 a day? $300? $1,000? Is it for current household income or to add a little return to a retirement or college account? Is this a long-term career choice or a transition? What do you want to achieve by trading?

- **Strategies.** Once the goals are in place, you need to create strategies to achieve them.

- **Rules.** Rules are part of trading strategies. They are personal guidelines you set for yourself through experience and that you follow consistently. For instance, exiting a trade that "goes bad" by a dime in five minutes is a good rule to follow.

- **Agreements.** Like with any other major decisions in life and marriage, share your plans with your partner, co-workers, business associates, and others to avoid any unpleasant surprises.

Use this list to take a personal inventory to help you decide whether to trade, how to trade, and what preparation might be necessary. It isn't essential to score "100 percent," but knowing your limitations and what to work on helps.

Initial Investments

The previous section covered the "personal capital" necessary to become a trader. This section gives an overview of the financial and physical capital required.

A Computer and a Connection

Today's trading is entirely premised on the availability of rea-time information and trading access to the markets. At a minimum you'll need a solid and consistently available Internet connection, with at least one computer serving as your trading workstation.

Broadband access—cable or DSL—is a very good investment and may cost as little as $30 a month above the costs of an ISP and a phone hookup. Some serious traders will spring for the $300 or so per month for a dedicated "T1" line to connect directly with trading platform servers, but it probably isn't necessary for most people.

Trading on a 56K modem works, but can be erratic and slow just when it shouldn't be. Murphy's Law is alive and well when it comes to computers and connections. For that reason, most serious traders have multiple access—redundant ISPs and extra computers, just in case.

Your computer should have a lot of memory, and your monitor should have a good screen resolution; these are cheap today. For all-day serious traders, a large high-resolution flat-panel monitor, for $700 (19-inch) or $900 to $1,100 (21-inch), is a good idea. Some traders are going still bigger, and some split their desktops across multiple monitors.

For traders "on the go" or doing other things, a laptop computer does the trick, but they can be physically demanding to use after a while.

Platform, Information, and Trading Costs

New traders should be prepared to shell out anywhere from a few hundred to a few thousand dollars to get information and trading access. Direct access and high-end information platforms charge monthly fees of up to $250; most waive all or part of these fees with sufficient trading volume. Level II NASDAQ quote access by itself will run $50 to $60 per month, but again, this cost can be waived if you trade actively. New traders face periods of a month to three months to "prove" trading activity, so expect to trade a lot and pay a lot of commissions before these services become cheaper.

Commissions have gotten cheaper and vary greatly, from about $5 per trade up to $19.95 (see Chapters 12 and 13). Most today are in the $10 per transaction range. Many brokers give discounts or offer "per share" commissions to active traders—again, once certain levels are met.

Bottom line: new traders will want to shop carefully and have some resources to spend for the first few months.

Trade Secrets

Whether or not you're a trader, if you're already established as a good brokerage customer, it is often possible to get started for much less. "Good customers" either trade a lot or have large accounts. At Charles Schwab, a $100,000 brokerage account brings "Signature Trader" status, which gives you access to their medium–high end StreetSmart Pro® tool.

Check with your broker—they may well have a product you can get into, and might even be willing to share some of the up-front cost because you're considered a good prospect.

Training Costs

Many new traders opt for some professional training. Self-paced training courses might run from $300 to $500, with full-week classroom courses available for $1,000 or more. Many of the high-end platform providers, like CyberTrader, offer certain training products free for subscribers. The assortment of packages available is too detailed to examine here, but know that they exist as an option—and an up-front cost.

Behind the Screen

Both new and experienced traders should consider attending the annual International Trader's Expo—a trade show dedicated to traders. Presenters demonstrate the latest in trading tools and training packages. Courses and breakout sessions are held on the premises. It's a good way to see what's out there and to acquire startup items—at attractive "show" prices. Shows are usually on the East or West Coast. Check out www.tradersexpo.com for more information.

Initial Stake

How much money does a trader need to get started? SEC regulations require $25,000 in available equity for active, or what they call "pattern," day traders (see Chapter 5) trading with borrowed funds, or *margin* (see Chapter 11). Many brokers and platform providers require more than that, and require a certain amount of overall net worth. Again, shopping around is important—as is being aware of the state of your own financial house. But no matter what the minimum is, it must be risk capital, that is, capital that can be affordably lost.

Alert!

After reading this chapter, many people will likely decide that day trading isn't for them. If trading is right for you, this book will help you to approach it with greater confidence and skill. And even if you decide not to trade, what you learn in this book should help with any form of investing.

The Least You Need to Know

♦ It takes a special combination of skills and personal traits to succeed as a trader.

♦ There are at least four major trading styles, each of which requires different levels of skill and commitment. Those styles include pure dealer, momentum trader, range trader, and pattern trader.

♦ Depending on the situation, some forms of trading may be practical while engaged in another activity, like a full-time job.

♦ A trader's earning potential depends on the frequency, size, and aggressiveness of the trades.

♦ Trading requires significant up-front investments.

Chapter 4

What Day Traders Trade

In This Chapter

- ◆ What you can day trade
- ◆ A comparison of stocks, options, and commodities
- ◆ Trading stock indexes
- ◆ Why we like stocks best

Sure, you could day trade just about anything—baseball cards, Beanie Babies, or even tulip bulbs (as they did back in the 1600s). But as a practical matter, these items might not work for day trading. Available markets, tools, and trading characteristics just don't support trading them.

For the purposes of this book (and most traders), trading refers to securities trading—that is, trading financial instruments representing companies or commodities. Such instruments have the most advanced markets and trading capabilities. This chapter explores the characteristics of good trading instruments and the markets for those instruments.

What Makes It Good to Trade

What makes a security a candidate for day or other short-term trading strategies?

As a pilot's best friends are altitude and airspeed, a day trader's best friends are *action* and *access*. As with flight, one without the other doesn't work. Today's trader needs both action and access to be able to trade profitably.

Action and access can be further broken down into the following elements:

- Liquidity

- Volume

- Movement

- Access to information

- Access to trade

One at a time:

Liquidity

We defined liquidity in Chapter 1 as "the availability of enough buyers and sellers to quickly and easily execute transactions in a market." Liquidity results in fast, reliable executions at predictable prices. In other words, it makes it possible for easy market entry and exit with little friction or delay.

There is no quantitative measure of liquidity. It is driven by a combination of …

- Nature of capitalization (number of shares outstanding).

- Trade volume or activity.

- Breadth of ownership—number of share or contract owners.

- Number of market makers.

- Familiarity of market players with the company or commodity.

Trade Secrets

Greater liquidity usually means smaller spreads, so "pure dealer" trading strategies (as introduced in Chapter 3) must be more active and precise to succeed.

For stocks, it's safe to assume that any stock in an index (Dow Jones averages, S&P 500, S&P 100) is liquid. Futures and options are generally less liquid, although many of the leading financial and commodity futures can be as liquid as the most liquid stocks. Liquidity of stocks may change over time, and liquidity of commodities may change with the seasons.

Volume

Volume is both an indicator and an element of liquidity, but unlike liquidity itself, volume is measurable. A good day trading stock should trade a minimum of 100,000 shares each day. For futures and options, 100 contracts or so passing through the market on any given day should be the minimum. The higher the volume, the better.

Movement

To make trading worthwhile, the security obviously has to move, and because it's a *day* trade, it should move reasonably quickly. That said, *predictable* volatility is better than unpredictable volatility, but volatility alone is a place to start.

Most traders like securities that move at least 5 to 10 times the normal spread in a day. That means that a stock that trades with a penny spread probably should move 10¢ or more in a day. An option or futures contract with a nickel or greater spread should move at least five times that much in a day to make it worthwhile.

More movement is better—a stock moving 50 cents or a dollar in a normal day is attractive from the view of potential profitability. However, such volatility also brings more risk; so it becomes more important to (1) watch closely; (2) use good risk management techniques; and (3) know what you're doing in general.

Trade Secrets _____

Yahoo!Finance (www.finance.yahoo.com) is our favorite quick charting tool for beginners—for stocks anyway. Type a symbol, bring up the quote, then click "Graph" and look at the "1-day" and "5-day" charts. Look for ups and downs—if there is some volatility, it's a good trading candidate. Flat as Kansas? Better look elsewhere.

Access to Information

It's difficult to make an informed trade if you can't get any information about a company or a commodity. If nobody's heard of it, chances are nobody's trading it, and when you want to get out, nobody's going to be buying it. Which leads to …

Easy Access to Trade

The stock, commodity, or option must be easy to trade at a moment's notice in real time. This is what rules out bulbs and Beanies as trading instruments. Essential is immediate access to electronic trading—up-to-the-minute quotes and push-button or mouse-click trading. Equally important is the ability to set fixed-price orders and use other techniques to help time trades and manage risk.

CAUTION

Alert!

Avoid the temptation to trade "penny stocks"—shares of very small, little-known companies usually trading for less than $1 per share. The idea of buying 10,000, 20,000, 50,000 shares is compelling, especially to "flip" them one penny higher for a few hundred dollars. But it isn't that easy—quotes, news information, and trade access are poor, as is liquidity. There are few players in the market, and electronic trading tools are limited.

Trading Stocks

When most people talk about day trading, they are talking about stocks. This book assumes that you have a basic knowledge of what stocks are—shares of ownership in a corporation whose value is determined in a stock market. Most stocks—at least those traded on major exchanges including the NYSE, NASDAQ, and American Stock Exchange (AMEX)—offer the advantages of liquidity, volume, movement, and electronic access to information and trading tools.

The Major Markets

We'll explore the inner workings of the major stock markets starting in Chapters 6 and 7. Both markets provide suitable liquidity, information, and access to trading for the day trader. In fact, both markets provide excellent real-time access to quote and activity data through computerized trading systems. The NASDAQ, being sort of an "open" electronic market, provides still greater visibility to underlying supply and demand through Level II access, which is useful to the serious or "high-performance" day trader. Chapters 6 and 7 explain how both of these markets operate, and how to use their information to your advantage.

Besides NYSE and NASDAQ: Other Markets

Although NYSE and NASDAQ command most of the attention and volume of the stock-trading world, there are other markets. The American Stock Exchange (AMEX, or "annex," as some Wall Streeters refer to it) is much smaller than the NYSE or NASDAQ. Most ordinary AMEX stocks trade at much lower volume levels with less liquidity and less electronic visibility. However, the AMEX has returned to the forefront of trading activity by trading the majority of "exchange traded funds," or ETFs—securitized baskets of stocks usually tied to market sectors or individual countries.

Regional markets also dot the landscape. The Philadelphia, Midwest, Cincinnati, and Pacific stock exchanges are the largest. For the most part, the stocks traded on these exchanges are also traded on the major exchanges, so these markets aren't part of the average day trader's strategy.

Behind the Screen

As brokers and platforms have consolidated, so have the major exchanges. The consolidations have been driven in large part by technology, competition, and the sheer volume of trading. It started in the late 1990s with the merger of NASDAQ—a dealer market—and AMEX—an auction market. Each wanted to capitalize on the capabilities of the other.

In addition, electronic communications networks have started to converge with the major markets. ECNs have emerged as sort of a trader-to-trader "parking lot" market where individual traders—and institutions—can trade with each other. NASDAQ has fully integrated ECNs into its trading mechanisms, and the "Archipelago" ECN has expanded into conventional market activity. Recently it announced the purchase of the Pacific Stock Exchange, and now it has gone mainstream in a much bigger way with the proposed NYSE merger.

Look for continued consolidation and shifts and improvements generally favorable to traders.

Options, Explained

An option is a contract giving the right to buy (or sell) something at or before a specific time at a specific price. This fairly simple idea has evolved into a major trading opportunity for institutional and individual investors.

Options come in three types: equity options, index options, and futures options. For simplicity, the following discussion is based on equity options. It is meant to be an overview only. Interested readers should study other resources before attempting option trading.

What Is an Equity Option?

An equity option contract is a contract to buy (or sell) 100 shares of a stock by a certain time (the expiration) at a certain price (strike price). A Dell JUNE 40 CALL is an option to buy 100 shares of Dell Computer between now and the third Friday in June at $40 per share. A Dell JUNE 30 PUT is an option, with the same expiration date, to *sell* 100 shares at $30 each. Options trade on several exchanges, the largest being the Chicago Board Options Exchange, or CBOE.

Behind the Screen

Most stock symbols bear some kind of relationship to the company name: MSFT for Microsoft, HWP for Hewlett-Packard, SCH for Charles Schwab. But when trading options on stocks, particularly NASDAQ stocks, there's a more complex alphabet at work. Traders should learn and become fluent with it. Option symbols reflect the underlying security, type of option, strike price and date, and exchange on which it trades. So MSQAJ.X becomes the symbol for a Microsoft January 25 call option traded on the CBOE. Most Internet broker and advanced trading platforms have easy links to option chains, that is, the series of options trading for a particular security.

Option Prices

Options are usually traded in strike-price increments of $5 for a price range relevant to the stock price. Higher volume options often have smaller strike-price increments of $2.50. For our Dell example, at the time of this writing put and call options are found at strike prices of $30, $32.50, $35, $37.50, $40, $42.50, and $45. The greater the volatility of the stock, the broader the band of option prices. The time horizon is usually monthly for the "closest in" three months, then quarterly for the next six months. For some stocks you can buy LEAPS (long-term equity appreciation options) with strike dates going out to two years.

A Transfer of Risk

An equity option is really no more than a transfer of risk from the seller to the buyer at a market price. A call writer (seller) gives up the potential for future price gains but gets a premium (the option price) for doing so. Cash is collected, reducing risk by lowering the effective cost of the security. It also gives the stockholder more protection in a downturn.

The call buyer, on the other hand, is taking on additional risk. An option price is inflated to account for the uncertainty of events and movement between the present and the expiration date. Unless the stock moves upward enough to cover this part of the premium, the call buyer will lose his or her investment (the usual outcome, by the way). On the other hand, a call buyer gets leverage—higher returns as a percent—if he or she does pick the right stock, strike price, and time period.

Equity Option Pricing

What should the price of an option be? What makes it move? Researchers have done a lot of mathematical modeling on the subject of option pricing and price behavior, particularly as option valuation questions have emerged in corporate financial reporting. In a nutshell, equity option prices are a function of the following three things:

♦ **Intrinsic value.** If Dell is trading today at $42, it is easy to see that a June 30 call is worth a lot more than a June 45 call. The intrinsic value is pretty simple: $12 for the former, zero for the latter.

♦ **Volatility.** Suppose Dell traded between $30 and $60 during the last six months, and Static Communications Inc., also selling today at $42, moved only between $41 and $45 during the same three-month period. Between a Dell June 40 Call and a Static June 40 Call, which is worth more? Which option appears to have the greatest profit potential given recent stock price history? The answer is … Dell, of course. Normally, the Dell option will sell for more than the Static option because of its volatility. When stocks, or markets in general, get more volatile, volatility premiums—the portion of the price driven by volatility—go higher. So do option prices.

♦ **Time until expiration.** The more time between the date of purchase and the expiration date, the more that can "go right" with this option. A June 40 call will be worth more than a May 40 call.

Trade Secrets

The Black-Scholes option pricing model calculates a theoretical option price based on intrinsic value, volatility, time to expiration, and the in-versus-out of the money factor. Many broker and trading platforms offer calculated Black-Scholes values. It can be a good indicator of what an option price should be.

At, In, or Out of the Money

Option prices behave differently depending on whether they are "in" or "out" of the money. Take Dell at $42. An in-the-money option would be a June 40 call. An out-of-the-money option would be the June 45 call. Why is this important? Because the behavior of intrinsic value, volatility, and time-premium components change. An out-of-the-money call has more leverage, a greater chance to "win big," percentage-wise, and will get a greater time and volatility premium as a result. "Deep" in-the-money call prices will owe more to the intrinsic value, less on volatility and time, and will trade more in lockstep with the underlying stock price.

About Trading Options

It would seem that options would be a pretty good trading vehicle—good volume, volatility, and price movements tied to *something*—in this case, the underlying stock. In practice, there are two downsides to equity option trading and option trading in general. First, the time premium tends to dampen price moves. Second, spreads are usually higher than for stocks, sometimes a quarter to half a point, so more has to "go right" for a trader to overcome the spread. And "pure dealer" spread trading doesn't work as well, because option markets aren't as liquid, meaning that there aren't as many buyers and sellers for a pure dealer to deal with.

A Different Risk Profile

When trading options with a months-away expiration, small gains and losses in the stock will be virtually invisible in the option price. As the expiration date approaches, the price is driven more by intrinsic value, so small underlying stock price changes will have greater effect. Because of this, many traders prefer buying equity options close to their expiration (less than one month) and in-the-money. Both will get you closer to the intrinsic value, which gets you closer to realizing point-for-point the moves of the stock. The advantage to this approach: less capital is risked than if you actually bought the stock, and similarly, some downside protection occurs in that you can only lose the amount invested in the option. There is little exposure to major downside moves in the stock. The disadvantage: some premium, and in most cases, the spread, must be paid.

Some traders prefer to buy out-of-the-money options as a highly leveraged bet on a major price move, either up or down. Such trades are of interest to the momentum trader. Most trades of this nature will lose, but the winners will win big.

Hedging and Risk Management

Traders sometimes use options to hedge other day trades. Traders can buy a put to get downside "disaster protection" on a particular stock while they trade that same stock daily for short upside moves. Similarly, they can buy a call if they are trading for downside stock moves, that is, selling the stock short. Finally, as mentioned above, options represent a way to take a short-term position in a security without risking as much capital up front.

Option Combinations

Finally, combinations of options can reduce risk and increase profit possibilities. Buy or sell a put *and* call at the same or different strike prices. Buy an in-the-money call and sell an out-of-the-money call. Buy a call with a long expiration, sell another with a short one. Option trading books refer to "straddles," "strangles," "spreads," and other option techniques for the more advanced trader.

Index Options

Index options have emerged in recent years as a good leveraged alternative to trading individual stocks or market basket securities. Traders can buy options tied to major stock indexes like the S&P 500, S&P 100, NASDAQ 100, Dow Jones Industrials, and many smaller sector indexes. Index option traders enjoy the same advantages of leverage and risk management inherent in equity options. In addition, the trader gets rid of some news or event risk—that is, the risk of unforeseen events affecting individual companies.

Index options are also commonly used as hedges; that is, traders might sell NASDAQ 100 index calls while trading "long" on individual NASDAQ stocks. Some traders prefer to focus on predicting market movements based on macroeconomic factors and news reports, and so will do most of their trading in index options and other index securities. Index options tend to be more liquid; that is, they have higher volumes and more players in the market, so some short-term "dealer" trades will work. Combination plays are popular on index options. The downsides: bid-ask spread and a relative lack of volatility compared to individual equity options.

Option Wrap-Up

Option trading adds depth to the trader's trading repertoire. Understanding options takes patience and experience. Traders should probably trade options only after getting experience trading stocks and reading up or taking training on the art of option trading. Most broker and trading platforms offer educational resources on options.

> **CAUTION**
>
> **Alert!**
>
> Not all brokers and trading platforms offer good packages for trading options. A broker offering attractive commissions for trading stocks may charge high commissions for trading options, and vice versa. If you decide to do a lot of option trading, shop the trading platform carefully for features and benefits related to options.

Trading Futures

Futures are a bit like equity options: they represent a contract to buy or deliver an amount of something at a specified price at or by a specified time. Like equity options, futures involve the transfer of risk and leverage from a seller to a buyer for a price. The pricing behavior of futures is similar to options, except that in many cases, there is even greater leverage.

Commodity Futures

People are probably most familiar with futures that are tied to agricultural commodities, including corn, wheat, soybeans, pork bellies, and orange juice. Energy futures include oil, gas, and heating oil, while metals futures include gold, silver, platinum, palladium, copper, and others. Producers use these futures to collect some cash and hedge against market downturns, buyers use them to hedge against price upturns or to speculate. For instance, Starbucks buys a lot of coffee futures in order to make sure it can buy coffee beans at fairly stable prices, which allows it to offer a stable price when a customer buys a latte this week, next week, or next month.

Some day traders trade commodity futures and do it quite well. Traders must understand the business—market internals (trends, directions, momentum) and market externals (what the weather is like in Iowa). Most commodity traders are professionals. Traders must be knowledgeable and on top of their game to make money at this, and this isn't where most day traders (or other investors, for that matter) are advised to start.

Behind the Screen
In several places in this book already the case has been made for high-end trading platforms to improve market visibility and trading performance. In futures trading, high-end platforms become a necessity: most e-broker platforms and even advanced hybrids like Schwab's StreetSmart Pro do not offer futures trading capability. As with options, there are many specialized analytics packages and even some customized futures-only trading platforms—more in Chapter 8.

Financial Futures

Financial futures represent underlying instruments and investments such as financial indexes, bonds and interest rates, and foreign exchange (known as "Forex"). Stock index futures are based on baskets of stocks. The S&P 500 and NASDAQ 100 broadly represent the market as a whole. (The NASDAQ 100 represents the top 100 stocks traded on NASDAQ by market capitalization, or total market value.) There are also sector-based indexes for semiconductors, technology, health care, pharmaceuticals, and other major sectors of industry.

Although the news coverage of topics affecting financial markets, foreign exchange, and similar investments is more widely available than that for pork bellies or corn, financial futures trading is equally as complex as commodities trading. It is also subject to unknown and unknowable forces, such as a nation's central bank's intent to stabilize a currency.

About Trading Futures

Trading futures offers considerable leverage, and like options, a different risk profile compared to trading stocks. It has become more mainstream in recent years as commodity prices in particular have entered the news and become more volatile.

In addition, futures markets have become more democratized. More information on more commodities has become available more quickly to more people, and the coming of advanced trading platforms to individuals has made commodity play more feasible. Many investors today incorporate commodities into their overall investing strategy. As with stock index trading, futures trading can involve somewhat less news and event risk exposure because individual companies are not involved. But as oil and gold traders know, geopolitical events and other supply and demand shocks can make markets move quickly.

Commodity and financial futures trading is explored in more detail in Chapter 8.

It Makes Sense to Start with Stocks

So, which sets of securities are best suited to day trading, particularly to the beginning trader? The short answer is ordinary equities—stocks. Stocks have what traders want: liquidity, volume, movement, breadth of ownership, access to information, trading access. Stocks are easier to understand. More professional advice and services are available to the small investor.

Stocks offer greater variety—slow movers, fast movers, highly volatile, less volatile, and so forth. Although there is some news and event risk for particular companies not inherent to broader securities, it is often easier to track the news and news headlines for a specific company. Finally, you can get started trading stocks using more commonly available trading tools, and while they help, you may get away without a specialized high-end direct-access trading platform, at least starting out. This means that up-front investments in training, information, and trading access will be higher for commodities and futures, and may be higher for options.

The Least You Need to Know

- Day traders look for action—liquidity, volume, and price movement—in whatever they trade.

- For most day trading strategies a good stock should trade at least 100,000 shares a day, and move at least four or five times the typical spread—the more the better.

- Not all stocks behave the same way; it is important to study how a particular stock moves in relationship to the market, other stocks, and company news.

- Options have limitations for day trading (high spread, dampened price movement) but can be used to hedge other trades.

- Commodity futures trading requires specialized knowledge and tools beyond normal stock trading.

5

Regulation and Taxes

In This Chapter

- Regulation of day trading—past and present
- New rules for "pattern" traders
- Tax treatment and strategies for traders

On July 26, 1999, a down-on-his-luck Atlanta trader named Mark Barton stormed into the offices of his trading firm and opened fire, then walked into another firm and continued shooting. By the time it was all over, nine people in those offices died, plus his wife and family, and eventually he himself by suicide. A professional chemist, he had largely put his career aside to become an active day trader. During the month before the tragedy, he racked up losses of $105,000, and he seems to have blamed his fellow traders for his troubles. Investigation later revealed that his troubles ran deeper than trading debts, but the damage was done.

The event brought regulatory and securities industry concern about day trading, which had already been brewing, to a crescendo. The question, already being asked by regulators, became top-of-mind: is day trading a good thing? Should it be allowed to continue? Should new regulations be put into place controlling *who* can trade and *how?* Are the services and claims of trading platform and service providers being sufficiently scrutinized?

This chapter explores the evolving regulatory environment in which today's trading is done. Public policy also dictates taxes, so while we're on the subject of external influences on trading, we'll touch on the influence of taxes and tax policy on traders.

The Regulatory View

The Mark Barton event and the general euphoria surrounding the stock market in 1999 and 2000 created considerable concern, both inside and outside the securities industry, about the practice of day trading and its effects. There were a number of calls from knowledgeable insiders, Congress, and the general public to pull in the reins of, or at least take a closer look at, the practice. Investigations into the practices and hazards of trading were launched with considerable fanfare.

The outcome of these investigations was not as precipitous as many expected. Generally, studies showed that existing securities law—if complied with—mitigated most of the hazards of the new age of trading. Some new focus was placed on compliance and some new rules were put in place, which we'll detail soon. Other than these relatively minor actions, little has happened since 2001 to affect individual traders. However, the discussions and context leading up to these new regulations provide an interesting insight into the world of day trading and its oversight by regulatory agencies.

The two major agencies involved in regulating trading are the Securities and Exchange Commission (SEC), a federal agency chartered with the enforcement of the securities laws created by Congress, and the National Association of Securities Dealers (NASD), a private self-regulatory agency representing the securities industry. The NASD works closely with the SEC if for no other reason than to make sure the federal government isn't *forced* to create laws that might not be in the best interests of the securities industry.

Let's begin by taking a closer look at each of these agencies and how they handled the concerns about trading that flared up in the 1999 to 2000 period.

The Securities and Exchange Commission (SEC)

The Securities and Exchange Commission has generally taken a laissez-faire view of trading, but they did take a close look at rules and compliance in the 1999 to 2000 period. Responding to a rise in complaints over a number of issues, including system delays and mishandled orders, then–SEC chairman Arthur Levitt Jr., once a career

Wall Streeter himself, placed responsibility squarely with the trader, not the broker, or for that matter, the regulators.

The (Former) Chairman's View

Levitt believed that traders should recognize that their profession entails certain risks and limitations, of which they must be fully aware and for which they must be fully responsible. He spelled out three primary hazards:

- ◆ Limitations of online trading technology: things can go wrong, and traders should always have a backup option.

- ◆ Risks associated with fast-moving securities: some stocks move up and down so quickly that online broker quotes may no longer be accurate by the time the order is executed.

- ◆ Risks associated with using margin to trade securities: traders should understand the rules, risks, and consequences of trading securities with borrowed funds.

In the end, Levitt and the SEC decided that the best course was to let things stand largely as they were. No changes in federal securities law came forth. The SEC accepted the role of the trader in the markets and stressed that traders should understand the importance of compliance with existing rules.

> **Behind the Screen**
>
> The most recent SEC study of day trading and broker dealer compliance was released in early 2000 and is titled "Report of Examinations of Day Trading Broker-Dealers." It is available online at www.sec.gov/news/ studies/daytrading.htm.

The National Association of Securities Dealers (NASD)

Although federal scrutiny of trading practices resulted in no major new securities laws, the SEC studies and recommendations did take hold with the NASD. As a result of SEC findings and recommendations, the NASD made a few changes, as detailed in the following sections.

New "Pattern" Day Trader Margin Requirements

In September 2001 the NASD, with SEC support, adopted new margin rules for day traders (see Chapter 11 for an explanation of margin). The rules stipulate minimum equity requirements of $25,000 for clients determined to be *pattern day traders*. If such a trader's account falls below this net equity requirement, they are not allowed to day trade with margin until the balance requirements are restored. There are some more details to this rule, readily available from brokers (and their websites), but what is included here is the essence. As your broker may have more stringent rules than those set forth by NASD, traders should become familiar with the rules used by their own broker.

The intentions of this rule are fairly obvious: to limit the influx of inexperienced but insufficiently funded beginners and to cut off existing traders before they lose everything.

The NASD also took steps to improve broker disclosure of the risks of day trading.

Trading Terms

The NASD defines a **pattern day trader** as any margin customer who "... buys then sells or sells short then buys the same security on the same day four or more times in five days." The definition goes on to stipulate that such trades are more than 6 percent of a customer's total trading activity for that same five-day period (thus ruling out swing or position traders who just happen to be very active).

Behind the Screen

Frank Zarb, for chairman of the National Association of Securities Dealers, said about trading in 1999: "Investors must be properly warned about the risks they may be taking in this environment with unprecedented levels of day trading." He was especially concerned about the vulnerability of potential traders with insufficient capital and investment knowledge.

Broker Disclosure

Acting in the interest of industry reputation and in the interests of its member firms, the NASD proposed a set of disclosure guidelines in early 1999 that are largely in place today. These guidelines urge the broker or trading firm to determine whether trading is appropriate for each potential investor and to disclose the risks of trading.

According to the NASD, in determining if trading is appropriate, the firm would have to ...

> weigh essential information about the investor, including his or her financial situation, investment experience, and investment objectives.

Then ...

> As part of the approval process, the proposed rules would require the firm to provide customers with a disclosure statement advising them to consider the following points before engaging in day trading:

- **That day trading can be extremely risky.** Customers should be prepared to lose all of the funds that they use for day trading. They should not fund their day trading activities with retirement savings, student loans, second mortgages, emergency funds, funds set aside for purposes such as education or home ownership, or funds required for current income;

- **That customers be cautious of claims of large profits from day trading.** Customers need to be wary of advertisements or other statements that emphasize the potential for large profits in day trading. Day trading can also lead to large and immediate financial losses;

- **That day trading requires knowledge of securities markets.** Day trading requires in-depth knowledge of the securities markets and trading techniques and strategies. In attempting to profit through day trading, an investor must compete with professional, licensed traders employed by securities firms. An investor should have appropriate experience before engaging in day trading;

- **That day trading requires knowledge of a firm's operations.** An investor should be familiar with a securities firm's business practices, including the operation of the firm's order execution systems, procedures, and should confirm that a firm has adequate systems capacity to permit customers to engage in day trading activities;

- **That day trading may result in large commissions.** Day trading may require an investor to trade his or her account aggressively, and pay commissions on each trade. The total daily commissions that he or she pays on trades may add to losses or significantly reduce earnings;

- **That day trading on margin or short selling may result in losses beyond the initial investment.** When customers day trade with funds borrowed from the firm or someone else, they can lose more than the funds originally placed at risk. A decline in the value of the securities that are purchased may require additional funds be paid to the firm to avoid the forced sale of those securities or other securities in an investor's account. Short selling as part of a day trading strategy also may lead to extraordinary losses, because stock may have to be purchased at a very high price in order to cover a short position.

Most brokerages and trading firms have incorporated this or similar language into their promotional materials and account setup agreements. Readers should examine these cautions and apply them to their own situation as well.

Licensing?

During the critical 1999 to 2000 period, several proposals were floated across the industry requiring prospective traders to be licensed. NASD policy requires most "professional" players in the securities industry to register and even to have some form of license. There were many calls to require "Series 7" retail broker licensing as a means of ensuring that prospective traders know how markets work and understand margin rules. Some who called for such licensing were traders and brokers who undoubtedly felt they were losing money to this new breed of trader.

As of this writing, however, no licensing regulations have been put in place for traders. Individual traders do not need licenses to engage in most types of trading. There are some exceptions: individuals trading on the premises of professional trading firms may be required by those firms to have a license.

> **Behind the Screen**
>
> While studying trading practices, regulators asked trading firms for information regarding client success rates. Some firms boldly responded by asking why they should have to prove that a majority of their clients make money when Merrill Lynch and other full-service firms don't have to meet such a requirement. Point well taken.

> **Behind the Screen**
>
> The NASD showed that it was serious about stricter compliance of existing regulations when, in 2001, it announced a fine of $380,000 against the day trading firm and platform provider All-Tech and its founders. The fines resulted from abuse of margin rules and misrepresentation of trading risks. One of All-Tech's founders is Harvey Houtkin, considered one of the fathers of individual electronic trading.

The Bottom Line for Traders

Today's regulatory climate continues to be characterized by a laissez-faire, let-the-trader-beware attitude. The bottom line: day trading shouldn't be eliminated or restricted, but emphasis should be placed on compliance with already-existing securities law, regulation, and industry standards. Traders should be advised of the risks of trading and using margin, all rules should be followed closely, and brokers should avoid misleading claims when advertising to prospective traders.

Time Out for Taxes

Income taxes may seem like a topic better suited for the end of the book—after one learns how to earn income from trading. But it's never too soon to consider taxes, particularly because knowledge of the tax laws will help you determine the style and level of trading activity most appropriate for your situation.

The basic tax decision anyone considering trading must make is whether they are trading as a *business* or as an *investor*. Trading as a business has certain tax advantages, which can be substantial, but also requires certain patterns of behavior and intent in order to qualify.

The tax code is decidedly ambiguous when it comes to traders and trading, although IRS rulings and bulletins over the past few years have clarified some issues. Traders are advised to study the tax laws carefully and get professional advice; what is shown here is neither legal advice nor necessarily completely up to date.

The Advantages of Trading as a Business

When a trading activity qualifies as a business, it is possible to deduct all related expenses against income, and it may be possible to deduct losses against other current income.

Traders set up as a business can deduct research costs, trading platform costs, and perhaps even expenses related to a portion of a home used for trading. Further, as a business, up-front capital investments (for computers, software, home offices, and so on) can be fully deducted using "Section 179" deduction rules.

Traders not set up as a business can only deduct direct expenses, subject to the Schedule A 2 percent floor on miscellaneous deductions. That is, investors can only deduct expenses that exceed 2 percent of their adjusted gross income. So for traders who earn $100,000 a year doing something besides trading, the first $2,000 of their expenses would not be deductible. In addition, traders not set up as a business generally cannot take a home office deduction.

How to Qualify as a Trading Business

When determining whether someone's trading activity qualifies as a business, the IRS looks at intent and activity and offers the following guidelines:

> A business is generally an activity carried on for a livelihood or in good faith to make a profit ... basically, if your day trading activity goal is to profit from short-term swings in the market rather than from long-term capital appreciation of investments, and is expected to be your primary income for meeting your

personal living expenses, i.e., you do not have a regular job, your trading activity *might be* a business.

The IRS goes on to state the following:

♦ You must seek to profit from daily market movements in the prices of securities and not from dividends, interest, or capital appreciation.

♦ Your activity must be substantial. Recent tax rulings suggest that one should engage at least 16 to 20 hours a week in dedicated research and trading and do at least some trading daily, and perhaps 500 to 1,000 trades per year.

♦ You must carry on the activity with continuity and regularity. No taking weeks, months, or summers off.

Trade Secrets

The IRS website (www.irs.gov) publishes articles and summaries for trading. Do a keyword search on "day trader" to find the relevant information.

Clearly the IRS is trying to separate the full-time trader from the investor who trades a little as a hobby or to enhance investing results.

Schedule C, Schedule D

Trading as a business brings up another tax anomaly. Typically, individual businesses report their revenues and expenses on Schedule C—Profit and Losses from Business. But trading income can be considered as *capital gains*, not "revenue" as such. Why is this important? Because individuals must pay *self-employment tax* (Social Security plus Medicare) on business income, but not on capital gains.

As a result of this anomaly, many traders elect to record their income as capital gains on Schedule D, and their expenses on Schedule C. Schedule C becomes an expense ledger. Most tax advisors recommend including an explanatory letter with a return when this type of reporting is used.

Generally, such reporting allows a maximum of $3,000 in losses to be used to offset other income. One cannot deduct losses and expenses indefinitely against income brought in from other sources.

Trade Secrets

When trying to define a trading activity as a business, it may help to set it up as a legal business—a limited liability corporation (LLC), or a "C" or "S" corporation. This costs money and time to do, the accounting will be more complex, and it may lead to double taxation of certain income amounts. But it may reduce total long-term tax liability and allow favorable treatment of many business and personal expenses. And you can save even more money if you set up such corporations in reduced-tax states like Nevada.

Mark-to-Market Election

The tax plot thickens when we consider another IRS option: the mark-to-market election. A trader already established as a trading business may elect to use mark-to-market accounting. That means that at the end of each year, taxes are paid on gain and loss positions even if the underlying security isn't sold.

This election allows traders to deduct all losses against income, and allows avoidance of tricky "wash sale" rules. Wash-sale rules hold that a loss cannot be taken on a position if the same or substantially similar security is bought back within 30 days.

Electing mark-to-market may mean you pay more taxes each year as ordinary income (instead of longer-term capital gains), but allows more advantageous use of losses. Note that mark-to-market rules have no real effect on the taxation of gains for true day traders. Their positions are sold out each day anyway; there are no year-end "holdings."

With mark-to-market accounting, you must report income on Schedule 4797—Sale of Business Property. You must file this election before the beginning of the tax year, and it is binding until the change is specifically requested from and granted by the IRS.

Alert!

Before making any tax decisions regarding your trading activities, consult with a tax professional to get advice tailored to your specific needs and to make sure you're aware of the latest rulings and interpretations. Some tax advisers specialize in this area of tax law; Traders Accounting (www.tradersaccounting.com) is one such firm.

The Least You Need to Know

◆ In the 1999 to 2000 period, day trading was the subject of considerable legal and regulatory attention.

◆ As a result of scrutiny and subsequent recommendations by the SEC, the NASD raised the minimum equity requirement for "pattern" day traders trading on margin to $25,000.

◆ Brokers are strongly encouraged to fully disclose the risks of trading to all potential customers.

◆ Tax treatment of trading activities is an important consideration for those planning to trade actively. It may make sense to qualify and set up trading activities as a business.

Part 2

A Trip to the Markets

Before you can really understand trading, you need to understand just how the securities markets function. Beyond understanding the markets themselves, it is important to learn the role and function of the critical players—the specialists, market makers, ECNs, and the like.

This section also examines the NYSE, NASDAQ, and commodities futures markets from the perspective of a trader. You'll learn how the various markets are better suited to different trading styles.

Chapter 6

Trading Places: The NYSE

In This Chapter

- ◆ A short history of the NYSE
- ◆ How the NYSE works
- ◆ Pros and cons of the specialist system
- ◆ How listed stock trades work
- ◆ NYSE for traders: present and future

The New York Stock Exchange is the grand old matriarch in today's family of trading markets. More than 210 years old, it represents the "old school" model of stock trading and investing. The NYSE and its regional brethren sponsor trading for more than 2,000 of America's most trusted and generally largest corporations.

Yet the NYSE gets mixed reviews from traders, and more recently, its traditional "specialist" system has come under fire for being outmoded and even, at times, unfair. In response, the NYSE is in the process of making changes, but the jury is still out on the success of the evolution. No matter what your opinion of the NYSE, it's essential that you understand how the NYSE works, how to trade *listed* stocks, and how recent developments may come to affect trading on the NYSE.

> **Trading Terms**
>
> **Listed** stocks are stocks listed and traded on the NYSE and other similar trading floors, like the American Stock Exchange (AMEX). This term is still widely used and contrasted with **unlisted** stocks, or **over-the-counter** stocks once dealt by individual securities dealers over the phone. Most larger unlisted companies now trade on the NASDAQ stock market, or just NASDAQ. Smaller companies still trade "OTC," but most of these aren't on the day trader's radar screen. Traders usually refer to stocks listed on the NYSE simply as "listed" and those on the NASDAQ as "NASDAQ."

A Star Is Born: A Brief History of the NYSE

In 1792, on a street corner in lowest Manhattan now known as the corner of Wall and Broad streets, a group of 24 traders got together to trade a few shares in two emerging companies. It was strictly trading alfresco—no limestone and marble buildings, no majestic columns. No IBM, no Xerox, Procter & Gamble, or Coke. These "name" companies were still 70 years or more away. The companies traded were small, nameless, local companies, long since faded into the mists of time. But it *is* where U.S. trading all got started.

What started in 1792 not only still exists, it continues to thrive. The NYSE grew at pace with capitalist America. New businesses formed, grew, and combined, and the NYSE is the place where they wanted to be. In fact, it was the only real trading place of any significant size and prestige available. Eventually the NYSE grew into today's classical shrine, with the Corinthian columns and carved marble trimmings of a grand statehouse. Somebody once called it the "Big Board," a name that has stuck. On that venerable trading floor the persistent dance of market activity continues through the 6½-hour trading day. Although many active traders set their eyes elsewhere, much of America—and the world—still watch to see what happens on the NYSE each day.

Prior to 2000

The history of the NYSE is remarkable. Through its advances one can see the growing strength of the business engine driving the U.S. economy.

Here are just a few early Big Board milestones:

◆ In 1865, the average daily volume was just above 34 *thousand* shares traded for 141 companies.

- By 1900, the volume had grown to 505,000 per day for 369 companies.

- By 1920, 825,000 shares for 689 companies were changing hands each day.

- Things slowed down after the stock market crash and Great Depression. In 1940 volume dropped to 750,000 per day for 862 companies.

Then things really took off:

- By 1960, the average daily volume rose to 3 *million* on 1,143 issues.

- In 1980, 44 million per day, 1,570 issues.

- In 1990, 157 million per day, 1,774 issues.

- In 1997, 525 million per day, 3,028 issues.

- The then-all-time record was 1.2 *billion* shares, traded on the post–October 19 minicrash day of October 27, 1997.

A few technology breakthroughs helped along the way:

- In 1878, the first telephone was installed.

- In 1978 the first electronic linkage to other exchanges was installed.

- In 1984, orders were electronically routed to the floor using SuperDot.

- In 1995, hundreds of old TV-style monitors were replaced with modern flat-panel displays in what may be the world's largest installation of this technology to date.

- In 1996, floor brokers started using handheld wireless information tools.

Beyond 2000

Like all stock markets, the NYSE handled the unwinding of the late 1990s bubble fairly well. Volume and volatility increased—the dramatic 1.2 billion–share day of 1987 now happens almost every day. The NYSE also made it through the destruction of the nearby World Trade Center, but that event certainly made clear the vulnerability of physical trading floors.

Beyond the threat of terrorist attacks, the bigger issue faced by the NYSE is the competitive threat posed by the faster-growing NASDAQ, the off-market ECNs, and electronic trading. When internal governance problems surfaced, highlighted by the departure of Chairman Richard Grasso and his $200-million-plus annual salary, the NYSE began to look like an outmoded, secretive boys club.

We'll take a closer look at the NYSE's response to the criticism and competitive threat later in this chapter, but first let's get a better sense of how the NYSE operates and how traders work it.

Who Gets Listed on the NYSE

The NYSE is mostly a venue for big, well-capitalized companies in American industry and for some foreign companies. Capitalization for all NYSE listings (price times total shares outstanding) must exceed $100 million. Approximately 2,800 companies are listed on the NYSE.

> **Behind the Screen**
>
> The specifics listing rules for the NYSE are complex because certain criteria may be substituted for others—for instance, cash flow for earnings, or revenue for cash flow. In addition, there are special listing requirements for foreign companies, fund companies, and spin-offs. The detail can be found at the NYSE website: www.nyse.com.

The NYSE has the most stringent listing rules of any market. To list on the NYSE, companies must meet minimum standards including number of shareholders, trading volume, revenues, market capitalization, and earnings/cash flow. For example, most companies must come to market with already $100 million in market capitalization, and must trade at least 100,000 shares per month. A company must post at least $75 million in annual revenues and $10 million in pretax profits during the last three years. The bottom line is that the NYSE seeks established companies.

The NYSE website: www.nyse.com.

How the NYSE Works

The NYSE is an auction market run by auctioneers, or specialists.

An auction market for securities is strikingly like one seen at the state fair or livestock auction market, except that most incoming information comes into and exits the market electronically. Like a conventional auction, the NYSE is a place where buyers and sellers get together to, well, buy and sell. The auctioneer, who is called a specialist, matches up buyers and sellers.

In the past, all sales went to the auction floor; however, the market has evolved and today some sales may occur through ECNs (discussed in the next chapter). As with any auction market, price is determined by supply and demand.

Setting the NYSE Stage

There are 17 trading posts, or stations, spread evenly throughout the NYSE trading floor, which itself is the size of an indoor sports arena. Each trading post is roughly circular and 15 feet across, with open windows surrounding it. Each post trades on average 150 different securities. Some windows are busy, others resemble a bank window on Christmas night. The specialists sit outside the posts in spots designated to them and the stocks they trade. The specialists' clerks sit inside the post window at whisper distance to the specialists. The clerk and specialist see a small flat-panel display cantilevered out from the post, so they can look at a customer (floor broker) and orders simultaneously. A series of large flat-panel displays faces out from the post above the windows, each showing quotes of the securities traded at that window. A series of conduits big enough to carry Alaskan crude rise up from the trading post, carrying myriad data lines to exchange computers.

The Big Apple Auction

In a live auction, the auctioneer has complete control over the auction because he or she sells one item at a time and is in charge of identifying the audience's bids and eventually accepting the highest. Such a scenario wouldn't be practical for a nationwide market with hundreds of buyers and sellers, so the NYSE auctioneer deals with both bids (offers to buy) and offers (to sell) at once.

Trade Secrets

The NYSE gives you some information about the traders, but not as much as does the NASDAQ (through Level II screens; more on them in the next chapter). This gives an edge to NASDAQ for the really serious trader.

Trading Terms

Transparency refers to visibility of the market—the whole market. Just as any chicken buyer would benefit from seeing *all* quotes in the proverbial poultry market, traders want to see all supply and demand, *at* and *away* from the current market price. Whereas away-from-the-market quotes are available on NASDAQ Level II screens, such quotes and orders are generally *not* visible for listed stocks, like those on the NYSE.

Also, whereas bids and offers from the audience are really *quoting* an intention to buy in a live auction, at the NYSE such intentions are declared by actual *orders.* That is, the specialist receives actual orders from the audience of investors and traders. Further, NYSE specialists/auctioneers do more than communicate and announce the sale when it happens—they instead seek to match orders and may come up with a few "chickens" of their own when necessary.

Who Has What Information

Part of the fun of attending an auction is the ability to see what's going on in real time—how the sellers and buyers behave, how many of each there are and how much they bring to market. When trading on the NYSE one doesn't attend in person, and far less information is available for everyone but the specialist.

In the case of the NYSE, the auctioneer sees the traders, and you see the results. You as the trader don't see other traders, except those at the best bid and ask price. You also see the actual trades that are made. The NYSE does disclose the order size, or number of shares available at the current inside, or best, bid and ask price. The rest of the order book is viewable only to the auctioneer. The NYSE is less *transparent* than its NASDAQ equivalent.

The Role of the Specialist

As already noted, an NYSE "auctioneer" is known as a "specialist." Understanding the specialist's work will give some insight to trading the NYSE.

A specialist specializes in making markets for one or more securities. The NYSE awards a specialist—or specialist firm, the privilege of doing so. The specialist spends his or her day matching existing and incoming orders.

Some larger orders come in directly and in person from a member firm's floor broker—a real person on the floor owning a *seat* or representing a seat holder. Most orders, and almost all individual or "retail" orders, show up electronically through SuperDot, the NYSE's electronic routing system. By share volume the split is about half and half; by number of orders, 90 percent or more are routed to the exchange floor electronically.

Trading Terms

A **seat** on the New York Stock Exchange is essentially a membership to this elite trading floor. It represents the right to buy and sell on the floor. In the early days individuals would buy a seat to make money trading securities for themselves. Today, seats are sold mainly to member firms—the big investment banks choosing to play in the market. Many of the people seen milling around on the trading floor work for a seat-holding member firm.

NYSE dominance in the mid-twentieth century made a seat a coveted item, some sold for upwards of $50 million. Thanks largely to increased concerns about competition and exchange integrity as well as the emergence of electronic trading, being a member of the NYSE isn't worth what it used to be: in 2004 a seat sold for under $1 million.

Creating Balance and Liquidity

The specialist is required to provide liquidity for the NYSE's public customers. If there aren't enough buy and sell orders, the specialist must still provide a fair market. This is where specialists perform a vital role: They balance the markets by trading from their firm's own "account"—that is, from its inventory of shares. Specialists can also achieve balance by delaying an opening or halting trading until the proper balance of buyers and sellers is achieved (often at a much different price). However, specialists are usually reluctant to delay trading because it can exacerbate the situation already causing the imbalance.

The Order Book

The specialist takes all orders coming to the floor and sequences them by price in an electronic order book. The specialist then matches buy and sell orders by price.

When a "market" order—that is, one without a specific price—arrives, the specialist matches that order with shares available from firm-price orders on the other side.

The specialist keeps order books for each price level, and quotes the current inside price to the investing world. Recall that the inside, or "at the market," price is the best (highest) bid and best (lowest) ask or offer price. The mechanics will become clearer in a later example (see the section titled "The Trader's View of the NYSE").

One very important NYSE rule holds that specialists must put customer orders in front of their own. That is, at the same price, an incoming order at a specified price must be sequenced *ahead of* any shares offered out of a specialist's inventory or intended for purchase by the specialist (bid side).

The Reward System

Specialists are expected to create fair markets and orderly price executions. In exchange for their efforts, successful specialists can get specialist status for more stocks. Specialists are rewarded financially by the opportunity to pocket the spread—the difference between the bid and ask price. Specialists also can trade for their own firm's accounts, buying low and selling high, within the rules, to make a profit. Such own-account trading, rather like a NASDAQ market maker (see Chapter 7), has become one of the lightning rods for recent unfavorable NYSE press.

Specialist Firms

Specialists usually work for one of many specialist firms—that is, companies that specialize in acting as NYSE specialists. There are many firms engaged in this specialty, including Fleet; LaBranche & Co.; Speer, Leeds & Kellogg; and Van der Moolen. LaBranche and Van der Moolen are independent publicly traded companies; the others are divisions of larger investment industry firms.

Behind the Screen

One of the bigger public embarrassments suffered by the NYSE is the 2004 settlement of five specialist firms caught trading their own accounts ahead of incoming market orders. Collectively, these firms were fined and penalized more than $240 million for violating NYSE rules and federal securities laws.

This event gave the NYSE a black eye from which it is still recovering, and has expanded the call for more electronic trading and more investigation of the specialist system.

Electronic Routing

The NYSE is only in the initial stages of implementing electronic, or automated trading, but it has been routing orders to the exchange floor electronically for years. Today the NYSE uses SuperDot, which stands for Super Designated-Order Turn-around, to route orders to the exchange floor.

The old paper-and-people system is still used for large, institutional, 10,000-share-plus orders represented in person on the floor for negotiation and handling.

Trade Secrets

Seen those old black-and-white photos of the floor of the stock exchange piled ankle-deep with small scraps of paper at the close of a trading day? Every transaction involved multiple pieces of paper—scribbled on, crumpled up, and tossed on the floor before moving on to the next transaction. Today's gallery visitors see a much tidier scene. It's not that today's traders are neater, it's just that more and more trades are paperless.

The Speed of NYSE Trading

Chances are that a day trader's orders are delivered through SuperDot from online or direct-access broker's systems. SuperDot is fast and reliable, both for order entry and trade reporting. Under most conditions entry occurs within seconds after the order is placed. Exceptions may occur on the very busiest days.

It's important to remember, though, that SuperDot is *not* a trading or automated execution system. Trades are still executed by specialists. If there is an *order imbalance*, or if you have placed a limit (fixed-price) order, SuperDot will only get it there; it won't guarantee fast execution—or any execution at all.

Although SuperDot has made the process faster and more reliable, many close-to-the-market "pure dealer" traders think it is far too slow. Studies suggest that round-trip trades—that is, order entry, execution, and reporting—average about 14 seconds. For many of today's fast traders, this is too slow.

Trading Terms

An **order imbalance** is an excess of buy or sell orders that makes it impossible to match up orders evenly. This may cause trading to be temporarily suspended.

Other Exchange Floors

The NYSE isn't the only exchange venue for trading listed stocks. While the majority of volume still goes through the NYSE, regional exchanges, ECNs, and more recently, even the NASDAQ, can trade listed stocks.

Regional Exchanges

Perhaps 5 to 10 percent of trading volume goes through "regional" exchanges—Philadelphia (PHS), Cincinnati (CSE), Pacific (PSE), and Boston (BSE), mainly when the NYSE is busy or there's a better chance for a member firm to obtain a more favorable execution faster or at a better price.

> **Trade Secrets**
>
> Regional exchange orders are displayed on more advanced trading platforms, giving some visibility to major supply or demand away from the inside market price. They are not displayed on standard online brokerage platforms.

ECNs

We'll cover ECNs in more detail in Chapter 7, but we have to mention them now because they do trade some listed stocks, and their role is expanding. An increasing volume of shares, perhaps approaching 20 percent, goes through electronic exchanges known as *electronic communications networks*, or ECNs.

Originally, ECN trading for listed stocks started out as a means for big institutional shareholders to trade directly with each other, often after regular trading hours, avoiding broker and market maker commissions and markups. ECNs have gradually become more available to the average investor seeking fast, automated, electronic executions at the best prices. ECN quotes from the Archipelago "ArcaEx" exchange show on advanced trading platforms, and some information sources show "INET"—the merged "Island" and "Instinet" ECNs—who handle large volumes of listed shares. The use of ECNs and the ECN concept is growing and, with the recently announced Archipelago/NYSE merger, will likely become even more important for listed stocks, as it already has for most NASDAQ stocks (see Chapter 7).

> **Trade Secrets**
>
> In late 2004 the Archipelago ECN announced the purchase of the Pacific Stock Exchange (PSE). In April 2005 it took a much bigger step in announcing the prospective merger with the NYSE. No doubt that Archipelago will become more active in trading listed stocks (and options—a PSE specialty). Eventually, the NYSE auction model may disappear altogether in favor of the electronic exchange model.

The Trader's View of the NYSE

Traders have a variety of trading platforms to choose from, and they vary in the kind of information they show and where they show it on the screen. The more advanced a trading platform is, the more information it will allow you to access. With regards to the NYSE, advanced trading platforms show the inside NYSE quote, plus quotes from other exchanges and a few ECNs. Online broker platforms typically show only the NYSE quote. For more on the difference between "online" and "advanced" platforms, see Chapters 12 and 13.

The following screenshot is from Charles Schwab's CyberTrader Pro, an advanced trading platform that has many of the same features as the same company's Street-Smart Pro hybrid platform. The screenshot shows the trading screen, which in turn shows real-time quotes from the market. This example is for an emerging automotive retailer known as CarMax, ticker symbol KMX. (Specific features of this screen and platform will become clearer in Chapter 13.)

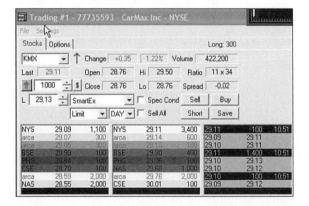

Screenshot from Charles Schwab's CyberTrader Pro trading platform, showing real-time quotes for CarMax (KMX).

© 2005 CyBerCorp Holdings, Inc. All rights reserved. Used with permission.

To the extent that "whole market" (away from inside, or best bid/ask) information is available, it appears in the lower-left-hand third of the window. The NYSE specialist is shown as "NYS" with 1,100 shares on the "bid" side at a price of 29.09 (top of lower left box, the "bid" side). Those may be customer orders, a "buy" indication placed outright by the specialist for his/her own account, or some combination of the two. Likewise, there are 3,400 shares for sale at 29.11 (lower center, the "offer" side). Other orders in the market include a few from the Archipelago ECN (ARCA), the Boston (BSE), Philadelphia (PHS), and Cincinnati (CSE) exchanges.

Most online brokerage platforms show less detail than what you see on the Cyber-Trader Pro screen. Most would only show the "inside" NYSE quote—29.09 × 1,100 shares bid, 29.11 × 3,400 shares offered.

What you will never see (at least, without a very expensive upgrade) when trading NYSE–listed stocks, no matter how advanced your trading platform, are orders away from this inside price. That is, there may be 100,000 more shares bid for purchase at 29.08, right behind the 1,100 share bid at 29.09—but you, as a trader, can't see it. Thus, while some more market detail is available using the advanced platform, market *depth* is largely invisible.

Trading Terms

Size refers to the amount of stock, or number of shares, available at a price. Using the KMX quote as an example, the *price* quote is 29.09 (bid) × 29.11 (ask), the size is 1,100 shares bid × 3,400 offered at those prices.

Executing the Trade

As a trader, let's say you decide to buy 1,000 shares of CarMax (KMX) at the market price. The market as quoted is 29.09 bid, 29.11 offered, with the last trade at 29.11. You enter the order. It is routed electronically by your broker directly to the trading floor by SuperDot. It ends up at the specialist's post along with all other market orders, which will likely be executed at the "ask" price of 29.11. Why? Because the *size* offered (3,400) at the ask price is sufficient to meet your 1,000 share order.

Back to the Order Book

Another trader may also have ordered 1,000 shares of KMX, but specified a limit price of 29.08—that is, the maximum he or she would pay is 29.08. This order isn't executable when it arrives because the current offer is greater—3 cents greater in this case—than the 29.08 limit. So the order goes into the electronic book. (Chapter 10 covers market and such fixed-price limit orders in greater detail.) All limit orders placed at 29.09 will be shown as part of the quote and size at that price (29.09 × 1,100 in this example). But you won't be able to see the limit order at 29.08—at least until the inside bid price drops to that level. (However, you would be able to see if it had been placed through the Archipelago ECN.)

The Other Side of the Trade

Let's say that another investor wants to buy a new BMW and needs to cash out of his KMX stock to pay for the car. He needs $29.11 per share to make his down payment, so he places a limit order at that price for 400 shares. That order shows up as part of the 3,400-shared-sized quote at 29.11. Your market order may or may not buy his shares directly at that price; it is up to the specialist to match your "buy" to what's available. Your order will be matched to someone's shares at 29.11, but you won't know who they belonged to.

When the Specialist Takes the Other Side

The specialist, for a variety of reasons, may also want to sell shares at 29.11, to clear inventory, or to pick up a few cents on shares bought half an hour ago at $29.06. So the specialist puts shares on the offer at 29.11. Perhaps the specialist wants to sell 3,000 shares—you'll never know. The current quote, at a size of 3,400 shares, combines the 400-share limit order already discussed, and invisibly, maybe the specialist's 3,000 shares. You'll never really know.

 Alert! _____

Keep in mind—NYSE rules require customer limit orders to be placed first, so your 1,000-share order would have been filled by the two limit orders on the offer for 400 and 100 shares, then 500 from the specialist.

What Makes the Price Move

So long as there are sufficient market and limit orders at the current bid/ask of 29.09 to 29.11, the price will stay there. As the orders on one side or the other dry up, the bid, ask, and trade price will start to move. Booked limit orders will be picked up at the quoted prices, either by matching limit orders or filling them with incoming market orders. Price movement may trigger other market orders from other customers eager to get in on the action. For an active stock, there is a steady stream of new orders at all prices, at and away from the market.

Alert! _____

It is easy to see how a specialist might manipulate bid and offer size at the current price to drive other traders into and out of the market. Suppose the specialist makes 19,000 more shares available on the offer at 29.11. As a trader, you don't know if this is real supply in the market, or just a specialist "feint" to get other buyers to back away.

Looking ahead, it's easy to see that "size" is at least a fair indicator of direction. While size only shows you shares offered or bid for at the current market (not away from the market—the distinct NASDAQ Level II advantage), it does give some indication of increases and decreases in buying or selling pressure at any given time. If the size on the bid suddenly jumps from 1,100 shares to 19,000, clearly someone is buying the stock. But if there are 19,000 shares bid at 29.08, a penny away from the market, only the specialist sees them. Advantage: specialist.

Is the NYSE Trader-Friendly?

Many traders find some of the NYSE's stocks—and trading patterns—too placid for their taste. Electric utilities and big consumer products firms, for instance, often don't move much during the day. On the other hand, the NYSE does offer traders plenty of liquidity and volume, publicly available company news, and fairly good trading access.

The NYSE's lack of transparency is a long-standing trader concern. Traders cannot see much if any supply and demand away from the current market price, which makes it more difficult to trade.

Lack of transparency, combined with the NYSE's specialist system, also introduces the possibility of abuse. Because only specialists have access to away-from-market information, the specialist has an advantage when it comes to trading stock.

Because of these concerns, many traders sidestep the Big Board, and even listed companies are starting to do so.

The NYSE sees the writing on the walls and is trying to fix some of these shortcomings. New transparency tools are coming onboard, albeit slowly and only for the biggest players. OpenBook is supposed to deliver full market transparency, and a miniversion known as LiquidityQuote (showing large size at price points near, but not at the inside market) is also in the works. Both are targeted towards the institutional trading market, and are extremely expensive and not widely available to individual traders.

Although traders shouldn't necessarily avoid trading NYSE stocks, they should be fully aware of its constraints and keep track of developments in listed stock trading.

The Least You Need to Know

- The NYSE trades listed stocks, primarily of large, well-qualified U.S. and foreign companies.

- The NYSE is an auction market, run by auctioneers known as specialists. Specialists match buy and sell orders.

- Only the specialist can see the complete order book. The "size" quoted at the current bid and ask is the main real clue to supply and demand.

- Size is based on actual limit, or fixed price, customer orders plus stock the specialist is willing to buy or sell from his or her own account.

- Specialists profit mainly from trading for their firm's own account.

- The NYSE specialists system has come under fire for being outmoded and faces competitive threats. Changes, including transparency and electronic trading, are likely in store.

Trading Places: The NASDAQ

In This Chapter

- ◆ What the NASDAQ is and how it works
- ◆ Who market makers are and what they do
- ◆ NASDAQ quote and information systems
- ◆ NASDAQ trading rules and systems
- ◆ What ECNs are and why they're important
- ◆ Anatomy of a NASDAQ trade

In Chapter 6 we examined the inner workings of listed stocks—the NYSE and its specialist system. In this chapter we turn to a newer and more modern stock exchange—the National Association of Securities Dealers and Automated Quotations, or NASDAQ.

Unlike the NYSE, the NASDAQ has only been around for a few decades, and it does not have a physical floor. What it lacks in age and atmosphere, however, it more than makes up for in volume. On a typical day, the NASDAQ trades 50 percent more volume than the NYSE. As an electronic dealer market, it is considered by most traders to be more liquid, more transparent, faster, and fairer than the NYSE. In this chapter we examine the NASDAQ and the closely related Electronic Communications Network, or ECN, markets.

The NASDAQ

The NASDAQ is essentially a giant computer-based system linking securities dealers ("market makers") together in a high-speed, state-of-the-art network. The central hub is in Rockville, Maryland, but there is little to see there. The real action is on the screen of any computer connected to the NASDAQ computer network.

In Chapter 6 we described the NYSE as an auction market. Buyers and sellers send orders to specialists, who match them together to execute trades. The orders determine the price, with a little help at times from the specialists. Whatever price matches the most orders is the price of the day. NASDAQ is different.

A Dealer Market

NASDAQ is known as a dealer, or negotiated, market. It is like an open-air market with lots of buyers and sellers, but no auctioneer. All buyers and sellers of a particular commodity post their bids (what they'll pay you), and asks or offers (what they'll charge you) as prices. The buyer paying the best (highest) price will get his or her order filled by sellers first. Likewise, the seller offering the best (lowest) price will attract the most buyer attention. In such a physical marketplace, a bunch of dealers might be gathered in a small space yelling out or displaying their prices to other dealers and to individual buyers and sellers. Both dealers and individuals would buy and sell to meet their needs.

Enter the Computer

Such an open-air market doesn't work so well on a national (or international) scale because of the sheer number of traders and securities involved. Until the 1970s, trading on "over-the-counter" securities was limited to smaller companies, usually with a handful of dealers trading them. The market—that is, the aggregate of buy and sell orders and their prices—consisted of a few dealers linked by phone. The market price could be obtained with a simple phone call or two to a market maker in a stock. The National Association of Securities Dealers (NASD) and its member dealers saw a great opportunity to expand this trading approach by computerizing it, which they did with foresight in 1971. It was, at the time, one of the "cutting-edge" applications of computer network technology, and it remains so today.

Instead of yelling out quotes on a market floor, dealers' and market makers' bids and offers are placed electronically into the computer network and displayed in real time on computer screens. The equivalent of the NYSE's order book is available and accessible online to all dealers in a stock. Dealers can see each other's bid and offer prices, and can post their own. The big difference: dealers and individuals with Level II access (more on that in a minute) to the NASDAQ computer network can see *all* bid and offer quotes, at and away from the market.

What Trades on NASDAQ

NASDAQ trades about 3,300 "NASDAQ-listed" stocks, which meet certain but less stringent listing requirements compared with the NYSE. These stocks are listed on the NMS (National Market System, or NASDAQ National Market), with about 600 of the 3,300 stocks listed separately in a small-cap (less than $50 million total capitalization) group known as the NASDAQ SmallCap Market for market capitalization under $100 million. Other "OTC"—or over-the-counter—stocks still trade under NASD auspices but don't trade on the NMS electronic market.

The NASDAQ trades about 1.8 billion shares per day—versus about 1.6 billion on the NYSE—in about two million transactions per day.

Behind the Screen
The NASDAQ advertises itself as being "faster-better-cheaper" than the NYSE or other listed exchanges. It claims to have faster executions at better prices at lower cost. Today NASDAQ faces competition mainly from the ECNs, which are discussed later in this chapter.

Market Makers

Market makers are the "dealers" who make the NASDAQ market work. They buy and sell stocks in the open NASDAQ market, providing liquidity and a conduit for their customers to buy and sell shares.

Market makers are actually securities firms that register to buy and sell a particular security. They follow NASDAQ rules to make a market. Large investment banks such as Goldman, Sachs & Co., and Morgan Stanley are market makers, but many smaller firms and securities wholesalers can also be market makers. There are about 2,500 market maker firms, large and small, give or take a few. Specially assigned employees in these firms actually do the job of making markets. Think of them as professional traders; in most cases, they trade the markets in much the same manner as individual day traders.

Market makers sit in the offices of their firms, armed with an array of computer screens and telephones. Traders will never know or see a market maker, but they will see his bid and ask quotes—his intentions—in the NASDAQ computerized market. A single human market maker may operate in one, a handful, or as many as 20 or 30 stocks at a time.

There are 60 or so prominent market maker firms trading the roughly 6,000 NASDAQ securities. Some lower-volume or "thinly traded" securities may only have three or four market makers. Other big names—Dell, Microsoft, Intel—may have 40 or more firms making a market in the stock.

Trade Secrets

NASDAQ disseminates important information about its inner workings through its websites. The primary website, NASDAQ.com (www.nasdaq.com), provides overview information about NASDAQ and current market activity. The NASDAQ–Trader site (www.nasdaqtrader.com) posts rules, lists, and trading information for market makers, but the information is useful for individual day traders, too. For example, traders can learn about NASDAQ system enhancements and download the list of current market makers from this site.

What Do Market Makers Do?

Market makers trade with the public, large institutions, and other market makers throughout the day. As dealers they serve two important masters. First, they execute buy and sell orders for their firms' customers—both individuals and institutional clients. Second, they try to make money for their firm by capturing spreads and trading swings in the market.

According to NASDAQ rules, market makers must create a "two-sided market," that is, always post a bid quote (or price) they will buy at, and an ask (or offer) quote they will sell at. Those quotes, however, do not have to be at or anywhere near the best prices available—the inside market.

Viewing Market Maker Action

Market makers create markets by posting their bid and ask prices into the NASDAQ computer system. They look at their own customers' orders as well as the rest of the market in deciding what price to post at. Market makers essentially bargain with each other, and the public, through their postings.

Traders can view these bid/ask postings through the NASDAQ *Level II screen.* Each posting has the market maker's four letter code, a price, and the number of shares that are represented by the bid or offer. It is often possible to figure out a market maker's "hand"—her intentions—by watching the sequence of bids and offers placed on NASDAQ. Chapters 15 and 18 cover this idea in greater detail.

Trading Terms

The **Level II screen** is the real-time screen showing the whole NASDAQ market—all posted bids and offers. NASDAQ also has "Level I" and "Level III" screens. Level I screens give only the inside quote—the best bid and ask price, with total size. Individual dealer quotes aren't shown. Level III screens are only available to registered market makers. In addition to viewing quotes, users have the capability to post them.

Trade Secrets

At one time, market makers made lots of easy money trading for their own accounts by capturing the spread, or markup, between bid and offer prices. An eighth or a quarter of a point on several million shares a day adds up quickly. This practice came under heavy criticism in the mid-1990s. Market makers were accused of colluding to keep spreads artificially high. Sometimes, customer orders between the spread (say, one sixteenth better than the current bid price) simply weren't posted! The SEC investigated, and since 1997 the limit order protection rule now forbids that practice. But the advent of decimal trading in 2000, where spreads on most stocks are only a penny or two, effectively curtailed these practices and made prices fairer for all.

A Dealer Market (Almost) Never Stops

Unlike the NYSE, where the specialist can stop trading if there is an imbalance of orders (more buys than sells, and vice versa), no NASDAQ market maker can stop trading. Even a flood of orders won't stop the market. A particular market maker may not choose to trade at or close to the current price, or inside price, but another market maker more determined to make a trade will. By definition, there is always an inside, or best bid and ask price, and so there is always a market.

Until recently, the NASDAQ would only shut down trading in an individual security in extraordinary circumstances, such as a major corporate announcement. Specific news from the company was required. On March 26, 1999, the NASD (NASDAQ's governing body) implemented a new rule allowing the NASDAQ to shut down trading in response to market news or rumors (in contrast to news submitted by the company). But it stopped short of allowing trading to be stopped due to volatility or severe price movements alone. The result? In most conditions of extreme volatility or price movement, market makers are left to play it out, often with drastic one-day effects on stock prices.

The Nuts and Bolts of NASDAQ

At the risk of oversimplification, NASDAQ consists of a quote management system and an order routing system. The quote management system provides what boils down to an electronic bulletin board for market makers to post quotes and for all market participants to view them. The order routing system, known as "Super-Montage," handles incoming orders from brokers and institutions and also enables market makers to trade with each other.

The NASDAQ Quote System

The best way to grasp the nature of NASDAQ quotes for a stock is to look at a computerized quote board through a Level II screen. The accompanying figure shows a trading screen, including a Level II display, for Starbucks Inc. (symbol SBUX).

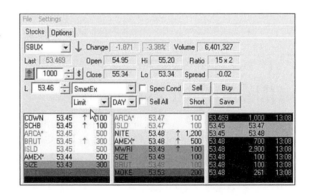

NASDAQ Level II screen showing quotes for Starbucks Corporation, as viewed on Charles Schwab's Cyber-Trader Pro trading platform.

© 2005 CyBerCorp Holdings, Inc. All rights reserved. Used with permission.

This all-important trading screen will be explained in greater detail in Chapter 13. For now all you need to do is focus on the bid and ask quotes, which appear in the lower-left and center portions of the screen. The lower-left portion represents the bid quotes; the lower-center portion represents the ask, or offer, quotes.

The Inside and Outside Market

The inside bid, or price available to buy shares, is 53.45, while the inside offer, or price available to sell, is 53.47. There are five players bidding 53.45. The top two are market makers. "COWN" is S. G. Cowen & Co, while "SCHB" is UBS Capital Markets. ARCA, BRUT, and ISLD are the Archipelago, Brut, and Island ECNs respectively. You'll learn more about ECNs later in this chapter; they aren't market makers, but bids or offers not matched within their own networks appear as available quotes on NASDAQ.

Note the size of the bids. The COWN and SCHB quote is only for 100 shares, while the three ECN quotes have bigger sizes. Will COWN limit their purchase to 100 shares? Maybe, maybe not—but this is the maximum they are committed to for automated trading purposes. More on that below, under the topic of the Small Order Execution System, or SOES.

Away from the inside quote sits AMEX at 53.44. This is a quote from the American Stock Exchange (where some floor trading occurs for NASDAQ stocks) and "SIZE" at 53.43. The appearance of "SIZE" among the market makers and ECNs is a relatively new thing. Recently NASDAQ implemented a series of changes allowing market makers to post anonymous quotes, and these quotes appear in the market as quotes from "SIZE."

On the offer side, the two ECNs hold the best offer at 53.47, followed by NITE (Knight Equity Markets), a big securities wholesaler, and AMEX. MWRI (McAdams, Wright, Ragen), SIZE, and the ECN Brut are 2¢ off the inside.

Note that this screenshot falls far short of showing the entire market, which goes several dozen quotes deeper away from the market. Quotes farther outside become visible when the screen is expanded.

Trading Terms

The four letter code identifying market makers is known as an MPID, or Market Participant Identification. There are thousands of them, and the NASDAQ now allows market maker firms to employ different MPIDs from different trading desks within the same firm. See Appendix B for a list of MPIDs from the larger players.

Trade Secrets _____

It may be getting a little ahead of the story, but it's worth noting the small arrows between the quote and size on the accompanying figure. The two up arrows on the bid for COWN and SCHB mean that these two market makers have just adjusted their quotes *toward* the inside, or best price, in the market. From such well-known and important market makers, such a move is usually bullish. If there were "down" arrows" (and there usually are, somewhere on the board) they would represent quotes that have moved away from the inside market.

What Do Market Makers Quote?

Unlike the NYSE, the postings on the NASDAQ are quotes rather than firm orders.

Market makers don't post all the shares they have available. They post just what they want to display in the market at that given time. As orders show up in the market, they may buy or sell far more shares than they indicate in their bid or offer quotes. And just because a market maker fills one order doesn't mean the quote will disappear; the quote is just that, not specific shares that, once gone, cause the quote to disappear. Interestingly, market makers may also buy or sell fewer shares than what they post on the NASDAQ—except for orders arriving through SOES (again, more on this in a minute). The only real requirement outside of honoring SOES is that a market maker must post at least one bid and one offer *somewhere* in the market.

NASDAQ Trading Systems

The full explanation of the systems employed by the NASDAQ to display and route orders is beyond the scope of this book. Driven in part by competition from ECNs and other trading venues, the NASDAQ strives constantly to keep its systems close to the state of the art, and to enable its dealer participants to prosper while giving the best executions and service to individual traders and institutions. As a result, NASDAQ systems are quite sophisticated and ever-changing. Most recent changes bring the NASDAQ beyond its role as an electronic quote board and closer to being a fully automated electronic market, similar to a giant ECN.

There are two NASDAQ features to introduce here: SuperMontage and SOES. Those wishing to keep up with the details and changes should become familiar with the NASDAQTrader website tool designed primarily for market makers and active traders at www.nasdaqtrader.com.

SuperMontage

SuperMontage is the NASDAQ's integrated order display and execution system. It enables market makers to post quotes, and it provides data feeds for quote displays. SuperMontage routes incoming market orders automatically to market makers and posts large orders into the market for market makers to review and act upon.

Execution Strategies

Market makers and the public can use SuperMontage to set automated execution rules, enabling them to execute a trading strategy automatically. For example, traders can preference specific market makers from advanced trading platforms, and Super-Montage manages the resulting order routing. SuperMontage also enables market makers to route orders and trade directly with each other.

TotalView

A recent enhancement to SuperMontage, TotalView allows market makers to quote anonymously (using the previously mentioned "SIZE" MPID) and allows market participants to more clearly see multiple quotes placed by single market makers. Refer back to the screenshot of the Starbucks posting earlier in this chapter. In that example, you can see that COWN has a bid for 100 shares at the inside market; you could use TotalView to group all of COWN's bids together at the top, giving you a clearer indication of COWN's total buy interest and liquidity.

Such features are probably beyond the need of new traders, but they are offered as an example of how the NASDAQ works to perfect trading and display capability.

SOES

SOES stands for Small Order Execution System, and it enables individual traders of modest size to trade directly and automatically with market makers. A market order placed for 1,000 shares or less will automatically "SOES" the lead market maker at the best, or inside, price. Most individual online trades for 1,000 shares or less are filled through SOES automatically and invisibly through a broker's software. SOES orders are usually filled in seconds. Very few take longer than 60 seconds.

Why SOES?

SOES—installed in the early 1980s—became important after the 1987 crash. At that time market makers had to be contacted, often by phone, to arrange a trade. When the market began to sink on that fateful October day, panicked market makers simply backed away from trade requests and refused to answer their phones. After the crash, the NASDAQ required market makers to honor all SOES orders with a few exceptions made clear in the rules, thereby providing customers with greater liquidity.

SOES rules

There are some important SOES rules for traders:

- ◆ SOES trades can only be executed in lots up to 1,000 shares. On some smaller stocks, this limit may be set lower.

- ◆ The same trader cannot trade on the same side (that is, the buy side or the sell side) of the same stock within a five-minute period. Otherwise, a trader could swamp the market with orders and take liquidity away from other traders.

- ◆ SOES is for customers only—no dealers or member-firm registered representatives (brokers) can use the system.

- ◆ SOES is mandatory—a market maker can't back away from an advertised price.

Behind the Screen

Ever hear of an "SOES bandit"? SOES gave rise to the first wave of new day traders, the so-called SOES bandits. SOES bandits took advantage of the almost instantaneous direct execution power to fast-trade with market makers. Often the strategy was simple: in a rapidly moving market, the SOES bandit simply picked up shares quoted to the market in outdated (by seconds, sometimes) market maker quotes. They would buy low from one market maker and sell high to another before they could react. The focused day trader could beat many a market maker, who often was watching more than one stock at a time. It still works but is much harder, with today's penny spreads and faster and more savvy market makers. For example, market makers can diffuse SOES by posting bids for only 100 shares, reducing their exposure to such automatic executions.

ECN: A New Trading Network

ECNs, or electronic communications networks, are an alternative trading path allowing market participants to trade directly with each other or to place orders directly into the market. In some cases, like Archipelago's "ArcaEx," ECNs have evolved into full-blown exchanges of their own. With modern technology and the attractive prospect of bypassing the market marker "middlemen," they are a growing force in today's markets and trading.

A Brief History of ECNs

ECNs were originally set up as closed trading systems for institutional traders and their brokers. They also provided a means for institutions to trade "after hours." For instance, Instinet, started by Reuters in 1969, provided a liquid after-hours market for big institutions.

Because of the buying power of these large institutions, they often got better prices than ordinary retail customers, in part by avoiding payment of dealer markups, or spreads.

Whereas in the past ECNs were usually limited to an exclusive few customers—big financial institutions, mutual funds, big traders—many more individuals have access to them through today's trading platforms. As a result, the volume of stocks traded on ECNs has risen dramatically, from 10 percent to 35 percent or more of NASDAQ share volume. Little wonder both the NYSE and NASDAQ consider ECNs to be a competitive threat.

ECN Trading

ECN customers can place orders to buy and sell from advanced trading platforms linked into the network. Anyone else on the network can see the order and fill it, or contact the originator to negotiate. Some networks match orders electronically, and some pass orders to the regular NASDAQ market if no fill is found inside its own network. You can see orders from these ECNs in the NASDAQ market Level II if you know their Market Participation ID; for instance, "INET" is the ID for Instinet, "ARCA" is the ID for Archipelago.

ECNs are used most to trade NASDAQ stocks, but INET, and increasingly ARCA, trade listed (NYSE) stocks, too.

Why ECNs Are Popular

ECN popularity stems from three factors: anonymity, automation, and economy:

- **Anonymity.** Most NASDAQ quotes indicate the market maker in full view of the marketplace and Level II public. However, the identity of ECN buyers and sellers isn't shown. Big traders and market makers actually use ECNs to hide their identity and motives. Recently NASDAQ began allowing traders to use the anonymous "SIZE" MPID to eliminate the competitive edge anonymous trading gave to ECNs.

- **Automation.** Orders matching in price and size are executed automatically, and market players can "self serve" by buying and selling shares against quotes posted on the board. There is no human intervention.

- **Economy.** ECNs are also economical: unlike when trading on the NASDAQ, customers don't pay the market maker's spread. Instead, they pay only a tiny per-share handling fee. On the downside: the smaller number of traders can mean less liquidity, especially for smaller stocks. In addition, order execution is not mandatory as it is for SOES. On an ECN, an order may never be executed.

Here's a description of some of the most popular ECNs in operation today:

- INET is the merger of the Island and Instinet ECNs, still referred to as "Instinet." Some NASDAQ quotes from Instinet are still placed under MPID "ISLD" and "CINN". INET is one of the largest and most liquid ECNs.

- ARCA is Archipelago, or ArcaEX, a growing and sophisticated combination of ECN and major market. An alliance with and recent purchase of the Pacific Stock Exchange gives this ECN greater resemblance to a full stock exchange. ARCA is the biggest player in listed, or NYSE, stocks.

- BTRD, Bloomberg Tradebook, is used mainly by institutional traders, brokers, and market makers.

- BRUT, Brass Utility LLC (BRUT), is owned and operated by a series of prominent Wall Street firms.

- RediBook (Speer, Leeds & Kellogg, REDI)

- ATTN is the Attain ECN, brought to market by All-Tech Investment Group, and provides trading access to individuals and some institutions and hedge funds.

Behind the Screen

Are we ready for 24-hour stock trading? No, says the NASDAQ, which has investigated it. No, says Archipelago (ArcaEx), feeling that the demand just isn't there right now. But in a recent change of direction, NYSE chairman John Thain indicated that opening the NYSE an hour or hour-and-a-half earlier was something that "they were looking into." In the stock exchange business, gaining competitive edge is what it's all about.

Anatomy of a Trade

Let's say you decide it's time to buy 500 shares of Starbucks.

First, you check the quote. The last trade was at 53.469 with an inside bid of 53.45 and an offer of 53.47. There are several bidders and offer quotes at the inside, and there are more away from the market. You launch the order as an ordinary market order (as opposed to a limit, or fixed price, order) through your firm. That order hits the NASDAQ computer system and is routed according to its size and size availability, per SOES rules. If there is enough size available, the order executes automatically and brings 500 shares at 53.47. Otherwise, the order is shown through SuperMontage and is picked up by another market maker, possibly at a price above 53.47.

Once the order is filled, the market maker has the option to maintain the offer price or take it down and post a new one. The execution is reported back to your broker and is updated in your account.

Fixed Price, or Limit Order

Suppose you want to buy for a better price, say 53.45. You enter the order as a limit order. If trading through an ordinary broker, your firm enters your order as a quote on the bid side. If your firm isn't a market maker, your order will be entered by a wholesaler like Knight Equity Markets (NITE) or through an ECN. If you trade using a direct access platform, the order is most likely entered through an ECN. The order won't fill until 53.45 becomes the inside price. At that point, it will be filled by the next arriving "market" sell order, or it may get picked up by a market maker. In either case you'll get 53.45 because that was the limit price you set.

Normally, you don't know or care who filled the order. But high-performance trading systems allow you to "preference" market makers or route orders to an ECN (usually Island) first, then automatically to NASDAQ and its market makers if an ECN fill is unavailable.

The Least You Need to Know

- The NASDAQ is a virtual market: it is computer-based and has no trading floor.

- The NASDAQ market consists of quotes from market makers—dealers—and some individuals through ECNs. The NASDAQ is fully transparent, meaning that all quotes can be seen on the Level II screen.

- NASDAQ trading systems route orders to market makers and work towards best-price execution. The Small Order Execution System (SOES) provides automatic execution with a market maker for 1,000 shares or less.

- Institutional and individual traders are able to bypass the dealer market by using electronic communications networks (ECNs). Orders not filled within the ECN are shown on the NASDAQ.

- ECNs are becoming more important as more individual traders seek direct access to markets.

Chapter **8**

Trading Places: Commodities and Futures

In This Chapter

◆ The case for trading commodities

◆ What futures are and where they trade

◆ The use of margin and leverage in futures trading

◆ Common futures trading tools and strategies

Today's more-level playing field and high-performance access tools have enabled many more players to access the stock markets. The resulting increase in the number of players, combined with an increase in trading activity, has led to a bit of overcrowding—too many players and too much competition in the game. In response, some traders have started to look for other securities to trade, and have found one such outlet in the commodities and futures markets. The increased rate of corporate scandals and "blowups" has also driven some players away from the market and into the futures and commodities. In addition, as the world industrializes, there has been an upsurge of demand—and interest—in commodities. Playing these three factors together, the commodities and futures markets have drawn a steady increase in the number of traders.

Commodities and futures trading has been around for as long as stock trading, perhaps longer. Yet these markets have typically appealed only to commodities producers and specialized professional investors focused on these markets. Contract size, leverage, and a relatively opaque trading environment have all restricted the number of Main Street investors and traders in these markets. Today, with visibility and popularity on the rise, public trust in corporations on the decline, and trading tools and technology becoming more available and user friendly, more traders are stepping in.

There are many similarities between stock and commodities trading, but there are also many important differences. This chapter gives a short overview of commodities and futures trading, and describes the main differences as compared to stock trading.

Why Trade Commodities and Futures?

Where there is volume, liquidity, and price movement, there is potential for profit. Modern futures markets have all three elements in abundance. Commodities traders recognize several advantages to trading futures markets in addition to, or instead of, equity markets.

Some of the primary advantages include leverage, a more defined information space, and certain tax benefits.

Leverage

Because of the large size and high value of futures contracts, commodities have always enjoyed high leverage trading—that is, small amounts of investor capital can control large amounts of a commodity.

Leverage comes from the use of margin. Commodities and futures margin requirements differ from those for trading stocks, effectively allowing traders to borrow more. The specifics of commodities margins are covered later in this chapter; stock margin trading is covered in Chapter 11.

More Defined Information Space

Futures can represent tangible commodities like oil, gold, grain, orange juice, or real but less-tangible things like currency exchange rates or equity indexes. In many cases, the information that drives price movements is more transparent and available to the futures trader than the equities trader. There tend to be fewer "surprises." Naturally, this depends somewhat on what is being traded—a trader heavily invested in orange juice futures would be surprised by an unexpected Florida storm.

Tax Benefits

While short-term equity trades are taxed using short-term tax rates, many futures are taxed at an advantaged rate. Futures based on commodities and security indexes comprising more than nine securities are taxed at a composite rate made up of 60 percent of the long-term capital gains tax rate and 40 percent of the applicable short-term tax rate. Since the long-term capital gains tax rate is capped at 15 percent (as of 2004), this presents a nice tax advantage. Qualifying futures are called "Section 1256" contracts. It should be noted that single security futures are taxed at the normal short-term capital gains rate.

> **Behind the Screen**
>
> "Gold will never preannounce bad earnings" and "crude oil does not suffer from accounting scandals" are popular sayings among commodities traders. In other words, trading in commodities eliminates a lot of "news risk"—the need to worry about corporate misconduct or mismanagement—a refreshing idea for many equity traders tired of corporate scandals.

As with stock trading, futures and commodities traders can elect to set up their trading as a business for tax purposes. They may be able to choose between reporting either on Schedule D (Capital Gains and Losses) or as ordinary capital gains/losses on IRS Form 4797 Part II (Sales of Business Property) if mark-to-market accounting is elected. The details are beyond the scope of this book and are material for a tax professional, but many traders play these two tax features to their benefit.

What Is a "Future"?

Futures are contracts for delivery of either a physical commodity or a financial value at a specified later date. Commodities futures provide for physical delivery of an actual commodity (wheat, oil, orange juice, for example) as a means of settlement. Financial futures (currency, stock index futures) are always settled in cash. Although commodity futures call for physical delivery, most are settled in cash by closing out before the settlement date.

The term "future" comes from the fact that each contract specifies some *future* date by which the settlement needs to take place. This is in contrast to the "spot price" of a commodity, which is the price at which a particular commodity is traded at currently on the open market.

Futures Exchanges

Most futures trade on one of the three primary futures exchanges: the Chicago Board of Trade (CBOT), the Chicago Mercantile Exchange (CME), or the New York Mercantile Exchange (NYMEX). The CBOT handles mainly agricultural commodities, the CME deals mainly in financial futures (stock and stock index futures, currencies), and the NYMEX deals mainly in metals and energy.

All three futures exchanges have a live trading floor but operate mainly as a dealer market (like the NASDAQ). Dealers and dealer representatives, known as floor traders, line a trading pit, and the market is the best bid and ask price quoted at the moment. Although there is no individual specialist, futures are bought and sold through the exchange—not by buyers and sellers trading with and delivering to each other. Some exchanges, like the Chicago Mercantile Exchange (CME) are moving towards electronic trading away from a physical pit or floor, but this is still evolving.

Kinds of Futures

The following table shows the most common futures and some key details about each. Note how the table is divided into seven major classes: Metals, Financials, Stock Indexes, Grains, "Softs" (like coffee, sugar, and lumber), Meats, and Energies.

Price Drivers

The column to the right of the symbols shows the primary price driver for the future. Traders must know what factors drive the price for any commodity they trade. Sometimes prices are driven by an underlying basket of securities, as in the case of stock index futures, but more often, they are driven by economic events, weather, and other signs of world supply-and-demand fluctuation. Traders must be keenly aware of the factors that influence long- and short-term futures price movement.

CHARACTERISTICS OF MAJOR COMMODITIES
March, 2005

	SYMBOL (note 1)	MARKET AND PRICE DRIVERS	CONTRACT SIZE	INITIAL MARGIN/ MARGIN MAINTANENCE (note 2)	APPROX. LEVERAGE RATIO (note 3)	LIQUIDITY	VOLATILITY	SUITABLE FOR DAY TRADING?
METALS								
Gold	GC *	inverse relationship to dollar	100 oz	$2025 / $1500	21	high	high	yes
Silver	SI *	gold movement & industrial demand	5000 oz	$2700 / $2000	13	low	high	no
Platinum	PL	Automotive / jewlery demand	50 oz	$2700 / $2000	16	low	med	no
Palladium	PA	Automotive demand	100 oz	$2700 / $2000	7	low	med	no
Copper	HG	Industral demand / economic growth	25,000 lbs.	$2700 / $2000	14	high	high	yes
FINANCIALS								
30 yr Treasury Bonds	US	inverse of int rates / economic growth	one 100,000 bond	$1700 / $1250	59	high	low	yes
Dollar Index	USD	US vs. world growth	1000 x $ Index	$2000 / $1500	44	high	high	yes
Japanese Yen	JY	trade deficit, economic growth	12,500,000 Y	$1800 / $1800	53	high	med	yes
Swiss Franc	SF	trade deficit, economic growth	125,000	$2000 / $1500	50	med	med	no
Canadian dollar	CD	trade deficit, economic growth	100,000	$1215 / $900	66	med	med	no
Euro	EC	trade deficit, economic growth	125,000	$2000 / $2000	81	high	high	yes
STOCK INDEXES								
Dow Jones mini	ZD	proxy for the DOW	5 x dow index	$2500 / $2000	22	high	med	yes
E-Nasdaq100 mini	NQ	proxy for the Nasdaq 100	20 x Nasdaq100	$3750 / $3000	7	high	high	yes
S&P 500 mini	ES	proxy for the S&P500	50 x S&P500	$3150 / $3150	19	high	high	yes
S&P 500	SP	proxy for the S&P500	250 x S&P500	$20000 / $20000	15	high	high	no
GRAINS								
Corn	C *	world demand & supply increase / decrease	5000 bu	$450 / $325	23	high	low	no
Soybeans	S *	world demand & supply increase / decrease	5000 bu	$1500 / $1100	21	high	low	yes
Wheat	W *	world demand & supply increase / decrease	5000 bu	$750 / $550	22	high	low	no
Oats	O	world demand & supply increase / decrease	5000 bu	$400 / $300	22	low	low	no
SOFTS								
Coffee	KC *	world demand & supply increase / decrease	37,500 lbs	$3000 / $2200	15	high	high	yes
Sugar	SB	world demand & supply increase / decrease	112.000 lbs	$840 / 600	14	high	low	no
Cotton	CT	world demand	50,000 lbs	$1000 / $750	24	med	low	no
Orange Juice	OJ	Florida weather conditions	15,000 lbs	$700 / $500	19	high	high	yes
Lumber	LB	Construction demand	110,000 BFT	$1650 / $1100	27	low	high	no
MEATS								
Live Cattle	LC	mad cow scares, weather conditions	40,000 lbs	$1500 / $1000	23	high	high	yes
Pork Bellies	PB	supply / demand	40,000 lbs	$ 1620 / $1200	22	high	low	no
ENERGIES								
Crude Oil	CL *	OPEC output, world demand, supply problems	1000 barrels	$2750 / $2500	19	high	high	yes
Natural Gas	NG *	weather	10,000 mmBTU	$7500 / $7000	9	high	high	no
Unleaded Gas	HU	economic conditions, oil prices	42,000 gallons	$4400 / $4000	15	high	high	yes
Heating Oil	HO	weather	42,000 gallons	$3850 / $3500	17	high	high	yes

NOTES:
Note 1:   (*) indicates available as a 'mini'; mini controls less than the amount shown in table
Note 2:   Margins quoted for positions held overnight. Margins for day traded positions are typically 50 percent of this value.
Note 3:   Using market prices as of March, 2005, number quoted should be interpreted as 'n':1

Contract Size

The Contract Size column on the table shows how big—how much "stuff"—each contract represents. A gold futures contract, for example, is for 100 ounces of gold (about $44,000 worth at the time of this writing).

Minis

The asterisk (*) next to the future symbol in the Symbol column means that a "mini" contract is available. These relatively new futures contracts are for smaller amounts, usually about one tenth of the base amount. The extensive use of leverage, mentioned above, allows traders to control large contracts with relatively small capital outlays. Still, the availability of minis makes it possible for traders to trade without large capital outlays while also avoiding some of the risks of high leverage.

Initial Margin, Margin Maintenance, and Leverage

Unlike stock trading, each future has its own initial margin and margin maintenance requirement. Initial margin is the amount of trader capital initially required to enter a trade; the margin maintenance requirement is the amount of net capital that must be maintained on the contract to continue it. (These terms are explained in more detail later in this chapter and again in Chapter 11.)

The Approximate Leverage Ratio column shows exactly how much leverage a trader can use, given the value of the contract and initial margin requirements. Gold has a leverage ratio of 21, meaning that each dollar invested can control $21 worth of the commodity. Note how highly leveraged the financial futures are, in particular the currency futures. High leverage and relatively controlled price movements with volatility within the price range make them popular among traders.

Behind the Screen

A full list of available futures contracts and specifications can be found at either of these two websites:

http://quotes.ino.com/exchanges/contracts

www.globaltradestation.com/futures_cm_online.asp

Liquidity and Volatility

Traders look for signs of liquidity and volatility in anything they trade; the last three columns subjectively evaluate both characteristics. Futures with high or medium ratings for *both* volatility and liquidity are considered most attractive for day trading. Some futures with high volatility and liquidity, but also with high initial margin requirements, are considered more difficult to trade than their "mini" counterparts—the S&P 500 stock index future is an example.

Who Trades Futures and Why?

To begin to understand how to trade futures, it is helpful to understand who the other players are in the market, and why they are there. Stocks and stock markets have many kinds of players—individuals, institutional investors investing on behalf of individuals, and big fund managers managing major endowments or other large bodies of assets. Although corporations whose securities are being traded own some shares of other companies or may participate from time to time buying back or selling stock, they generally are not big players.

Commodities futures, on the other hand, are heavily traded by the producers and users of those commodities. In fact, if these players weren't in the market, it might not exist at all. Commodities producers use futures to hedge variations in the price of the commodity they produce and to generate some extra income off of it. Big commodities buyers—like food manufacturers or airlines—also use futures to hedge against future price increases. The following table expands on this idea:

Market Players and Motives

	Reasons for Buying	Reasons for Selling
Industry/Hedgers	Lock in a price for a commodity used in the production of a product	Lock in the price at which to sell a commodity, thereby allowing better planning
Speculators/Traders	Hope to profit from rising prices	Hope to profit from falling prices

It is important to note that in the futures markets specific buyers and sellers are not matched up. The exchange acts as a dealer and middleman for these contracts. And keep in mind that very few contracts actually result in physical delivery (there are a few very notable historical exceptions), as not many traders want to take delivery of 320 pounds of silver or 5,000 bushels of grain. Therefore, commodity contracts are nearly always settled in cash *before* the settlement date by buying or selling the contract on the open market.

Behind the Screen

In the mid and late '70s, a group of investors associated with the Hunt Brothers (members of the H. L. Hunt family Texas oil dynasty) bought futures contracts in silver as speculators and actually requested deliveries of massive quantities of the precious metal, hoping to create a shortage in the process. In fact, the group took delivery of 55 million ounces at one time, and stored the silver both in the United States and in Switzerland at an estimated annual storage cost of $3 million. It ultimately ended badly when the price of silver crashed. This story has become legendary among futures traders.

Quoting and Trading Futures

Quote information and trading access to futures is available mainly through specialized futures trading platforms. Many, but not all, advanced stock-trading platforms (discussed in Chapter 13) offer some futures quote and trading capability. To get a better handle on futures, it's worth examining a futures quote and trade screen.

Sample futures quote table for copper.

Copper - High Grade											
Data retrieved on 02/03/05 08:41:23 - All quotes are in exchange local time - Data provided by FutureSource											
Contract	Month	Last	Change	Open	High	Low	Volume	OpenInt	Exch	Date	Time
Copper - High Grade	Feb 05	141.30	-2.05	142.40	142.50	140.00	350	2729	COMX	2/3/05	10:58:01
Copper - High Grade	Mar 05	137.20	-2.15	139.65	139.70	135.60	11747	52603	COMX	2/3/05	11:10:31
Copper - High Grade	Apr 05	138.70	-1.75	136.70	136.70	136.70	52	2022	COMX	2/3/05	10:42:39
Copper - High Grade	May 05	135.90	-1.65	137.60	137.60	134.40	2540	12109	COMX	2/3/05	11:07:05
Copper - High Grade	Jun 05	133.90	-1.65	133.90	133.90	133.90	5	1791	COMX	2/3/05	10:40:59
Copper - High Grade	Jul 05	132.50	-1.95	134.60	134.60	132.50	342	6302	COMX	2/3/05	10:49:05
Copper - High Grade	Aug 05	132.45 y						789	COMX	2/3/05	13:38:41
Copper - High Grade	Sep 05	131.45 y					175	5305	COMX	2/3/05	13:38:41
Copper - High Grade	Oct 05	129.60 y						501	COMX	2/3/05	13:38:39
Copper - High Grade	Nov 05	128.35 y					11	416	COMX	2/3/05	13:38:39
Copper - High Grade	Dec 05	125.60	-1.60	125.00	125.00	125.00	24	3417	COMX	2/3/05	10:30:55

Shown is a portion of the futures quote table for copper. Each line in the table shows a different expiration month and the market prices for that month. For example, the last line of the table shows the last trade price for a contract to buy a unit of copper at the price of 125.60 in December 2005 (referred to as "December copper"). As time progresses, the "future price" to buy a unit of December copper will change frequently through the day.

Trade Secrets _____

A close look at the copper quote table reveals something interesting about prices and settlement dates. The further out in the future, the lower the price. Such a structure is called *backwardization*. Backwardization occurs when the market believes short-term price pressures on the commodity will be relieved over time. Examples include supply disruptions caused by hurricanes in the Gulf of Mexico (affecting oil), and late freezes in Florida (affecting orange juice). With many commodities, demand today creates supply tomorrow, as more of the commodity is planted or mined. Traders use backwardization as a signal that a commodity is overbought in the short term.

A Futures Trading Window

The following screens were captured from futures trading platform Refco (www.refco. com), using a simulated trading account. Beginning futures traders would be wise to start with such a simulator.

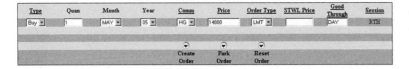

Sample futures order setup screen.

Suppose a trader wants to buy one copper contract with a May expiration. The symbol for copper is HG. The trader wants to pay no more than the equivalent of $1.40 per pound for the contract. How is that amount quoted? The accompanying figure shows that quote at 14000, thus that is the price at which the order is entered.

Each quote is given with an implied two decimal places. Quotes for copper are in cents, so the 14000 quote is 140.00 cents per pound, or $1.40. Traders must become familiar with how each commodity is priced and traded.

A look at the Characteristics of Major Commodities table at the beginning of this chapter reveals that a copper contract is for 25,000 pounds, so the trader is committing to approximately a $35,000 contract. Since the initial margin requirement is $2,700, the trader is able to control a large amount of copper for a relatively small amount of invested capital.

Once the order is set up, the trader sees a submission screen:

Sample order submission screen.

Type	Qty	Month/Year	Comm	Price	Option	New Offset	Order Type	Stop Limit Price	Good Through	Session
Buy	1	MAY05	Copper	14000			LMT		DAY	RTH

Symbol	Open	High	Low	Last	Chng	Bid	Ask	Volume	O.I.	Time
HG KDS	N/A	14460	14260	14410	+5	14305	14420	7391	N/A	09.11

Submit New Order   Escape

The submission screen gives the trader one last chance to check the order. It is very important to double-check all fields, as it is easy to enter futures orders incorrectly, particularly because of the implied decimal convention.

Futures Order Types

The following sections cover the types of orders most commonly used by day traders in the futures and currency markets. Trading order types are more generally discussed for stocks in Chapter 10, and many of the same order types apply to futures.

Market Orders (MKT)

Traders use them when they want to get into a market immediately, and they are the most common type of order for trading. Market orders specify quantity, but not price. Market orders expose traders to bad fills in illiquid markets, as contracts may only be available at much higher or lower prices than most recently quoted. But they tend to get better prices in highly liquid markets, since at any given moment enough contracts are available at the current price.

CAUTION

Alert! _____

In fast or illiquid markets, stop orders may lead to unfavorable entries or exits from positions. Stop orders guarantee an execution when a target price is reached, but *not* a price. They only activate the order, which may actually be filled at a price far higher or lower than the trigger price.

Stop Orders

Stop orders become active when the market hits a certain price, and behave as market orders when that happens. A buy stop is placed above the market and a sell stop is placed below the market. Once the market trades at the stop price, the order is treated like a market order and will be filled at the best possible price.

Stop orders are used frequently in futures trading, both on the buy and sell side. These orders are typically used at price points just above (or below) a trading range, to play possible breakout or breakdown situations. Stop orders are used more often in thinner (less actively traded, less liquid) markets to avoid the risk of prices falling right through specific limit levels.

Limit Orders

Limit orders are used for both buys and sells. Limit orders to buy are placed *below* the market, and limit orders to sell are placed *above* the market. These types of orders may never be filled, as typically the market must trade at or better than the limit price to fill the order. Such orders can take a long time to fill and may not be a good option in some situations.

Or Better Orders

Or Better, or OB, orders tell the floor trader to execute the trade at or better than the specified price. Technically, it is no different than a limit order. In practice, a limit order entered when the market is already much better than the limit price can lead to delays as the pit broker may question the order. OB is typically used in relatively illiquid markets as a way to say: market order, but no higher than "X" price.

Fill or Kill

The fill or kill ("FOK") order is used by customers wishing an immediate fill, but at a specified price. The order will be shopped on the floor for a short period of time. The order is killed if there are no takers. It's often used by day traders, who may not want to wait till the end of the day for a fill.

Margin in Futures Trading

Margin, or funds borrowed from a broker, is widely used for stock trading and is covered as a topic in Chapter 11. Because of the size of futures contracts, margin is a much more important and widely used tool in futures trading.

Margins requirements differ for each future and are set by the commodity exchange. They can vary over time.

Initial Margin

Initial margin is the amount of money that must be in a trader's account at the close of business on the day a new position is established. Interestingly, and very important for the day trader, for contracts *not* held through the close of the day trading, only half the initial margin may be required, depending on the contract traded and the experience level of the trader. To get this extra leverage, the broker must be informed (and approve of) a trader's intentions to day trade.

Maintenance Margin

Maintenance margin is the amount of money that must be in the trader's account on subsequent days *after* establishing a position. This is always less than the initial margin. When account equity falls below the combined required maintenance margins for all positions in the account, a margin call occurs. Margin calls must be met immediately with more cash or by liquidating positions.

Margin and Leverage: An E-Mini Example

Gains and losses in futures trading are very highly leveraged, perhaps more so than any other common form of investment, making futures trading very attractive to the day trader. Obviously it is important for the futures day trader to understand the relationship between leverage, required margins, and account funding.

Using the E-Mini S&P 500 futures contract (ES) as an example, a single E-Mini S&P 500 contract is valued at $50 times the value of the S&P 500 index. If, on a given day, the S&P 500 is at 1,500, then a single contract of the E-Mini S&P 500 future is valued at $75,000. The required initial margin for this contract is approximately $4,000. So, for $4,000 the trader controls a $75,000 future. The minimum price movement of the future ("tick") is .25 points or $12.50 per contract. If the S&P 500 were to move just 1 percent or from 1,500 to 1,515, a single E-Mini contract moves $50 × 15, or $750.

Remember that only $4,000 is tied up in this contract as required by the initial margin, so the 1 percent movement in the futures value represents more than an 18 percent gain on invested capital. Of course, it works the other way—a small downtick, in this case, about 5.33 percent (15 points × $50 × 5.33 = $4,000) would cause the trader to lose the entire investment.

Since true day traders enjoy a 50 percent initial margin requirement for futures, leverage is increased further—the S&P 500 contract can be controlled for $2,000. Unlimited leveraged gains for limited losses—not a bad thing at all. But as with options, the advantage of leverage is, at least to a degree, paid for in the futures price.

Margin and Leverage: Full Contract Example

Now, looking at the full-size S&P 500 index future, the power of leverage is even more impressive. For an initial margin of around $10,000, a trader can purchase and control a futures contract covering the S&P 500 valued at $375,000 or more. The value of the S&P 500 futures contract is $250 times the S&P 500 index. Suppose the trader purchases the current month's contract with the S&P 500 index currently trading at 1500. It moves from 1500 to 1540 (less than 3 percent). This 40-point move corresponds to a $10,000 move in the value (40 × $250). The return on the initial $10,000 investment is 100 percent with a 3 percent move in the index. Unfortunately the same leverage can work to the downside—a 40-point down move loses everything.

Common Trading Strategies

Futures trading can be highly complex and difficult to grasp at first. New traders must learn it a step at a time.

What Day Traders Trade

Most day traders look for highly liquid markets that tend to be volatile in the short term. The table at the beginning of this chapter notes the contracts most popular with day traders. Many traders migrating from stock trading use gold, euros, S&P 500 minis, or crude oil as their first foray into the futures markets.

Assisted Trading

Traders have a choice between going it alone and getting assistance. Commodity trading firms are eager to get new traders started, and offer services not always found among their stock counterparts.

Do-it-yourself traders, as the name implies, trade their account without the aid or advice of a broker. Traders are responsible for analysis, trading, and managing the funds in their accounts. Going it alone requires complete attention and complete understanding of the trading logistics of the market.

Broker-assisted accounts let traders trade their own accounts, but a broker is available to advise and help set up complex trades. Commissions are higher, but many new traders find the help worth the additional cost.

Trade Secrets _____

Some commodities brokers and trading platform providers offer both do-it-yourself and broker-assisted accounts. A few examples:

Cannon Trading Company (www.e-futures.com)

Peacock Trading (www.peacocktrading.com)

First Direct Futures (www.firstdirectfutures.com)

Optimus Futures (www.optimusfutures.com)

Evaluating the Trade

Like stock traders, commodity traders must become intimately familiar with the market and trading patterns of the commodity being traded. They must understand what drives the price and how much influence different factors have over price. They watch for repeatable trading patterns (discussed as "technical analysis" in Chapters 16 and 17).

Traders look for price liquidity, margin leverage, price movement, and predictable patterns for trading. Poor liquidity and weak price movements can cause trades to fail, as fills can be hard to obtain. Since there is less transparency in the total market, traders must be able to see a price and get the price they see. Likewise, there are many commodities where daily price movements are scarcely greater than the bid-ask spread; generally these won't work either. Traders may adopt a "pure dealer" strategy, buying on the bid and selling on the offer—but without sufficient activity, they won't profit very much.

Time Horizon

Unlike stocks, a trader isn't done after identifying the market to trade. He or she also must decide which month in the future to trade. Current months are usually more liquid and have greater price movement. Months further out tend to be more stable and represent the long-term expectations of price and so do not have the volatility most day and even swing traders look for.

Choosing an Entry Point

Once the target futures market is found, it is time to determine how and when to trade. Technical signals—support resistance, patterns—give many traders the signs they need.

Playing an Established Trend

Playing an established trend can be a relatively comfortable way to approach day trading. Trading the same upward or downward trend provides a consistent trade target, and over time, can yield nice profits. Traders find the overriding trend, which can be more definite and less fickle than stocks. Why? Because commodity demand/supply balances can stay constant for a reasonable amount of time, and when an imbalance is perceived, it not only persists but can drive itself, as it did for oil from 2004 to 2005. Some trends may not create enough price movement over short periods of time.

Trend Reversals

Trading trend reversals can be more difficult, but much more profitable, since trend reversals tend to be violent and quick. The key to this strategy is to understand the primary trend and then watch for technical indicators such as a trend line break, or topping or bottoming patterns, and then time an entry to coincide with the trend reversal. Chapters 16, 17, and 18 explore this idea further.

Trading Ranges

Playing a trading range break in futures trading is very similar to that in the stock market. Use trend lines and resistance and support levels to determine when a future has broken the current trend. This idea, too, is discussed again in Chapters 16 through 18.

Technical Analysis Tools

There are many technical analysis tools specific to commodities and futures. Trading platforms provide good technical tools, and many sophisticated software packages can turn a desktop computer into a statistics and graphics workstation.

One of the simpler sets of tools is available at www.barchart.com. This tool provides visual charts but also interprets them for key indicators. Charts can be found at www2.barchart.com/mktcom.asp?section=indices.

The Commitment of Traders Report

The Commodity Futures Trading Commission, an independent governmental agency created by Congress in 1974 to regulate futures trading, provides a report known as the Commitment of Traders, or COT report. This report breaks down supply and demand to identify potential trends and trend reversal points. For more on the CFTC, see www.cftc.gov.

Using the COT Report

When choosing a position to take, it is sometimes helpful to know what both speculators and the commercial traders are doing in the market. The theory behind this is to look for divergences in bullish/bearishness between the "smart" money and the "hot" money, and possibly take a position in a market in which an extreme is seen. Extremes tend to signal a coming trend change.

The Commitment of Traders Report.

Source: Commodity Futures Trading Commission.

SILVER - COMMODITY EXCHANGE INC. CFTC Commitment of Traders *Combined Futures and Options* Feb 08, 2005								
Reportable Positions as of Feb 08, 2005							Non- Reportable Positions	
Speculators			Commercial		Total			
Long	Short	Spreading	Long	Short	Long	Short	Long	Short
38951	11127	21677	22744	72516	83372	105320	34387	12439
Changes from last report - Change in Open Interest: -356								
-2142	769	1089	296	-3387	-757	-1529	401	1173
Percent of Open Interest for each category of traders								
33.1	9.4	18.4	19.3	61.6	70.8	89.4	29.2	10.6
Number of traders in each category; Total Traders: 170								
97	30	53	25	35	142	102		
(CONTRACTS OF 5,000 TROY OUNCES)							Open Interest: 117759	

The COT table lists the different kinds of positions taken in a commodity. Non-Reportable Positions are very small traders, most likely individuals. Speculators are those with large positions and are technically driven, most likely money managers and funds like hedge funds, pension funds, and so on. Commercials have large positions and their business is involved with the production or consumption of the commodity.

The COT table makes the most sense when viewed in a historical context, so it is important to watch what each type of trader is doing over time. A good trader will track such data versus price over time for any interesting market. One familiar with the silver market would note that the table is *not* overly extreme on either the long or short side, so one may conclude that the market may continue to follow the short-term trend. A trader looking to make a big score in this market may wait until the ratio is more like 10:1 long specs versus 10:1 short commercials, then watch for the break, potentially using either market or stop orders. Alternatively, the trader may be more comfortable following the short-term trend with the current COT standing, knowing that a significant reversal may not be immediately imminent.

COT reports for all futures can be found at www.cftc.gov/cftc/cftccotreports.htm. A more thorough discussion of the history and meaning of the COT report can be found at www.cftc.gov/opa/backgrounder/opacot596.htm.

Short Selling

Short selling is very common in commodities trading. Because of the relatively steady moves in commodity prices, short sellers aren't as exposed to the unlimited upside as they are in stocks. Nobody has ever announced a surprise "takeover" of a commodity.

Spreading

Traders won't be involved with futures for long before they hear about spreads. Spreads combine purchases and sales of contracts into strategic combinations. A spread is a purchase of one futures contract and the sale of another, different, futures contract. The purpose of the spread is to profit from the expected change in the price relationship between the two contracts. To exit (or unwind) this position, both sides are closed out. Spreads are not used that commonly by a day trader because the daily profit potential is relatively low.

Spreaders may "spread" the same commodity using different settlement prices and/or expiration dates. If a trader thinks that oil futures are overpriced, he or she could short July crude and go long on December crude oil futures. Money is made if the prices come back in line, but this may not occur within very short trading horizons. Some traders "spread" across commodities, playing gold against silver, for instance, if the price relationship between the two suggests it. Spreads tend to reduce risk for longer-term commodity plays, but again, may not meet a day trader's expectations for price movement.

Trading Currencies

Outside of the stock market, the most popular market for day traders is the spot foreign exchange market (Forex, or FX). The Forex market is the world's largest market, with over one trillion equivalent U.S. dollars traded per day. Currency markets are highly liquid, provide massive leverage opportunity (on the order of 100:1), and on any given day there will always be currencies that are rapidly moving up and down. Currency trading occurs 24 hours per day, seven days a week. For these reasons, the currency market is a big favorite of day traders.

New currency traders must be aware of how currencies are quoted, and how transaction costs are incurred. The U.S. dollar is considered the base currency and other currencies are quoted in dollar and cents terms (how many Japanese yen or Canadian dollars to a U.S. dollar, for example).

Transaction Costs

The transaction cost of establishing a position in the Forex market is equal to the spread, and prices are always quoted using five numbers, the final digit of which is referred to as a "pip." For example, if the U.S. dollar/Canadian dollar exchange was trading at bid of 123.75 and an ask of 123.80, the spread (5 pip) is the cost of trading the position.

Spot and Futures Markets

The Forex market offers currency futures in addition to the ability to trade the "spot," or cash market. Like other futures, currency futures are quoted against the U.S. dollar. For instance, if the May05 Euro FX future is quoted at 1.2372, this means that 1.2372 U.S. dollars buys 1 euro. Again, there is a lot of leverage in this market.

Currency Trading Platforms

There are many established and emerging platforms from which to trade currencies. Two of the most popular are Refco Group (www.refcofx.com) and Forex Capital Markets (www.fxcm.com).

Each of these sites has tools and contacts that will help you get started commodities trading.

Futures Trading Pitfalls

Futures trading requires a steady eye and hand on the markets being traded. Those trading agricultural commodities must watch the news for any signs of bad weather or changes in demand or supply. Commodity market internals (bid, ask, demand, and supply away from the inside price) are relatively less transparent than some others, particularly the NASDAQ. The good news: there is no veil of corporate secrecy or insider information to lift. Factors that affect commodity prices are available for public consumption though they might not show up in everybody's newspaper.

Less Platform Standardization

The evolution of brokers specializing in commodities has not progressed as far as for stockbrokers and trading platforms. Be careful when choosing a brokerage with whom to trade futures, as not all are "ready for prime time." Evaluation and references are a must. The list of commodities and forex brokers changes frequently as brokers combine or merge and new brokers enter the scene. CommoditiesLinks.com, a commodities trading portal, offers a list of brokerages and trading services at www.commoditieslinks.com/brokers.html.

Transparency

Getting the real-time bid/ask may be more difficult for a futures market than for the stock market. There are no quotes or show of supply and demand away from the inside market. Quotes, when they are available, may be out of date. Accuracy and frequency of refresh can be a problem. If you are not confident in the bid/ask information from your quoting service, then call your broker!

Overleveraging

Leverage is a beautiful thing and promises riches for all traders, but beware—it is a two-edged sword. Although traders can profit more and profit faster, they can also lose faster and more often. Like any high-performance instrument, traders must make sure they understand leverage and its impact and avoid excessive temptation.

The Least You Need to Know

◆ Commodities and futures attract traders because of leverage, tax advantages, and relatively less news risk.

◆ Commodities futures control tangible assets like agricultural products, metals, and energy, while financial futures track stock indexes and currencies.

◆ Commodities have different margin rules. While stocks can be bought with 50 percent margin, commodities futures can be bought with capital amounts of usually 5 to 10 percent. and as little as 1 percent of the contract value.

◆ Commodities can be traded on many advanced stock-trading platforms. Specialized commodity-trading platforms are emerging rapidly.

◆ Commodity-trading strategies are not unlike stock-trading strategies, except that they usually employ more leverage.

Part  3

Tools of the Trade

This part covers the tools traders use to stay informed and to execute trades.

Not surprisingly, traders have an enormous appetite for real-time information—mainly news, quotes, and analysis. Chapter 9 describes the various information sources, the kinds of data they provide, what they cost, and how they compare.

Chapter 10 covers the different types of orders all traders use, and Chapter 11 explains how to get more bang for your buck by trading using borrowed funds—by trading on margin.

Traders can choose between three levels of trading platforms: relatively inexpensive basic platforms, high-performance advanced platforms, and so-called "hybrid" platforms, which offer some of the features found on advanced platforms for a lot less money. Chapters 12 and 13 feature these platform types and discuss the pros and cons of using each one.

Chapter 9

Staying Informed

In This Chapter

- ◆ The importance—and advantage—of information
- ◆ The types of trading information available
- ◆ How to select information sources
- ◆ Getting the most information for the least amount of money

Trading can be looked at as a three-step process: (1) get the information; (2) make the decision; and (3) make the trade. This sequence makes it obvious that, without good information, the trader is leaving everything to chance.

In this chapter we identify the kinds of information that are important to traders and tell you where you can find it. We also help you avoid information overload by focusing only on the information you need.

As you read through this chapter, keep in mind that there are far more sources available than can possibly be presented here, and that the sources we do tell you about are examples, not specific recommendations.

What Do We Mean By "Information"?

The amount of information available to today's trader can be overwhelming. With the advent of the Internet and the rapid growth in active investing and trading, there has been a boom in the availability of information services. Many of these services have been around for a long time, but were only available to professional traders.

The information traders need generally falls into one of four categories: news, quotes, charts, and analysis.

News

By "news" we mean both "macro" news from the business and geopolitical world and "micro" news specific to a company or industry. Traders must stay tuned in to news from a number of sources at both levels to follow events that affect market direction and the behavior of specific securities.

Quotes

Trading close to the market requires being able to closely track quotes and the "pulse" of the market in a specific security. Naturally, real-time quotes are important for fast trading strategies. Traders further distinguish between two different kinds of real-time quotes:

◆ **Summary quotes** show only the "inside" market—the best bid and ask prices available in the market. NASDAQ Level I shows only summary quotes.

◆ **In-depth quotes** show the inside market quotes as well as all quotes away from the market, that is, those less than the best bid or greater than the lowest offer. NASDAQ Level II provides in-depth quotes showing the entire market.

Charts

Charts are graphs showing historical behavior and patterns for a security, index, or some other measurable piece of the market.

Analysis

Analysis takes raw data and history and searches for patterns useful to the trader. Technical analysis uses historical data to identify quantifiable trading patterns, ranges, and momentum. Analysis helps a sophisticated numbers-oriented trader set entry and exit points to or from a position.

Analysis software packages range from fairly basic varieties integrated into data source packages and trading platforms, to highly sophisticated mathematical modeling and so-called *data mining* software packages. These tools and trading systems support advanced trading strategies—and advanced traders.

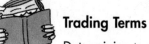

Trading Terms

Data mining tools attempt to find patterns and relationships—any patterns—crunched from huge bases of seemingly unrelated data. In the words of one data-mining professional, it is "ideally suited for domains characterized by large amounts of noisy data, and the absence of general theories or hypotheses about the data," which is as good a description of today's markets as any!

Selection Criteria

How does a trader go about choosing information sources? Traders need information to profit from their trades. But one never knows for sure exactly what little gem of data will lead to a profit on a particular day. So, unfortunately, traders must "drink from a firehose" of information to get those few "gems" that lead to success.

Too much information, however, will take too much time to sort through and overwhelm one's capability to process it. So the trader's dilemma is to get enough information, without getting too much, and to get it at a cost that's not prohibitive.

Trade Secrets

The whole point of information is *advantage*. Competing successfully in the securities markets means traders must …

♦ Know *more* than most.
♦ Know it *sooner* than most.

At the end of the day, traders get paid for knowing more, knowing it sooner, and making the right decision from the information. Information is first converted to knowledge, then to advantage.

Remember: knowledge is power.

Fee or Free

Thanks to the economics and broadcast capabilities of the Internet, a lot of good information is available for free—or darned close.

Mainly through financial portals like Yahoo!Finance (finance.yahoo.com), a great deal of news and trading information is packaged in a well-organized format through acquisition and linkage to other sites. The coverage is broad, but mostly centered on stocks.

The downside to these free Internet portals is that they lack depth, and more importantly, aren't real time or streaming—that is, traders must hit "refresh" on a browser to get the latest updates. Still, free portals represent a great place to start, and combined with other free or low-cost media including radio, television, and print media, give the trader a solid information base on which to build.

> ### Behind the Screen
>
> It's expensive to produce and provide so many wire feeds and so much research, so why is it that so much great information is free? The answer: *Advertisers.*

> ### Trade Secrets
>
> While most "free" portals don't offer exchange-originated real-time quotes, many do offer windows to ECN quotes (because ECNs issue their quotes in real time for free), which represent the market minus market makers and specialists. For actively traded stocks they are a good approximation. Go to Yahoo!Finance, get a quote, and then click on "Real Time ECN" quotes for a sample.

Fee services range from simple subscription services, like briefing.com, costing $10 to $25 per month, to advanced news, quote, and analysis feeds costing upwards of $300 per month. The latter are designed mainly for professionals, but are also packaged in "consumer" editions. Driving the costs of some of these platforms are not only the fees paid to the data service or platform providers, but also to the data feed originators, such as the stock exchanges, who garner a great deal of income off of data feeds.

Delivery

Timing is a big part of trading, and trading strategies, particularly close-to-the-market strategies, require real-time, up-to-the-minute news and, particularly, quotes. Timeliness of information is very important for traders.

The best information is real-time and streaming. Real time means that there is no delay built into the transmission of the data. This mostly applies to quotes. Free Level I NASDAQ quotes are intentionally delayed 15 minutes, while comparable NYSE quotes are delayed 20 minutes. Although such delays might once have been a function of technology, today they are a function of the desire of exchanges to produce more revenue: the data originators use the alternative real-time quotes as a profit center.

Streaming information comes across a network and into a client computer automatically without refreshing a browser window. Each piece of new information pops up on a screen without the need for the trader to "refresh" the screen. Advanced trading platforms have several windows open at once with information streaming to them.

Breadth and Depth

Information sources and platforms can be judged by their breadth and depth. Breadth means variety: Does a quote platform give wide coverage to different securities, options, indexes, commodities, or industries? Does a news platform bring in feeds from a variety of wire services? Does a charting platform give a wide selection of chart types and technical analysis tools?

Depth refers to the completeness of the data offering. Are Level II NASDAQ quotes, reflecting the entire market, available? Does a quote feed come with real-time minute-by-minute streaming chart capability? Does a trading platform show real-time, up-to-the-minute portfolio performance? Does a news feed offer links to the full story?

Trade Secrets _____

To get complete market coverage beyond the stock markets into international stock markets, commodities, forex (foreign exchange), and other complex securities, traders must "trade up" to an advanced platform. These advanced data feeds are more expensive, and these venues aren't as popular with the general public. Hence the advertising revenue isn't there to support inclusion on more basic platforms.

Selectivity

One way to avoid information overload is to "filter" news and quote feeds. Many advanced data services allow you to elect to receive news items just for particular securities and industries. Similarly, it is important to be able to set "watch lists"—groups of securities you want to watch closely—for portfolios, potential trades, and markets or market sectors.

Single or Multichannel

Most portals, online brokers, and trading platforms are set up to let traders watch a portfolio or some form of watch list. But only the advanced platforms allow traders to watch "deep" information—i.e., Level II quotes or up-to-the-minute news feeds—for more than one security at a time.

Data to Information

Good information platforms allow you to set alerts when certain conditions occur. At the most basic level are news feeds that beep when a news story comes across for a particular security or market. More advanced alerts go off when certain price or volume conditions are met for a certain security. Still more advanced alerts will actually set up an order—or even enter it—if certain conditions are met. Alerts can be set as an alarm on a computer screen, or as a beep or page on a wireless device.

Customization

The best information sources are the most customizable. Highly customizable platforms allow traders to change the layout, selection criteria, and the degree of detail shown. They are capable of tracking multiple securities, setting multiple and customizable alerts, and delivering the information wherever needed, whether that's a home computer or a mobile device.

Information Sources by Price

As you might imagine, it's usually the case that the more breadth and depth your information source has, and the more customizable it is, the more you'll have to pay for it. However, a lot of good information can be had for free or for a pittance. In the following sections we break information sources down according to cost, beginning with the freebies.

Free or Nearly Free

It wasn't that long ago that the morning newspaper provided the only investment information available outside a trip to your broker's office. You could open to the business section and find out yesterday's closing prices and, if you had a paper specializing in business, maybe high, low, volume, and a few news stories. There was no way to keep track of price changes or news events as they happened, so unless you were set up as a professional trader with a Quotron terminal and a bank of telephones, day trading as we know it today wasn't possible.

Today, the combination of print media, cable and satellite television, and the Internet bring a broad assortment of free or almost-free information well suited to keeping traders aware of the markets, developments in particular companies and securities, and reasonably good market data and quote information. Although such sources won't support an advanced day trader, they are sufficient for some trading strategies. And even advanced traders use these sources to stay informed of the general economic and political climate.

Print Media

Although it's not the aim of this chapter to make specific recommendations, here's one piece of advice: traders should read at least one financial newspaper and one good business/economics magazine on a regular basis. These sources circulate so widely that they won't necessarily give a trader an advantage, but they are important tools for assessing the general business climate and the climate in certain companies and industries.

Here are the favored choices:

- *The Wall Street Journal* is a venerable favorite that provides data on a wide range of markets and summarizes the past day's action. Beyond financial information, it provides good insight to what's happening to companies in the marketplace.

- *Investor's Business Daily* is similar to the *Journal* but with more of an investing and trading focus. IBD tracks trading trends and factors driving trading activity. "Relative Strength," "Industry Relative Strength," and volume percentage change indications for each company are among some of the analysis offered.

- *Business Week* provides solid information about companies and insight into the effects of political actions on markets.

- *The Economist* gives an objective, deeply focused, and often biting view of world and national business, politics, and economics, as well as business and economic trends, interest rates, and so forth. Those trading international securities or currencies will find it especially useful.

TV/Radio Media

We count cable and satellite TV among the free or nearly free category because many households subscribe to these services already. The late-1990s market boom gave rise to several cable TV and radio outlets for market data and commentary. The post-boom consolidation has claimed a few, but several others survived with some adjustment.

♦ **CNBC** was one of the cable channels to survive market consolidation, with its well-known crawler (ticker), *Morning Call, Power Lunch, Squawk Box,* and Joe Kernan commentary. Most active day traders have CNBC on throughout the day to keep up with breaking news and commentary. CNBC broadcasts market news throughout the day, and a breaking CNBC news story will certainly move a stock.

♦ **Bloomberg Financial Network** has more of an academic tone to its news and analysis. It's a good way to follow market activity after hours, as it tracks S&P, Dow, and NASDAQ futures around the clock as well as international markets.

♦ *The Nightly Business Report* is a long-running PBS show that offers a half-hour summary of the day's business and market activity and the day's big movers. It's a good nightcap to a trading or working day.

♦ *Marketplace* is National Public Radio's equivalent to *Nightly Business Report,* with insightful commentaries and a brief summary of the day's markets.

Web Portals

Of all the Web portals (and among all free information, for that matter), the Yahoo!Finance Web portal (finance.yahoo.com) is probably the best. It is well designed, easy to use, fast, and packed with information and links to other resources. It is free, though you have to put up with banner advertising. Through linkages, it provides a window into breaking market news, including continuous market updates and "In Play" summaries from Briefing.com. It also provides an effective way to keep up with the business and economic calendar for economic reports, earnings news, and broker upgrades and downgrades. For those who don't want to pay for their online information, this is probably the best source.

Market Update   MY YAHOO!

11:00AM: Buyers remain in control of the action despite oil prices climbing to their highs of session... Crude oil futures ($46.50/bbl -$0.68), which was off more than 2.0% earlier after Iraq's elections ended without serious incident and no reports showed disruptions to major oil pipelines, have rebounded somewhat in the last half hour, subsequently turning many energy stocks positive... OPEC's decision to maintain its current rate of oil production at 27 mln barrels a day has also added selling pressure to the commodity in the early going...XOI +0.4, NYSE Adv/Dec 2168/853, Nasdaq Adv/Dec 2051/775

10:30AM: Stocks continue to hold their own and sport solid gains after dissecting this morning's economic data... Jan Chicago PMI has recently checked in at 62.4, better than expectations of 59.8 and indicative of continued manufacturing expansion, while Dec New Home Sales increased 8.9% to 1.09 mln units, slightly less than forecasts of 1.2 mln, further suggesting a leveling off in the housing market... Earlier, the Commerce Dept.'s personal income and consumption figures came in as expected...

While Dec personal spending rose 0.8%, roughly in line with expectations of 0.9%, personal income posted a record 3.7% gain (consensus 3.3%), due primarily to a 3.1% gain related to Microsoft's (MSFT 26.39 +0.21) $32 bln dividend payment...NYSE Adv/Dec 2217/706, Nasdaq Adv/Dec 2091/662

10:00AM: Little change since the last update as virtually every sector continues to attract buyers in the early going... Technology has led the charge to the upside as semiconductor, software, hardware and networking have all surged roughly 1.0%... Also showing strength have been airline, financial, biotech, retail, transportation, materials and utility...

more...

Yahoo!Finance Market Update Screen.

In Play® MY YAHOO!

12:54PM Saflink Receives Follow On Order for Physical Access and Biometric Products to Secure State Prison System (SFLK) 1.49 -0.06:...

12:46PM Longs Drug Stores announces new $150 mln share repurchase program (LDG) 42.00 +0.25:

12:39PM Crude Oil edges to best levels of the day... $49.50 +0.34... Dow -44 about 8 pts above lows of day :

more...

Yahoo!Finance "In Play" feature. The "In Play" screen shows news stories about stocks with major news or price movements.

Today's Highlights

Upgrades

Company Name	Symbol	Details	Analyst
United Micro	UMC	Buy	Deutsche Securities
Benchmark Elec	BHE	Buy	KeyBanc Capital Mkts / McDonald
ADC Telecom	ADCT	Outperform	Morgan Keegan

more...

Downgrades

Company Name	Symbol	Details	Analyst
LKQ Corp	LKQX	Mkt Perform	Barrington Research
A. Schulman	SHLM	Underweight	KeyBanc Capital Mkts / McDonald
PolyOne	POL	Hold	KeyBanc Capital Mkts / McDonald

more...

Splits

Company Name	Symbol	Split Ratio
Adobe Systems	ADBE	2-1
JB Hunt Trans	JBHT	2-1
Genlyte Group	GLYT	2-1

more...

Earnings

Company Name	Symbol	EPS Estimate	Call
MEDTRONIC INC	MDT	0.53	Call
SCOTTISH PWR ADS	SPI	N/A	N/A
NETWORK APPLIANCE	NTAP	0.17	N/A

Economic

Statistic	For/Time	Actual	Prior
FOMC Minutes	May 3/2:00 pm	-	-
Existing Home Sales	Apr/10:00 am	7.18M	6.87M

more...

Yahoo!Finance "Today's Highlights" feature. "Today's Highlights" shows analyst rating changes, announced splits, earnings announcements, and economic calendar events that might influence individual stocks or markets.

The main drawbacks of Yahoo!Finance and similar free portals can be summed up as follows:

- They are screen based, not streaming. Internet portals require you to refresh to get the latest information.

- They only provide delayed quotes. For active traders, delayed quote resources are almost useless. The "Real Time ECN" available on Yahoo!Finance and similar portals gives some depth and watch capability for the cubicle day trader, but it's far from perfect.

- They offer little in the way of customization. Although users can set a watch list for last trade quotes, that's about all you can do.

Yahoo!Finance is a good tool for the casual trader, but more advanced and active traders will need a higher level of coverage.

Online brokers

All online brokerages offer free quotes and news service in some form. News services usually include the standard newswires—BusinessWire, Reuters, Associated Press, Dow Jones, and Marketwatch. But the news feeds aren't streaming, meaning that browser refresh is required. They aren't very customizable, either. About all you can do is select headlines for a particular company.

Delayed quotes like those found in the Web portals such as Yahoo!Finance are furnished for free, and an increasing number supply real-time quotes for free, especially to larger account holders. However, these quotes are simple bid/ask quotes and require browser refresh. Size is only available on "detailed" quote screens. No Level II, and no streaming quotes, unless you're willing to part with $50 a month or more and/or you trade actively.

Brokers do provide some access to investment research, although most of it is geared to long-term investors rather than traders. Broker sites offer alerts, and most can be set up to send an e-mail or screen alert when a condition is met.

More and more brokers and information portals offer simple streaming quotes as an advanced feature for a small fee, and often for free. Traders can select a handful of stocks and watch inside bid, offer, size, and last trades for stocks, often at little to no charge. Such simple windows are a good way to track stocks closely without using an advanced platform, although they still lack the breadth and depth required for sophisticated trading.

We take a closer look at the most popular online broker platforms in Chapter 12.

> **Trade Secrets**
>
> With all of the shortcomings of free or low-cost trading information sources, one might wonder what good they are. The reality: many traders use such simpler sources to spot trading *opportunities:* what's hot, what's not, what's changing. True, stock selection can be done on advanced platforms, too. But sometimes less is more—simpler, friendlier media can often do the job while a trader is otherwise occupied, not to mention with reduced eye and brain strain.

$10–$25 Per Month

Next on the list are the specialized information sources and feeds that cost money but don't represent a major investment. Most of these products cost $10 to $25 per month, but "souped-up" versions can cost considerably more. The latest competitive focus is on streaming quotes *and* news through normal Internet connections; most low-cost providers offer such service. There are many to choose from; a few examples follow.

Briefing.com

Briefing.com provides refresh and streaming feeds of news, headlines, and basic analysis through the day. It provides a regularly updated list of "In Play" stocks; that is, stocks "likely to experience sharp moves or heavy volume"—in other words, short-term trading opportunities. It issues advisories for stocks reaching certain technical conditions, such as resistance or support levels. Briefing also covers broker/analyst upgrades and downgrades, so-called "story" stocks—financial journalist centerpieces for the day—and the business and economic calendar.

The basic Briefing.com "Silver" offering is free, and allows browser access to a variety of information and reports, but little of it in real time. For $9.95 a month ($100 per year), "Gold" subscribers get e-mail alerts and hourly "In Play" lists, while a "Platinum" subscription for $24.95 a month ($250 per year) brings streaming real-time "In Play" and other alerts.

Briefing.com offers well-packaged, clear, concise, and timely information. Note that some briefing.com information is available through the Yahoo!Finance portal for free, and some of the more advanced information, like real-time analyst actions, is available through advanced trading platforms. More detail can be found at www. briefing.com.

Briefing.com's services.

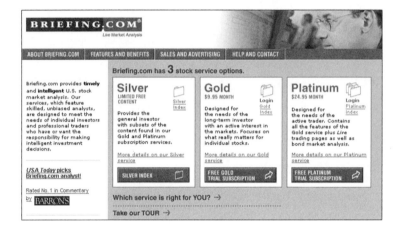

Yahoo!Finance Real-Time Quotes

Not surprisingly, Yahoo!Finance has entered the fray with a streaming news and quote service of its own for $13.95 a month.

Yahoo!Finance Yahoo! Real-Time Quotes.

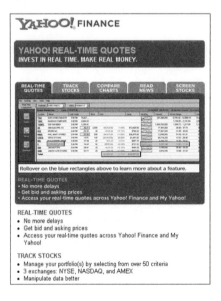

Tradingmarkets.com

Tradingmarkets.com directs its analysis and daily commentary to serious traders. Daily opportunities are identified, with alerts and analysis and commentary from trading specialists. The service also offers training courses and packaged trading systems, which are quantitative methodologies for identifying securities and entry/exit points. Tradingmarkets also covers commodities, futures, and foreign markets. Tradingmarkets is a big step up in sophistication when compared to Yahoo!Finance and Briefing.com.

Subscriptions are $29.95 a month (with a hefty 40 percent discount to $265 for a yearly subscription). The streaming version, at $99 a month, provides hourly audio analysis in addition to the usual streaming news and analysis. Some Tradingmarkets features are displayed for free through Yahoo!Finance.

> **Trade Secrets**
>
> The investment information industry is extremely competitive, and information providers live and die by the size of their subscriber base. As a result, traders can usually find offers for free trial subscriptions and deep discounts for yearly subscriptions.

Expensive: Advanced Information Platforms

Advanced information platforms started out serving the needs of professional traders and market makers. The growing market of individual traders has induced platform providers to package consumer versions of their products.

These platforms are very sophisticated, with continuous streaming feeds into multiple, highly customizable windows. Advanced platforms bring broad and deep data from multiple markets, including options, futures, and foreign markets. They offer highly customizable news and trading alerts, and most offer charting, technical analysis, and software tools. Most also offer access from most mobile devices.

Advanced *information* platforms stop just short of advanced *trading* platforms in that they don't offer a trading window. However, users can easily keep open a separate broker window with trading capability on their computer screen.

Advanced platforms give broad and deep information both for markets and individual securities. Most can give Level II quotes for more than one security. The following illustration is an example of how a screen could be set up to watch markets and Microsoft stock individually.

Sample advanced platform desktop layout.

Set Alerts Screen	Real Time Intraday Chart
Real Time News Feed	
Stock Watch List	
	News Feed - MSFT
U.S. Major Market Indexes	NASDAQ Level II MSFT / NASDAQ Time/Sales MSFT
U.S. Sector and Commodity Indexes	

eSignal

eSignal (www.esignal.com) offers a complex assortment of platforms with differing levels of sophistication. The "flagship" package is called eSignal, and offers four levels. The top level (eSignal Platinum) offers the most advanced technical and software capability to go with high-end news feeds. Costs range from $75 a month ($49 with a one-year commitment) for the "Basic" version up to $395 per month ($320 with a one-year commitment)—*plus* exchange fees (fees charged by exchanges for real-time data access). Users can purchase tiered packages and add-ons for tracking multiple securities at once; for instance, a $100 add-on gives deep-quote coverage on 100 securities at once. The somewhat simpler and mobile-device oriented Quotrek offering costs $49 a month.

eSignal main page.

Alert!

Watch out for exchange fees, which can be substantial and are often passed on as add-ons to the subscription price. The NASDAQ charges a modest $1 per month for Level I quotes and $9 for Level II ($30 for "professional" traders). But the TotalView feature (see Chapter 7) costs $14 a month. The NYSE Openview feature costs $50 a month. Chicago Mercantile Exchange real-time deep quotes cost $38 a month, and Chicago Board of Trade fees run $43 (though both commodity exchanges charge far less for their "e-mini" products). Deep and very broad information coverage can get quite expensive. Shop carefully, and make sure you are aware of all fees before subscribing to a service.

Very Expensive: Analysis Software

Finally, on the long list of information sources are the many software packages that convert data—lots of it—into information by analyzing it for tradable patterns. Most "back-test" series of historical data—that is, they run models on previous history to see if certain models fit. They run patterns on their own or test patterns specified by a trader. Such patterns can be extremely complex and are beyond the scope of this chapter.

Among the more well-known providers are TC2000 (www.tc2000.com) and Prophet (www.prophet.net), but there are dozens of offerings. Expect to pay up to $400 for software packages, with add-ons for data feeds to support them. Some packages operate off an existing data feed from the likes of eSignal or an advanced trading platform.

Trade Secrets

A good resource for finding advanced information and analysis providers is *Technical Analysis of Stocks and Commodities, The Traders Magazine*, a publication of traders. com. It's available at many bookstore newsstands and is a good technical learning tool for the math-oriented trader.

Very Expensive: Specialized Day Trading Resources

Traders will run across numerous tools of varying quality designed specifically for pure day traders. There are newsletters, magazines, bulletins, chat rooms, simulation sites, and other resources too numerous to explore here. As you begin to trade, you'll encounter many of these sources. Most traders should stick with mainstream packages and trading platforms. Too much information can be overwhelming, and some of it can be misleading, not to mention expensive.

> **CAUTION**
>
> **Alert!** _____
>
> Traders should be particularly wary of chat rooms and "message boards" available in popular portals. Rogue traders and even securities dealers can run "pump and dump" schemes pretty much at will, although recent SEC crackdowns have had some effect. Traders generally should not trade off of rumors, and should use informal information sources only after gaining some experience with them.

The Least You Need to Know

♦ Data—converted to information, converted to knowledge, delivered in real time—is necessary to give traders an advantage.

♦ Traders should seek information from news, quotes, charts, and analysis.

♦ A good source of information should offer traders depth, breadth, speedy delivery, and customizability of information sources. Streaming information is far better than browser-refresh delivery.

♦ The cost of trading information ranges from free to hundreds of dollars each month.

♦ Traders should shop carefully for information, acquiring what they need using a return-on-investment approach. They should seek that which gives advantage while avoiding unproven sources.

Chapter 10

Buying and Selling

In This Chapter

- ◆ How to place an order
- ◆ All about order timing and conditions
- ◆ Making market, limit, and stop orders
- ◆ Short selling
- ◆ After-hours trading

This chapter is the first of a series of chapters designed to explain the tools of trading. By the time you finish reading Chapters 10 through 13, you'll know about order placement, margins, online broker platforms, and advanced trading platforms.

In this chapter we introduce the basic set of tools for making the trade—that is, order placement and the different types of orders used in today's markets.

More Than Just Buy and Sell

If it were simply a matter of placing "buy" and "sell" orders, there wouldn't be much reason to construct a whole chapter around the concept of placing orders. But the order-entry process is necessarily more complex so that the investor can time and price orders to gain advantage.

Orders can defined by *time*—that is, how long until they expire—and they can be defined by *price*—that is, with a specifically stated price or simply the current state of the market. Especially with more advanced trading platforms, additional features and combinations of features are available to put orders into play at specific times and prices.

Order Timing

Time in force (TIF) refers to the length of time an order is left open in the market. Most orders are placed as "DAY" orders; that is, they are good through the end of the trading day. However, most online broker and advanced trading platforms also allow traders to time their orders in the following ways:

- **GTC/good till canceled** orders stay open indefinitely (although many brokers have time limits of 30 days, 90 days, and so on).

- **FOK/fill or kill** orders must be filled immediately, or else they are canceled. These are used to try to hit very specific price points, usually on a fast-moving stock. The trader doesn't want to have to cancel before placing another order at a different price.

- **IOC/immediate or cancel** orders work like FOK for listed (NYSE) stocks.

Traders can use TIF strategically in a lot of ways. For example, a trader might place a FOK order to try to pick up (or dispose of) a security right away at a particular price, either away from or at the market. Or if a trader can't watch a stock closely but hopes to protect against an adverse move or catch a low (or high), they can leave an order open for a day or longer.

Special Conditions

Traders may place special conditions on their order. Typically these conditions specify whether an order must be filled completely or if partial fills are acceptable. A trader may want to buy 1,000 shares at a certain price, but understandably may not want to accept only 100 shares if that is all that's available (a situation that usually only arises on less liquid or actively traded securities). So a trader can specify "AON," which stands for "All or None," on the order or specify a minimum acceptable quantity to fill.

In some cases, traders will have to go to a "special conditions" screen to find TIF and other Special Conditions options. The default is typically "DAY" with no other special conditions, but traders can save a designated order-entry condition, often for a single security, on an advanced trading platform.

Order Pricing

The ability to specify price in an order is a key component of most trading strategies. While price-unspecified market orders have their place in the trader's playbook, price-specific limit orders are used more often. Market and limit orders can be entered into the market as active orders, or set up to enter when certain price conditions are met.

Market Orders

The simplest, most basic form of order is the market order. A market order must be executed at the best price available when the order reaches the market maker or trading floor. A market order looks like this:

> **Buy 500 shares INTC at the market.**

Notice that no price is specified. The market order says, "Just execute me now, I don't care about the price." The trader is trying to buy (or sell) stock *now*. Although price is important, it's secondary. Presumably the quoted bid and ask price and size are close enough to meet the trader's objectives.

The pitfall, of course, is that the stock could easily move away from your price before it's executed. The only guarantee is that the order will be filled. Most of the time market orders trade at or near the price the trader anticipates, but surprises can and do happen, particularly if the stock is volatile, and/or the trading system isn't very fast. A minute gap between the time an order is placed and the time it hits the market can cost a lot in a fast-moving stock.

Trading Terms

Slippage is the movement of the actual trade price away from the price at the time the order is placed. It is a function of volatility and speed of order transmission and execution. TIF and special conditions parameters help avoid slippage. High-performance trading systems with direct access, such as SOES and SuperDot, are fast enough to reduce the risk of slippage with market orders.

High-performance momentum day traders often use market orders. Although they may endure some price *slippage*, they won't miss out on the larger price move. Every trader alive has experienced missing a point move because they set a fixed "limit" price a penny below the market—and the order never got filled.

But what if a trader wants to control price? What if a trader wants to trade as a pure trader in a very active market, where a penny or two means the difference between profit and loss? Even though they're fast, market orders and SOES won't do it.

Or what if a trader is watching several stocks at a time, or even trying to do a full-time job from his or her cubicle? The ability to set a fixed price, so as not to be blindsided by market moves, becomes very important.

Alert!

The nice thing about market orders is that they get filled right away. But complications arise when there's insufficient size in the market, for price can slip away as the order moves farther away from the inside market to get the number of shares specified. Launch an order to buy 1,000 LCAV, a less active stock, and you may get 200 shares at the inside ask of 26.45, but the next 200 shares might come at 26.55, the next at 26.65, and so forth. Read the market closely by looking at size at and away from the market where possible before launching a large market order.

Limit Orders

Market orders guarantee an execution but not a price. Limit orders guarantee a price but not an execution. A limit order sets a limit on the price paid to buy or the price received to sell a security. The limit isn't absolute—if the price is *better* (lower for a buy limit, higher for a sell limit) the order will fill at that better price.

Technically, a limit order becomes *eligible* for execution when a price is reached. It may not be filled automatically. Why? There may not be enough size available at the price, and there may be other orders ahead of yours at the same price (this is called "stock ahead"). If the supply of stock dries up at that price before your buy limit order is executed, your order gets left out. *Note:* With NYSE orders, your limit order is always sequenced ahead of the specialist's own account, so chances of a fill are better.

> **Alert!** _____
>
> It is usually very risky to enter a market order after hours or before a market opens. Why? If you have after-hours trading capability, you're entering less liquid markets. If not, the order will execute automatically at the next open market price—which could move significantly by the time the market opens. Such market orders entail too much event and price risk to be worthwhile. Always use limit orders to trade when the market isn't fully in session.

Buy Limit Orders

The buy limit order is an order to buy shares at a limit price, usually at the bid price or lower than the current market. When (and if!) the stock hits that lower price, the order is executed.

The details are actually more complex. The trader's buy limit order becomes part of the bid size at the limit price. If it is at the best bid price, it is part of the inside, and is likely to be filled quickly. If it is "off" the inside, it will sit until the price moves down toward the limit price.

Let's suppose it is at the inside, or best, bid price. What happens then depends on market dynamics. It could be that the next market sell order arriving in the market will be filled at that price, depending on (NASDAQ) order routing or (NYSE) other orders on the book. Or, the specialist (NYSE) or another market maker (NASDAQ) might decide to sell you those shares at the limit price. Either way, the trader gets the shares at the limit price. If the limit buy order is placed on an ECN, a fill may happen on the ECN, and if not, it will be introduced into the NASDAQ or NYSE (if ARCA ECN) markets as a limit order.

Buy Limit Scenario

So the order might look like this:

Buy 500 shares INTC limit 22.47.

This order will show up as 500 shares of size at a price of $22.47, and may be shown together with other limit orders by a market maker representing the trader's order (unless placed directly using direct access or an ECN). Assuming the inside market is bid 22.47, offer 22.48, the next market sell order for 500 shares could execute at 22.47, thus filling the trader's "buy" at that price. Or another market maker could let the trader buy at 22.47, even though the current market offer is 22.48—a good sign that the market is headed lower. Traders observing a lot of fast fills at the bid price might take this as just such a signal.

Bottom line: the limit buy for 500 shares at 22.47 won't execute unless someone else wants to sell at that price. That may be never, or at least not during that trading day, so if it is a "DAY" order, it will expire at the end of the trading session.

Sell Limit Orders

Sell limit orders are similar to buy limit orders, except that they set a sell-price target instead of a buy-price target. Naturally, a sell-price target will be higher than the current trading price. Using the our same example, we might place a sell limit order that looks like this:

> **Sell 500 shares INTC limit 22.48.**

This order places 500 shares on the offer at 22.48 and will execute when a market buy order shows up or if a market maker decides to hit the trader's offer.

Using Limit Orders

Traders use limit orders to improve buy or sell prices or to manage positions that can't be followed closely in "real time."

Without watching in real time, a trader could potentially "catch" a buy of Intel at 22.47 or get a more lucrative 22.48 on a sale. Again, there is a risk of not entering or exiting the position *at all*.

Trade Secrets

Most experienced traders will advise using limit orders to gain control and price advantage. However, today's penny spreads on liquid, active stocks, have somewhat diminished the limit-order-only approach to trading. In the pre-2000 "old days," limit orders captured price differences of sixteenths (6.25 cents), eighths (12.5 cents), or even larger. Now the difference between a limit order and a well-timed market order might be a penny. The penny gained might not trade off well against the risk of not getting filled at all. For those looking to buy on a dip or sell on a spike, the limit order is still the way to go.

Stop Orders

Combining features of market and limit orders, stop orders provide yet another tool for the trader's kit. Stop orders say, in effect, when the market hits a certain price, "Stop here and enter a market order." The market order, as above, executes immediately at the best available price. The result is a guaranteed fill, and with liquidity and a sane market, somewhat of a guaranteed price.

Traders use stop orders mainly as risk management tools to exit positions quickly on the downside and occasionally to enter them (or cover short sales) on the upside. The downside protection offered by the sell stop is used most, so that will be examined first.

Sell Stop Orders

Sell stops, or stop loss orders, are often set to safety net a *long* position—a purchased security position held in your account. You bought Intel at 22.48 and now it's risen to 22.95. A trader wants to lock in 40 cents of profit, so he places a stop loss. The following, often referred to as a "trailing stop," is placed:

> **Sell 500 INTC at 22.88 stop.**

So what happens if the stock goes to 23.10? Nothing—the profit on the position grows. Conversely, a hiccup sending the stock tumbling in price will trigger the stop, launch a market order, and bring a market execution at or near (hopefully) 22.88, locking in most of the profit. It's a useful risk management tool for profitable positions, but it's not without pitfalls. Slippage may cause further price deterioration (remember, it's a guaranteed fill, but not a guaranteed price). But as the next sidebar illustrates, stop loss orders can be used by market makers on the other side to pick up "cheap" stock.

Alert!

Visible stop loss orders placed through most online brokers and trading platforms have a major pitfall: market makers and specialists can shake them out to pick up cheap stock. Market makers, especially in less liquid stocks, will drop their bids in an effort to trigger stops, what in trading jargon is called a "shake out." On the NYSE such orders actually show up on the order book, so likewise, specialists can trade to pick up the lower "stop" price if they believe the security is headed higher.

Many traders using stop loss orders indiscriminately find their stop price winding up to be the low for the day, not a good thing for a sell order. The solution is to use them carefully, and consider automated trailing stop features on advanced platforms. Automated trailing stops don't send the order into the market until the stop price is reached, so nobody in the market can see or grab cheap shares.

Buy Stop Orders

A buy stop becomes an active market order when the stock rises to a specified "stop" price. Suppose Intel is trading at 22.47 bid, 22.48 ask, and the trader is interested in capturing a strong upward move. They might place the following:

Buy 500 INTC at 22.55 stop.

Nothing will happen until Intel hits 22.55, then a market order is placed. The trader feels that is a strong enough percentage move to jump onboard. A trader may feel that, so long as the stock is trading in a quiet range, there's no sense in committing capital, but if it rises, they want to be onboard. The 8¢ price penalty is worth it to keep risk capital out of the market until a *breakout* occurs.

> **Trading Terms**
>
> A **breakout** occurs when a stock or other security makes a sharp, sudden move away from a static trading pattern. Usually the term is used in conjunction with sharp upside moves, but can describe moves in both directions.

Buy stops are most often used by day traders to protect short positions. A short position may have been entered at 22.50; that is, the trader borrowed and sold stock anticipating a down move. The buy stop might be placed at 22.55, providing a safety net against loss should the stock take off to the upside.

Stop Limit Orders

There is another refinement in the world of limit and stop orders—a combination of a stop order and a limit order known as a stop limit order.

> **Alert!**
>
> Some brokers and trading firms still charge higher commissions or fees for using limit and stop orders, although the practice has declined somewhat as brokers have consolidated and trading platforms have become more competitive. It's worth checking out when selecting a platform.

When a stop limit order is used, a limit order (not a market order) is triggered when a stop price is reached. For example:

Buy 500 INTC stop 22.55, limit 22.49.

Intel is still at 22.47. The trader is saying, in effect: "If Intel 'breaks resistance' (or makes a move through its apparent resistance level of 22.55), then I'm a buyer at 22.49 or better if the stock retreats again." It's a buy stop order with more price control. The trader isn't exposed to the price uncertainty of a market order, but obviously picks up some risk of nonfill. It's used by traders playing a stock with a large upside breakout potential (or conversely a big downside potential if placed as a sell). A day trader able to watch every pulse of the market for a stock may not need this type of order, but it's good to know about.

Canceling or Changing Orders

Markets change fast, and traders must be able to change or cancel orders quickly and easily to meet changing conditions.

Backing Out

All brokerages and trading platforms allow traders to cancel orders. Simply identify the order and hit the cancel button. Some platforms require paging through a list of open orders, right-clicking on a mouse, etc.; "fast" traders will want to learn and test cancellation and change procedures carefully before selecting a platform. Note also that NASDAQ charges a 25¢ cancellation fee, and that some brokers still charge one as well.

Cancellation normally works just as fast as the original order placement. Orders reaching an exchange in seconds can be canceled in seconds—when things are working right. But when markets and electronic trading systems become extremely busy, cancellations can be painfully slow. A cancellation may arrive after the order is filled. It's nobody's fault—just the nature of the animal. Your broker or platform should warn you when trading activity is heavy and things are moving slowly. An order already filled cannot be canceled; another opposing order must be entered to close out a position.

Change Orders

Traders often want to change an open order. (Obviously, this is more of an issue with limit orders; market orders generally will have executed before you can process the change.) Traders can change limit or stop prices or the timing of an order. It should be a short, simple series of mouse clicks, but will encounter response time issues similar to cancellations.

Selling Short

Most investors talk about buying stock with money, holding it, and selling it back for money. Known as "going long," or holding a "long" position, success in this type of strategy requires the stock price to go *up*. But what if a trader thinks a stock or security is headed lower? Traders can sell short—that is, borrow shares and sell them, hoping to buy them back later at a lower price.

The Short-Selling Mechanism

The markets and brokerages have provided a mechanism to play an anticipated downward move, known as the short sale. In a short sale, the trader borrows the stock from his or her broker or trading firm and sells it into the market. If the broker doesn't own shares of the stock, the trader can be obtained from wholesalers or other middlemen. The trader receives cash but pays interest (margin) on the shares borrowed.

Short-Selling Rules

There are a few key rules governing short sales which all traders must know:

- ◆ **Uptick rule.** Short sales can only be "opened" when the market is on an "uptick" or "plus tick." That is, the last sale price or inside bid price must be above the previous one.

  Why is there an uptick rule? It's a leftover from the '29 crash. The major exchanges, in the interest of security and stability, wanted to prevent a selling "snowball," or "dogpile" as some traders call it.

Trading Terms

A **zero-plus tick** is a minor exception to the "uptick" rule: It occurs when the last trade was made at the same price as the previous one, but the previous one was higher than the trade two or more trades ago. Traders can sell short on a zero-plus tick.

The upshot: the stock must be going up, even if very briefly, for the short sale to be executed. Some trading systems won't even accept a short sale order on a downtick. Traders may want to play shorts while the stock is ascending—but shouldn't wait too long to find a top, because they may become boxed out by the uptick rule on the subsequent descent.

In May 2005 the SEC announced a temporary one-year suspension of the uptick rule in a pilot program involving about half of the issues traded on the NYSE and NASDAQ. The intent of rule suspension is to allow "free movement of prices." The intent of the pilot is to see if it has any real effect on trading. Many market commentators think it will give short sellers more power and lead to stronger downside moves, but we'll see.

- **Minimum price.** To short a stock it must be above $5 in price.

- **30-day rule.** New issues can't be shorted during the first 30 days of public trading

- **Availability.** Not so much a rule as a supply-demand condition, there must be stock available to borrow. Shorting doesn't work or may be barred from very thinly traded or illiquid stocks. Some stocks might be barred from shorting by a broker or trading firm.

Trade Secrets _____

Goody to remember: brokers often won't charge margin interest on a short trade unless the position is held overnight. So true day shorting can be free (of interest, anyway). Every little bit helps.

Entering a Short Sale

Short sale orders can be entered on all electronic trading systems provided the rules are met. The order is coded on the trading screen as a "sell short," usually one of the three choices (buy, sell, sell short). To close out a short sale—that is, to buy back or cover the short—a "buy to cover" choice appears on the ordering screen. Selecting "buy to cover" tells the order entry system to close out the short position instead of buying another "long" position in the security.

Short Sales Use Margin

A short sale is always handled as a margin transaction. Whereas a typical purchase transaction using margin involves borrowing funds to buy shares, a short sale involves borrowing shares to sell. The current margin interest rate is applied for the length of time the short position is open. The margin maintenance requirement (details coming next chapter) is often a little higher, meaning that a slightly greater account-equity percentage is required to borrow stocks for shorting than to borrow cash to buy long. In addition to paying interest, traders must also pay any dividends forgone by the lending party.

Trading Terms

Short squeezes occur when a number of short traders get pushed to the exits all at once. A modest up-move in a volatile, heavily shorted stock can get it started. Then it's like a herd trapped in a fire—orders fly in and automatic margin-related closeouts add fuel to the fire. Market makers and big traders see the opportunity and capitalize on it. It's a bad place to be.

Short-Selling Risks

The pervasive risk of short trading is the possibility of infinite loss. Going long means risking the price of the stock: buy a stock at $30 and a trader can lose all $30, but that's it, and it's unlikely that much will be lost unless the company goes belly up. The short seller, on the other hand, shorting a stock at $30, risks any and all loss as the price climbs higher, while all they can make is 100 percent—the price of the shares originally sold. There is also a risk—albeit minor—that the original shareowner will call the loaned shares back, and you'll have to go to market to buy them at whatever price they may have risen to. Markets can be quite cruel to a short position gone wrong; emotion-driven *short squeezes* can be devastating.

Shorting as a Strategy

Many stock traders are incurable optimists: anything they buy is sure to go up. People—most people, anyway—are just conditioned to think that way. But the astute and experienced day trader balances long trades with a few short ones. Not all markets go up all the time. A balanced approach makes the income stream more consistent while avoiding being caught on one side of the market.

It's a little harder to deploy short trading with the uptick rule, but it's a club that every day trader should have in his or her bag. There's more coverage of short selling strategy in Chapter 18.

After-Hours Trading

The rapid growth of trading has led to increased trading outside the normal U.S. market hours of 9:30 A.M. to 4 P.M. Eastern time. Mainly due to the advent of ECNs and advanced trading platforms, after-hours and premarket trading have become available to Main Street investors, and of course, active traders.

Another compelling reason for the growth of after-hours trading is that many news events—and most earnings announcements—are made after hours. In fact, the majority of earnings announcements are made 5 to 30 minutes after the market close, and some are made just prior to the market opening, to allow investors and analysts to digest news before taking action.

As a result, and combined with lower liquidity driven by fewer participants, after-hours trading can be quite volatile. This, of course, can be a good thing for traders, but it also makes after-hours trading more risky.

After-hours orders can typically be placed as limit orders between 4 and 8 P.M. Eastern Standard Time. After-hours activity on most markets ceases at 6:30 P.M. EST. Premarket orders can be entered at any time after the previous market close, with the trading session beginning in most markets at 7:30 A.M. EST. After-hours orders are routed to ECNs, and each ECN has its own trading hours.

The Least You Need to Know

- Most orders are "DAY" orders, but they can be set up for immediate fill ("fill or kill", or "FOK") or to stay in effect indefinitely ("good till canceled" or "GTC").

- Market orders will execute almost immediately at the inside market price. Traders can use them to achieve fast fills but must pay the spread and risk price movement.

- Limit orders are fixed-price orders used to either improve buy or sell prices, or to manage positions that can't be followed in real time.

- Stop orders become market orders at the "stop" price. A trailing stop order protects a trader against sharp downside moves, but may be vulnerable to specialist or market maker attempts to trade securities at prices favorable to them.

- Short sellers borrow securities to sell into the market, hoping to buy them back later at a lower price. Traders engaging in short sales must follow special rules.

Using Margin

In This Chapter

- ◆ Understanding margin trading
- ◆ Important margin terminology and rules
- ◆ Margin maintenance requirements and how they work
- ◆ The cost of using margin

Without a reasonably sized stake, it's difficult to turn a profit from trading. You need to make enough money to cover fixed information and trading costs and still have enough money left over to pay yourself. A 25¢ gain on a 100-share investment yields only $25. When commissions are factored in, the profit drops to near zero. That same 25¢ on 1,000 shares yields $250. But trading 1,000 shares requires a fair amount of capital (penny stocks aside), and presents a challenge to the average trader.

How does the trader put enough capital into play to succeed? The simple answer for all but the well-heeled trader is margin. In the world of trading, the term "margin" refers to funds loaned by a broker or trading platform provider to invest or trade in securities. This chapter explores the use of margin as a trading tool, including its rules and risks.

What Is Margin?

Margin is a form of credit. The brokerage house or trading firm loans traders money to buy securities. The lenders benefit from this practice in two ways: They earn commissions on all trades and they earn interest on the loan.

The amount loaned by the broker is called the debit balance. It is the amount owed plus accumulated interest on the loan. The debit balance rises daily or monthly, depending on how the broker charges interest.

The rules regarding margin trading are somewhat complex. In order to protect traders, the broker, and the economy, the Federal Reserve Board, the exchanges (NYSE and NASDAQ), and the brokers themselves have established a series of rules to regulate credit exposure. These rules cover how much can be borrowed on what securities. They also provide safety mechanisms to help curb leveraged accounts gone sour before all is lost.

Terms and Conditions

Traders need to be familiar with the terms, rules, and variables involved with using margin funds.

Current Market Value

The current market value of an account is the total value of the securities in the account as of the close of the last trading day. Brokers update the value of each account at the close of the market each market day. The term used in the industry to describe this process is "mark to the market."

Initial Margin Requirement

The initial margin requirement is the amount that must be deposited up front to purchase *marginable* securities. This requirement is set by the Federal Reserve Board and is called "Regulation T." These requirements can and will change as the market conditions change.

Trading Terms _____

Marginable securities are securities that a broker (with the help of the SEC) deems appropriate for margin buying. These are typically securities of known companies with a record of some stability and some intrinsic value. Generally, the list excludes shares under $5, many IPO shares, companies in bankruptcy, or companies simply deemed too speculative. Most brokerage quote and trading window displays will indicate if a security is marginable; this information is usually included on account statements as well.

To satisfy the initial margin requirement, a trader must make a minimum initial deposit. This is an initial amount that must be deposited and cleared into the account. As of this writing, the initial deposit required by the feds to establish a margin account for standard investing is $2,000. For "pattern" day trading, as discussed in Chapter 2, the requirement is boosted to $25,000 when the active trading "pattern" is established. Most trading platform brokers require this much or more to even start using their platforms.

In addition, a trader must meet a minimum equity percentage. The *equity* percentage is the value of the equity as a percentage of the current market value. Currently, the minimum equity percentage is set at 50 percent. This means for any marginable securities purchased, the equity percentage must be 50 percent. So an initial deposit of $2,000 means that a trader can buy up to $4,000 worth of securities.

Trading Terms _____

Equity is the difference between the current market value and the debit balance of the account. This figure rises and falls with the value of the securities holdings. In the original example this figure is also $2,000 ($4,000 current market value less $2,000 margin debt = $2,000 in equity).

As the stock moves (and as interest accrues) the equity percentage will change. In the preceding example, the equity percentage is 50 percent ($2,000/$4,000). But suppose a bad trade knocks $1,000 off of current market value, bringing it down to $3,000. The margin debt is still $2,000, so equity sinks to $1,000. The equity percentage drops to 33 percent ($1,000/$3,000). In this scenario, the trader must bring the account to a sufficient equity position by adding another $1,000 to his account.

Buying Power

Buying power is simply the total amount of securities that can be purchased, combining uninvested funds or funds already invested in marginable securities with the amount still available to be borrowed. In the earlier example, the initial $2,000 deposit brought $4,000 in buying power. But if the trader bought $1,000 of a security deemed unmarginable, that would reduce the buying power by $500 (50 percent of the $1,000). Buying power is used by many traders to gauge the overall success or failure of their trading activities.

Alert! _____

In 2001 the SEC revised its equity requirements rules for so-called "pattern" day traders. Traders are required to maintain an equity position of $25,000. If their equity falls below this amount, an additional deposit is required, otherwise short-term trading capability is suspended. For more on this rule, look up "Rule 2520" on any brokerage site or at the SEC (www.sec.gov).

Excess Equity

Suppose the $4,000 security position grows to a $5,000 position. The "debit balance" remains $2,000 (omitting accrued interest for the sake of simplicity). Equity rises to $3,000, up $1,000 from the start. In this situation, a trader can purchase more stock on margin. A $1,000 increase in equity means that a trader can purchase $2,000 worth of stock on margin (the newly acquired $1,000 excess equity turns into $2,000 of buying power because of the Regulation T 50 percent rule). However, keep in mind that the increase in equity doesn't repay the debit balance unless the security is sold and converted to cash. The only thing that repays the debit is cash—either from selling stock or from a new deposit.

Minimum Maintenance Requirement

So far the discussion has covered initial margin requirements and "buying power" limitations. Entering a stock position requires 50 percent equity. If the stock stays at the same price, the debit balance and equity stay the same, and everything is okay. If the stock increases in value and the debit stays the same, the equity increases, and everything is better. But what if the stock goes down?

Brokers and clearing houses, sometimes with guidance from exchanges, set rules to cover the minimum equity percent traders must maintain after the initial purchase. If the account drops below this minimum, the broker will require the trader to repay part of the loan in order to maintain satisfactory equity in the account. The broker issues a margin call to the trader.

The minimum equity is known as a minimum maintenance requirement (MMR). Most online brokers today have a 35 percent minimum maintenance requirement for ordinary marginable securities. That requirement may be higher when exceptionally risky or speculative investments are involved.

If a broker has a minimum maintenance requirement of 35 percent and if equity falls below 35 percent of current market value, the trader gets a margin call from the broker. Returning to our previous example, if the $4,000 investment becomes $2,500, the debit is still $2,000 and the equity is $500. That's only 20 percent equity ($500/$2,500), so the account is below the minimum maintenance requirement.

Why is there a minimum maintenance requirement, and why is it different from the initial 50 percent mandated requirement? It is intended to give the investor some cushion. Imagine buying 100 shares on 50 percent margin. The stock goes down 10¢—should that trigger a margin call? That would be too much of a nuisance for brokers and traders alike, and would accomplish little.

And what about the trader with a $1,000 gain—can he withdraw that money from his account? Yes, it does work out. The current account value is now $5,000, and the minimum maintenance requirement at 35 percent is $1,750. So a $1,000 withdrawal would reduce the equity position from $3,000 back to $2,000, which is above the minimum maintenance requirement of $1,750. It should be noted that once the withdrawal is complete, the account resets; that is, with a value of $4,000 and equity of $2,000, the 35 percent MMR drops to $1,400 going forward.

Trade Secrets

Exceptions to ordinary margin maintenance requirement rules emerged in the late 1990s as Internet stocks brought a new wave of volatility and speculation. Brokers responded by creating lists of stocks for which marginability—and minimum maintenance requirements—would be calculated differently. Such stocks required, instead of a 35 percent MMR, a 40, 50, or even up to 100 percent maintenance. Margin calls became more frequent, and it became difficult to predict exactly when portfolio activity would trigger that call, with so many stocks at different maintenance thresholds. Fortunately, that scenario has subsided today, but some brokers still maintain exception stock lists.

Trade Secrets

Free money! Doesn't that have a great sound to it? Don't laugh, some brokerage houses really offer free money—for a limited time, anyway. If you trade in and out of a trade during the same day, avoiding the nightly mark-to-market, interest won't be charged on margin funds used to make the purchase. Check with your brokerage house to see if it charges interest on intraday trades. Regardless of charges, initial margin requirement and margin maintenance rules still apply, even for day trades.

Why Use Margin?

Margin is important, not only to enable traders to purchase substantial amounts of securities, but also to achieve leverage. Leverage is the expansion of the earning power of capital.

Behind the Screen

Commodities traders will find a different set of rules and regulations for borrowing on margin. Generally they allow borrowing of greater percentages of the security value. These margin rules appear in detail in Chapter 8, and prospective commodities traders should become familiar with them.

Suppose a trader buys $4,000 in stock and pays $4,000 in cash, and it goes up $1,000. She makes $1,000 on $4,000 invested, a 25 percent return. Not bad. But with the maximum 50 percent initial margin, only $2,000 of trader capital was invested. A $1,000 profit was still earned, now representing a return of 50 percent.

But the power of the lever works both ways. Suppose the stock goes *down* $2,000. In the first scenario, you lose 50 percent. Bad. If you used margin, guess what? You lose 100 percent. Worse. What's more, your broker will be phoning you with a margin call.

What Does Margin Cost?

The price tag for a margin loan, like any other loan, is interest, referred to as margin interest. Margin interest rates tend to run a little higher than some secured loan rates, like mortgages, but lower than others, such as auto loans. Margin interest rates are typically tiered—that is, preferred customers who borrow a lot are charged lower rates. Lower margin rates may also be available to active traders, as commissions contribute to their value to the firm.

As of this writing, the current industry norm for margin rates runs from 6 to 9 percent for ordinary customers, and from 4 to 7 percent for very active traders. By comparison, current home mortgages run just under 6 percent, and shorter-term equity lines are at about 5 percent. All things considered, it is fairly cheap money, considering the broker's risk.

Sample Margin Rates

Following is a sample margin rate table for rates offered by E-Trade, a popular online broker, in early 2005. Rates are usually tiered from a recognized standard known as the broker call loan rate. The Power E-Trade rates are available to eligible traders trading at least 27 trades per quarter. Note that the rate is determined by margin debit balance, not by the total value of the account.

Debit Balance	Standard Rates	Power E-Trade
Less than $50,000	8.99%	6.99%
$50,000–$99,999	7.99%	5.99%
$100,000–$249,999	6.99%	4.99%
$250,000 or more	5.99% (base rate)	3.99% (base rate)

Calculating Margin Interest

Interest is figured daily. Actually, as pointed out earlier in this chapter, it is figured *nightly*—interest is usually not assessed on debit positions closed out before the end of the day. Margin interest compounds, and some brokers may charge interest monthly while others debit accounts daily.

Tax Treatment of Margin Interest

Many investors can get a tax break on charged margin interest. Traders set up as a trading business (those who use Schedule C or a corporate tax form) can deduct the interest as a business expense (see Chapter 5). Individual traders can also deduct investment interest as a Schedule A itemized deduction, provided it is exceeded by investment income (which can include dividends and interest received elsewhere besides the trading account) and provided that they can itemize deductions in the first place. It's a good idea to get professional tax advice on such matters.

The Margin Call

"Dear, your broker is on the phone." Not good news for a trader with a few bad trades and a declining account balance. It's probably a margin call, which happens when the value of your account no longer has enough equity to support the loan.

Resolving a Margin Call

Returning to our previous example, suppose the equity drops to $500 on a now-$2,500 portfolio. The minimum maintenance requirement is 35 percent for all stocks contained in the portfolio.

The minimum equity required is 35 percent of $2,500, or $875. Thus the broker asks for $375, which, when combined with your $500 existing equity, will bring your equity up to $875. If there are stocks in the account with higher minimum maintenance requirements, the broker may ask for more. Each broker has a margin "department" that manages mark to market, evaluates margin calls, and calls the customer.

There are two ways to meet a margin call:

◆ Deposit more funds

◆ Liquidate positions

The simplest way to bring an account into MMR compliance is to send or transfer funds to the account. A trader also can elect to sell (liquidate) stocks to generate cash. Of course, a trader must sell enough shares to generate cash proceeds sufficient to bring the equity back up to minimum requirements. Furthermore, if the stock doesn't sell within a reasonable time period, usually the same day, the brokerage house has the right to sell some of the trader's securities—any securities they choose. This is called a "sell out."

Trade Secrets

A margin squeeze is bad news for traders with long positions on a declining stock, especially if they used margin to enter the position. The squeeze will cause the decline to accelerate. But it can also present a great buying opportunity. Look for securities with accelerating downward momentum, and wait for the momentum to subside just a bit—the margin-related selling may have abated.

Sell outs can hit traders particularly hard, because brokers will often dump the riskiest securities, which may have been the ones that got the trader in trouble in the first place. Often these sell outs occur at a market bottom. Why? Because other margin traders may have been caught in the same downdraft, and are forced to the exits at the same time. Such a rush is called a margin squeeze.

Should a Trader Use Margin?

So should a trader use margin? It depends. Margin is a tool that, when used properly, can help the trader play more sizeable positions and to leverage original risk capital. But leverage is a two-edged sword; it can take a trader out of the game more quickly. Use of a moderate amount of margin, perhaps 10 to 20 percent (instead of the 50 percent allowable) probably makes sense for most traders.

Traders should also factor in their financial situation outside the trading account. If a trader's other financial needs are met and funds are easily available elsewhere to cover losses, trading on margin is less of an issue. When it comes to trading on margin, an old financial maxim applies: loans are for people who don't need them.

The Least You Need to Know

♦ Margin is a form of credit extended by a broker, who will charge interest on the loan. Margin expands trading power and leverage, improving trading performance but increasing trading risk.

♦ To use margin, an account must have a minimum balance of $2,000 and meet an initial margin requirement of 50 percent—that is, a trader can borrow up to 50 percent of the value of most stocks.

♦ Account equity must remain above a minimum maintenance requirement, usually 35 percent of the current total account balance.

♦ Margin rules for commodities trading differ: initial margin requirements and margin maintenance requirements generally allow a greater percentage of the security value to be borrowed.

♦ Pattern day traders must maintain at least $25,000 equity in a margin account to maintain day trading activity.

♦ Accounts falling below the minimum maintenance requirement will receive a margin call from the broker. Accounts can be brought into compliance by depositing funds or selling securities.

♦ Margin interest is generally not charged for balances closed out before the end of the day.

Chapter 12

Online Brokers

In This Chapter

- How online brokers operate
- Advantages and disadvantages of using online brokers
- Online broker features and services
- Selecting and using an online broker

Online, or "Internet," brokers offer a versatile and cost-effective way for beginning traders to get started. All one needs is a computer, an Internet connection, and an Internet browser such as Netscape, Firefox, or Internet Explorer.

In this chapter we examine the features, benefits, and costs of online broker platforms and how traders can effectively use them for trading.

The online broker market is extremely competitive, and new services and pricing are announced almost daily. For these reasons, this chapter can't go into detail on specific broker offerings. Naturally, online brokers list the specifics on their websites and have telephone sales and support agents readily available to answer questions about their services.

What Is an Online Broker?

Online brokers are a low cost, easy-to-use way to get started in trading. Although basic online platforms may not offer enough speed and advanced features for the true day trader, most online brokers offer sets of features on more advanced or "hybrid" platforms that appeal to fast traders. Traders often migrate towards these more advanced platforms as they gain experience.

Online brokerage services are provided by true Internet brokers, firms such as E-Trade, Ameritrade, or TD Waterhouse. Online services are also provided by traditional discount brokerage firms, like Fidelity and Charles Schwab, as a part of a wider range of services, and they are also available through traditional brokers like Merrill Lynch and Morgan Stanley. These platforms and their technologies are fairly standard, giving a similar look and feel. But each platform will have slightly different features, somewhat different costs, account management tools, and research tools to support trading and investing activities. At the end of the day, they are more similar than different.

The "Pros" of Using Online Brokers

Online brokers offer a cheap, flexible way to get into trading. Here are the key advantages:

- **Cost.** Online brokers' relatively low commissions and fees make it feasible for many people to get started trading. In addition, brokers provide a wide array of free information services. And some of the important fee-based services, like streaming quotes, are available at modest prices.

- **Room to grow.** Most of today's online brokers have some advanced platform offerings, either developed in-house or acquired from a direct-access platform provider. As traders gain experience and begin moving into advanced trading, they can migrate to their brokers' "hybrid" platforms, like Schwab's StreetSmart Pro and Ameritrade's Apex, which offer advanced tools in a browser-based package.

- **Flexible offerings.** Traders can get the services they need to manage their entire portfolio, not just the active trading portion. Retirement accounts and other "cornerstone" portfolio segments can be established with the same broker, and most brokers offer packages that include professional research and advice services.

The "Cons" of Using Online Brokers

Online brokers lack the breadth, depth, and delivery capabilities required by most serious traders. Hybrid platforms go a long way to fill the gap, but still fall short for many serious traders in these areas:

- ◆ **Breadth.** Although online platforms, and even most hybrids, allow trading of all stocks and most options, they do not support commodities or futures trading. Most also do not allow users to track or trade multiple stocks at a time.

- ◆ **Depth.** Basic online broker platforms do not have deep market access, i.e., NASDAQ Level II quotes. Such services can be purchased as add-ons for many platforms, but in many cases traders must establish themselves as active before they can access them, creating sort of a chicken-and-egg quandary.

- ◆ **Delivery.** All online broker platforms are browser-based, and basic platforms have no streaming data. Result: all news, quotes, charts, and so on must be refreshed.

> ### Behind the Screen
>
> Most online brokers do offer advanced features, such as streaming quotes, news, Level II access, discounted commissions, and even complete trading platforms. But traders must establish themselves as an "active" trader to qualify for these features, particularly if they want the features for no additional charge. Such requirements—to trade at least 10 times a month, for example—can cost a trader a lot in commissions, not to mention losses, just to get started. Most firms now offer some sort of trial period, but once past, traders must still pay their "dues," in the form of commission trades, regularly, which may interfere with what they really want to do. Some providers offer some advanced features at no additional charge if the account is large enough—usually $100,000, but sometimes lower.

Online Broker Features

The kinds of services brokers offer can be broken down into three broad categories: information, trading, and support. In the following sections we'll explore each of these service categories in detail.

Information

As you read this section, keep in mind that almost all information offered by online brokers requires browser refresh (it's not streaming), and the speed at which it is delivered depends on the speed and quality of your Internet connection.

Quotes

Most online platforms offer simple, browser-refreshed NASDAQ Level I quotes—that is, last trade and inside bid and ask. Most show size at the inside level. All platforms offer delayed quotes (15 minutes NASDAQ, 20 minutes NYSE). Some platforms offer real-time (though not streaming) Level I quotes, but to access them you might have to meet an account minimum or a certain level of activity. Most offer option equity market index quotes but do not offer foreign stock or commodity quotes.

As an add-on feature to their basic packages, most providers offer some form of Level II access, some with streaming quote windows. Generally these features are fee-based or require traders to meet activity minimums.

News

Most platforms provide both general and company-specific news coverage, but most of it is not streaming. One must keep a quote window open for the security to get news on that security. It isn't very flexible or dynamic, but it works.

Advanced hybrid platforms (discussed later in this chapter) offer much better news services.

Charts

Online brokers offer flexible charting packages even with the most basic platforms. They typically offer a variety of chart horizons, chart types, technical indicators, and comparative charting. Traders can set up charts to show price and volume activity for stocks of interest to them. However, these charts are not streaming, so they cannot easily be used to track minute-by-minute activity. (Chapters 16 and 17 discuss charts in detail.)

Research

When it comes to research, online platforms are geared to the long-term investor. Most brokers offer an assortment of investing tools and reports from Standard and Poor's, Argus, Morningstar, and some brokerages, particularly in platforms designed for larger or more active accounts. At least one provider—Fidelity—offers analysis software to its active traders. But for trading purposes, the best resources are mainly found in advanced trading platforms and the information sources that support them.

Alerts

Most online platforms offer some form of alert service, although you probably won't be surprised to learn that some of the more advanced alerts require active account status. Alerts cover a range of action, from minute-to-minute price behavior and news stories to daily and weekly portfolio and news summaries. Most basic platforms send such alerts by e-mail—which tends to not be a fast-enough delivery method for very active traders. Some alerts can be set up to transmit to a wireless device such as a PDA or pager. Price alerts—perhaps the most useful alert service for active traders—can be customized on basic platforms, but the range of options is more limited on basic platforms than it is on advanced platforms.

Online platform alerts, in general, are useful but not as real-time, customizable, or actionable as those available on advanced trading platforms.

Account Status and History

All online platforms provide summaries of account activity, balances, and gains and losses, although not always on a real-time basis.

Schwab Signature Trading™ screen for setting up stock price alerts

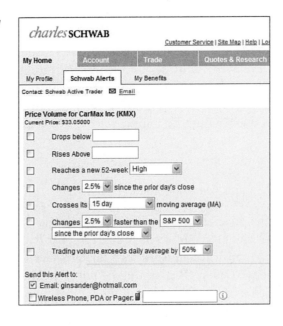

Trading

Online brokers provide fast executions at competitive prices. The trading capabilities aren't state of the art, but they are good enough to enable traders to execute a number of trading strategies.

Alert!

Read the fine print before signing on with a broker who advertises extremely low commissions and fees. Brokers may charge quarterly or annual account maintenance fees for smaller accounts, and at least one broker charges extra to place limit orders. Make sure you *fully* understand the commission and fee schedule before signing up.

Discounted Commissions

Discounted commissions are a key feature of online brokers and, naturally, a highly competitive battleground. As of this writing, commissions range from as low as $5 for some very active traders on platforms which may also lack many features and support, but most range from $9.95 to $19.95, with lower price structures for more active traders.

Ordering Features

Most platforms incorporate the ordering features most traders would expect to find—the ability to place market and limit orders, fill or kill orders, and all-or-none orders. Beyond these features, most online platforms are set up to require traders to review their orders before they are placed. Particularly with slow browser connections, this consumes time, and may expose the trader to slippage. Although some hybrid platforms allow more advanced order logic, such as platform-generated trailing stops, such advanced tools are generally not found on online broker sites.

Fast Execution

Online brokers are in a race to see who can offer the fastest order executions. Most have improved their systems—and eliminated the middlemen—to get orders to and confirmations from the market very quickly. E-Trade offers a two-second guarantee for SOES-size market orders (1,000 shares or fewer), and most of the others offer an order execution speed of less than 10 seconds. At the time of this writing, Schwab was offering a match-the-competition guarantee—if a trader can prove someone would have been faster, the commission is free.

Margin

Online brokers provide competitive margin offerings. Very active traders—or traders with sufficient account balances—often get preferred margin rates. See Chapter 11 for a more detailed discussion of margin, including a list of typical interest rates.

Options Trading

Most online brokerage platforms offer equity and index option trading, but that's as far as they go beyond standard equity trading. Some online brokerages, among them DT Futures (www.dtfutures.com) and The Linn Group's "Smart" platform (www. smtfutures.com), specialize in futures trading. However, as of this writing, those services have not been integrated into the typical online brokerage offering.

The best online option trading platforms offer quotes on complete options chains, as introduced in Chapter 4. Each option is arranged in series by expiration and price. Many include option analysis tools such as displayed theoretical option prices based on the Black-Scholes option pricing model.

Options Expiration: February 19, 2005

	Symbol	Open Interest	Volume	Net Change	Last	Bid	Ask	Strike Price	Bid	Ask	Last	Net Change	Volume	Open Interest	Symbol	
		Calls								Puts						
Trade	SQXBV	71	0	0.00	7.40	8.00	8.40	42.5	0.00	0.05	0.10	0.00	0	81	SQXNV	Trade
Trade	SQXBI	207	0	0.00	4.50	5.60	5.80	45	0.00	0.05	0.10	0.00	0	1,202	SQXNI	Trade
Trade	SQXBT	1,063	21	0.50	2.90	3.20	3.50	47.5	0.10	0.15	0.15	-0.20	310	2,535	SQXNT	Trade
Trade	SQXBJ	4,556	1884	0.45	1.35	1.30	1.45	50	0.60	0.70	0.70	-0.55	2712	10,091	SQXNJ	Trade
Trade	SQXBK	11,878	316	0.05	0.10	0.05	0.10	55	4.20	4.50	4.20	-1.50	294	11,839	SQXNK	Trade
Trade	SQXBL	7,174	0	0.00	0.05	0.00	0.05	60	9.10	9.50	9.20	-0.80	19	2,884	SQXNL	Trade
Trade	SQXBM	5,053	5	0.00	0.05	0.00	0.05	65	14.10	14.60	10.40	-4.79	0	148	SQXNM	Trade

Sample Option Chain, from E-Trade, displaying the series of put and call options available for a stock.

Service and Support

Most online brokers offer telephone and online support to help with questions about trading platforms, account status, or basic securities-related questions. Today, most support services are open 24 hours a day, although some require certain account status to get round-the-clock support. Many offer broader arrays of financial planning services to accompany basic platform support. Active traders today can expect to get privileged access to dedicated support teams and account managers, increasing the breadth, depth, and quality of support services.

Active Trader Add-ons and Features

Most online brokers offer some form of a "hybrid" trading platform, incorporating many tools from more advanced and specialized direct-access trading platforms.

> **Trade Secrets**
>
> Active trader qualifications vary from broker to broker, and if a trader trades 10 times per month or has $100,000, some set of "first-class" features are usually available. Read the fine print, and realize this arena is extremely competitive and changes constantly.

What Is an Active Trader?

Different online brokers define "active trader" differently, but the distinction is usually based on the level of trading activity or some combination of trading activity and account size. Charles Schwab has the lowest trading threshold to qualify as an active trader—four trades per month—but may charge monthly account fees if the account falls below $50,000. Ameritrade requires 10 trades per month or an account balance of $100,000. E-Trade's minimum requirements are similar to Ameritrade's, although it makes available to all traders some high-performance information tools, like streaming quotes.

Commission Discounts

Most online brokers give their most active traders a break on trading commissions. As noted previously, the typical "base" commission ranges from $14.95 to $19.95 per trade. With active trader status, the range drops to $12.95 to $9.95, and sometimes even lower.

Options traders should be sure to review option commissions. Without preferred status, option trades can be very costly, up to $40 or $50 per trade. However, today's preferred rates typically run $9.95, plus $1 or $1.50 per contract.

Streaming News and Quotes

Active trader status qualifies clients for some form of streaming news and quote service, most often through a hybrid platform like Schwab StreetSmart Pro, E-Trade Power Etrade Pro, or Ameritrade Apex. Note that E-Trade offers a streaming quote service for free to *all* accounts.

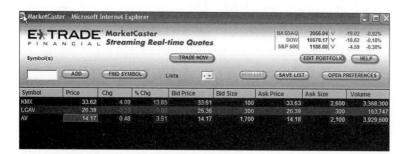

E-Trade MarketCaster Streaming Real Time Quotes free streaming quote service.

Dedicated Service and Support

Increasingly, the larger online broker players are offering their more active traders a higher level of dedicated support, and even training. Most now offer dedicated toll-free round-the-clock access to some form of "Client Services" desk. An account balance of $250,000 gets a "relationship manager" at E-Trade, and Charles Schwab dedicated support brings strategic advice for trading and for all parts of a trader's portfolio.

Software Tools

Most online trading and "hybrid" platforms offer some technical analysis capability, usually in the form of fitting trend lines and oscillators to historical data (see Chapter 16). More advanced software packages, which examine deeper patterns and "back test" for entry and exit points, must be acquired from other sources. However, in late 2004 Fidelity began to offer its new Wealth-Lab Pro—a fairly advanced analytic package—as part of its Active Trader Services platform. It's likely that others will soon follow suit.

Hybrid Platforms

Hybrid platforms incorporate *most* of the features of advanced direct-access trading platforms, usually at a fraction of the cost. They represent an ideal way for people to migrate towards serious trading.

Hybrid platforms are browser-based, but they incorporate streaming information and direct-access tools from advanced, direct-access platforms. They offer real-time Level II quotes, real-time charting capability, direct access and advanced order routing for trading, and sophisticated customizable alert setups. Devoted traders can run them continuously on their desktops, while those doing something else can run them in the background with a set of effective alerts. Specific hybrid platform features will be discussed in the context of advanced platforms in the next chapter.

Schwab's StreetSmart Pro standard desktop layout.

Although hybrid platforms offer most of what serious active and day traders need, they still have a few shortcomings.

Probably the biggest shortcoming for traders is that hybrid platforms are web-based and are subject to its limitations, including delays and unwanted interruptions. Broadband goes a long way to reducing connection problems, but it doesn't eliminate them altogether.

Hybrid platforms also limit the kinds of securities one can trade. They do not allow trading in commodities or other specialized securities, for example.

Finally, some hybrid platforms may only allow Level II access and trading on one stock at a time.

Many traders use hybrid platforms as an excellent set of "training wheels" to advance further.

Choosing an Online Broker

Traders will need to determine their own needs based on their expected trading activity, their knowledge, and their broader financial needs. The following sections detail some common selection criteria.

Features and Services

Look for …

- **Quote services.** All online brokers provide delayed quotes. Are real-time quotes available and free? Are streaming quotes available? For free? What about Level II quotes? At what cost?

- **Charting and technical analysis.** Do sites provide easy-to-use charting tools? How good are the technical analysis overlays? Are real-time intraday charts available? How long does the browser refresh take?

- **News services.** Are there real-time streaming news stories from the major wire services (Reuters, AP, Business Wire, Dow Jones)?

- **Alerts and other tools.** Are alerts available, and are they customizable? Can they be delivered in such a way that a trader can react in real time?

Ease of Use

Screen design and layout should be simple and easy to read, as should navigation among pages. Complex screens take a long time to refresh, and complex navigation takes precious time away from trades and important confirmations. Look for simple layouts and easy buttons to access trading and information tools.

Trade Secrets

Desktop "real estate" is at a premium for most traders. Many traders use 19-inch or 21-inch (or larger) monitors, and some technically savvy traders split their trading screen among multiple monitors to keep everything in view.

Trade Secrets

Traders are wise to think not only of today but also tomorrow. What features and services are available at what cost for more advanced trading?

Cost

Look at the total cost picture, including commissions, cost of information and quote access, margin rates, and other fees. Brokers are like retailers—each offers a value proposition with loss leaders and profit generators. Each trader has specific needs and trade-offs, and should look for the set of choices that best suits their needs and read the fine print.

Minimum Trader Requirements

Each online broker will have minimum requirements for opening an account. These requirements, along with cost, performance, and features, are an important part of a broker's "mix." The key, for active and day traders, is what the break points are for premium active trader services.

Performance and Dependability

Performance and dependability can mean everything to the very active trader. Here are some key performance characteristics to look for:

- **Execution speed.** Trades should be executed and confirmed in 5 to 10 seconds, faster in hybrid platforms.

- **Dependability, reliability.** Look for clean, fast, dependable websites. Complex sites with lots of pop-up windows and ads add to the burden of browser refresh.

- **Order routing.** Does the firm execute and clear its own orders? Or does it send them through another intermediary? Does it offer any kind of "smart" routing to get the best execution prices? What about direct access in a hybrid platform?

- **Rapid account updates.** Money management is an important part of trading, and good platforms should give rapid access to real-time or near–real-time account balances and positions.

Manual Backup

Redundancy is essential when it comes to trading. If something happens to a broker's server or a trader's Internet service, it can cause huge headaches, especially for very active traders. The best active trader services provide one or more of the following "backup" ways to get information and trade:

- ◆ **Agent backup.** It's essential that you have someone you can call to execute a trade "by hand," even though commissions might be higher.

- ◆ **Touchtone backup.** Most older online traders got started with touchtone trading with the likes of Schwab Telebroker™. It's still a good backup, particularly for travelers.

- ◆ **Wireless trading.** Today's wireless technology brings a lot to the PDA enthusiast. Frequent travelers should check out PDA alerts, information, and trading capabilities.

Service and Support

Customer-service quality is hard to judge objectively, but you can get a good first impression by calling various brokerages' active trader desks. Do the agents seem knowledgeable and willing to help? Can they explain features and offerings in plain English?

Migration Path to Advanced or Hybrid Platforms

Does the broker have more advanced hybrid platforms, and even a fully advanced platform? Can a trader acquire some features of these platforms as "training wheels" as they progress? Does a trader have to spend hundreds in commissions to qualify, or are trial periods available? Are account transitions seamless, or does the trader have to "start over" with another platform?

> **Behind the Screen**
>
> *Consumer Reports, SmartMoney,* and *The Wall Street Journal,* among others, publish ratings of online brokers. Firms specializing in Internet performance also review online broker performance—studies of service and features appear regularly on Gomez (www.gomez.com).

The Least You Need to Know

- ◆ Online brokers offer an inexpensive way to get started trading, but offer only browser-based platforms, which may lack features many serious traders seek.

- ◆ Most online brokers offer advanced trading services and migration paths to more advanced trading platforms. New "hybrid" platforms provide a cost-effective way for new traders to access advanced trading tools.

- ◆ Online brokers compete intensively on features, service and price. Traders, especially active traders or those with large balances, are advised to shop carefully.

- ◆ Many online brokers offer real-time, streaming news and quotes for modest prices or even free.

Chapter 13

Advanced Trading Platforms

In This Chapter

- ◆ What high-performance trading platforms do
- ◆ Advanced information features
- ◆ Choosing a trading platform
- ◆ Today's advanced platform providers

In today's fast-paced, dynamic, and competitive trading environment, you need effective tools to achieve results. Success depends on knowing more, knowing it sooner, and being able to act very quickly on that knowledge.

Fortunately, technology advances and brokerage firms' energetic pursuit of the more lucrative "trader" segment of the retail brokerage market have brought forth an assortment of high-quality advanced trading platforms. They evolved from professional trading platforms that were originally designed for high-end computer networks and workstations.

Today, the best performance still comes with direct network connections, and most serious traders use them. But these advanced platforms can now be run on ordinary computers with an Internet connection, subject to some of the reliability issues mentioned in the previous chapter. As such, they provide sophisticated capability with increasingly low cost and technical complexity, and can be used from anywhere.

That said, these platforms are still far from free. As you might expect, high performance still comes at a price. Advanced platforms are geared to the very active trader—those placing anywhere from 25 to 40 (and more) trades per month—and are priced accordingly. If you're a part-time or swing trader, an advanced platform won't "earn its keep." (Fortunately, many of the better features on advanced platforms have been incorporated into the so-called "hybrid" platforms introduced in Chapter 12.)

In this chapter, you'll learn about the features found on most advanced platforms. By the time you reach the end of this chapter, you should have all the information you'll need to decide whether they will be of value to you.

Sample advanced trading platform from CyberTrader.

© 2005 CyBerCorp Holdings, Inc. All rights reserved. Used with permission.

What Makes Advanced Platforms "Advanced"

Advanced platforms provide the best in broad and deep-streaming, real-time news, quotes, and other information feeds. They help traders grasp the mountains of input by providing graphics and user-friendly data layouts and windows.

They also enable traders to trade in the markets rapidly and flexibly. They provide direct access to markets and launch orders into the market with precision guidance and timing, so the trader can hit the market with the right type of order. Advanced tools allow traders to stay invisible to the market until the right

> **⚠ CAUTION Alert!**
>
> Keep in mind that features will vary somewhat by platform. Like any high-performance tool, you must learn to use it before charging forward.

moment. Such tools put the day trader on a level playing field with professional traders, offering premium performance through combining the best information and trading tools in a single package.

Finally, advanced trading platforms' up-to-the-minute account-management tools enable traders to gauge performance and manage risk properly.

Advanced Platform Technology

When advanced platforms were originally introduced, connecting to them required a direct dial-up connection to a host computer. Today, the increased speed and reliability of the Internet has made it possible for traders to connect to many of these platforms via the Internet, making it possible to access them from multiple locations while at the same time saving a lot in phone charges.

> ### Behind the Screen
>
> Literally, "behind the screen" of an advanced platform is a high performance Java-based server and communications software programs. At the time this book went to press, there were about a dozen different versions on the market. Originally these high performance engines were developed for professional traders. Interestingly, the technology, and particularly some of the screen designs, are derived from battlefield defense technology systems.

The Complete Picture

Desktop components and the overall desktop "look" vary somewhat among providers but are more similar than different. The first time you look at the screen of an advanced trading platform, it will probably look very complex and "busy." Rest assured that the seemingly bewildering array of information, quote, and trading windows will become more familiar over time.

For ease of use, each feature has a separate window. You can change the size and shape of these windows to suit your needs. Advanced platforms also make ample use of color and enable users to configure fonts to help ease eye strain and distinguish between features. Drop-down menus and storable defaults make it easy to change information feeds and streamline trading actions.

You can save or store different configurations and settings for individual windows as well as for the entire desktop.

Another advanced/hybrid platform look: Ameritrade Apex.

Source: Ameritrade, Inc.

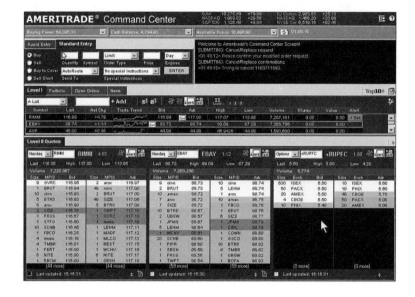

Information Tools

News and data on advanced platforms are broad, deep, and customizable. Traders get raw data and have access to a number of tools to help process it:

- ◆ **News feeds** can be set up to capture all breaking market and business news or just news for a specific company or group of companies.

- ◆ **Watch lists** can be customized to help traders follow specific stocks or portfolios of stocks.

- ◆ **Specialized tickers** can be set to watch certain kinds of quote and trading activity, such as the activity of a specific market maker or of a group of selected stocks.

- ◆ **Screening** tools enable the trader to capture lists of securities meeting certain price, quote, or technical conditions.

The following sections describe these features in more detail.

News

Traders watch news along several fronts to stay informed of general business and economic news as well as specific information affecting the companies and commodities being traded.

Hot Stories

Traders can set a streaming news window to capture and display "Hot Stories." Although they're not always "hot," the up-to-the-minute news releases follow the general pulse of business and the economy by capturing the major business and financial newswires—the Associated Press, PR Newswire, Businesswire, Reuters, Dow Jones, Comtex, and a number of smaller news sources. The stories can be *very* hot—such as the latest Federal Reserve Board announcements—or quite unrelated to the fortunes of most traders, as in the latest price and output of Turkish cotton. Significant announcements and regular market updates, including sector winners and losers, arrive through this window. There's a lot of "noise," but the window bears watching—if only out of the corner of your eye.

News Queries

The news window can also be set up to watch for news items on a specific security, sector, or commodity. You can set up this window to sound alerts or even to enact a trade if a qualifying news item comes across. News items appear in summary form with links to the full story.

Portfolio Watch

Slightly broader than the "query" feature, news windows can be set up to catch news on a series of stocks or other securities—like your portfolio, for instance. You can set up customized lists of securities or indexes to watch, like selected stocks in a market sector. Alerts can be set, and multiple windows and "baskets" can be tracked.

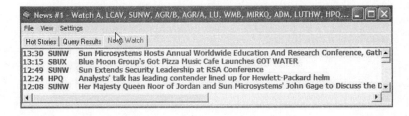

Sample portfolio news watch for Starbucks (SBUX), Hewlett-Packard (HPQ), and Sun Microsystems (SUNW).

Quotes

Advanced platforms provide full, deep, real-time quotes on securities and deliver those quotes in many ways.

Trading Window

The trading window is where the real action takes place. This is where quotes—both Level I and Level II—are displayed in greatest detail and where all of the order placement tools are located.

Sample trading window displaying Level I and Level II quotes with order entry, for Starbucks, Inc.

© 2005 CyBerCorp Holdings, Inc. All rights reserved. Used with permission.

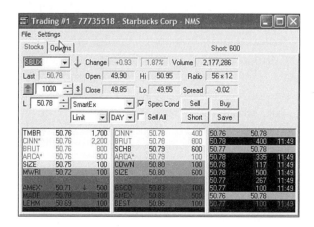

Level I Quotes

Recall that Level I quotes represent the best bid and offer price and size in the market for a security. Level I quotes are displayed in the trading window and elsewhere throughout the platform in watchlists and portfolio lists. These quotes are in real time and refreshed continuously.

Trade Secrets

All advanced platforms can support multiple open trading windows, whereas many "hybrid" platforms support only one. This can be one of the key differences between advanced and hybrid platforms.

Among the handy Level I features are the *ratio* and *spread* figures reported in the upper-right-hand corner of the trading screen (see the preceding figure):

◆ The **ratio** is the accumulated total of bid and ask size at the inside price and is an indication of a stock's immediate strength or weakness. The ratio "56 × 12" in the example indicates that more shares (5,600) are to be bought on the bid than sold on the offer (1,200), indicating that this stock has some strength.

- ◆ **Spread** captures the difference between the best bid and offer prices. Large spreads can indicate "scalping" opportunities; that is, the chance to capture a larger markup, and can also foretell rapid price movement. Why? Because when a security moves rapidly, bid and offer quotes (or orders on listed stocks) may not keep up with the change, hence the gap.

Level II Quotes

Level II quotes, which were introduced in Chapters 6 and 7, show quotes away from the inside market and are most important for trading NASDAQ stocks. By observing full away-from-the-market activity, it's possible to get a better picture of supply and demand. On the preceding Level II screen, the lower-left column represents bid quotes and the lower-center column represents ask, or offer, quotes. The market maker, or ECN, is listed to the left of the quote, and the size is listed to the right of the quote.

Trading windows highlight each price level away from the inside price in color (users can choose what colors to use). It's hard to illustrate this in a black-and-white book, but such color distinctions make it easier to pick up market depth. Additionally, ECN quote detail can be changed so that traders can see all ECN quotes, or just the inside quote from a particular ECN.

Chapter 15 goes deeper into reading the activity and intent of market players through the Level II screen.

Time and Sales

The Time and Sales screen is one of the most closely watched tools of the active trader. Simply, this screen shows the price and time of actual trade executions, called "prints" in trading jargon (the term carries over from the days when trades were printed on ticker tape).

Time and sales windows can also be set up to immediately show changes in the inside bid and offer price. For instance, in the preceding figure, the inside bid dropped to 50.76 immediately after the last print at 50.78, possibly indicating a slowdown in incoming market "buy" orders.

Many "fast" traders use nothing but Level II and time and sales screens to pick up instantaneous changes in market direction.

Watchlists

Traders can set up one or many groups of securities—or indexes—to watch. Data is fed into these lists as real-time quotes. Most platforms—advanced or hybrid—allow users to create and watch more than one list at a time.

Customized stock watchlist for the Standard & Poor's Specialty Retail Index ($RLX) and five specialty retailers.

© 2005 CyBerCorp Holdings, Inc. All rights reserved. Used with permission.

The accompanying watchlist has been set to track a selection of specialty retailers and the Standard & Poor's Retailers Index ($RLX). It has been saved under the name "PJSspecialtyretail," so it can be recalled at any time.

Note the tiny "newspaper" symbols in the second column to the left ("N ...", or "News"). These are clickable links to news stories on the wire that day for those securities.

Real-Time Charts

Advanced and hybrid products provide full charting capability, enabling traders to create charts depicting price behavior over a selected period of time. Several types of charts are available, including the popular candlestick variety illustrated here. Technical analysis "studies" can be added as overlays to the price history, and up and down price movements—and volume during such time intervals—appear in different colors on these charts.

Importantly, charts are real time; that is, intraday charts (depicting price history during the trading day) are updated as trades occur.

For more on charts and technical analysis, see Chapter 16.

Real Time Intraday Chart for Starbucks, Inc.

Alerts

Alerts can be a trader's best friend. As watchdogs, they track the data and "bark" when certain conditions are met, making it easier for traders to track many securities at once. Unlike online brokerage platform alerts—which only beep or send an e-mail when something happens—advanced platform alerts can be customized to set up or even launch a trade.

Alerts can be set to signal a wide variety of conditions and actions. Traders can set as many alerts as they wish, and they can be set to last through the trading session and stored for repeated use.

Alerts consist of a condition—that is, a definition of the circumstance the trader is watching for—and an action—that is, what happens when the condition is met.

Alert Conditions

Here are some of the many kinds of alert conditions available on advanced trading platforms:

- **Price,** or **print,** alerts indicate when a stock trades at a selected price or when the bid or ask reaches a certain level. Conditions can either specify a price or a price increase or decrease amount, which can be set as a dollar amount or as a percentage.

- **Volume** alerts are fired when the volume reaches a certain level (possibly indicating momentum or a momentum change).

- **Spread** or **straddle** alerts indicate when the gap between the inside bid and inside ask expands or contracts by a certain amount, potentially foretelling a price move or an opportunity to capture a spread.

- **Trailing stop** alerts are clever tools allowing a "stop" price (set by the trader) to shadow the stock price. For instance, a trailing stop set at 10¢ below the current price will rise so long as a stock is rising, then stay put to fire the alert if the stock falls.

- **Position** alerts are based on the level of profit attained. For instance, a trader can set an alarm to sound when a position has earned—or lost—$300 from the initial investment. Such alerts assist traders in managing money and risk.

- **Combination** alerts allow a trader to set multiple conditions as criteria. As an example, a trader could set an alert if price increases a certain amount with an increase in volume, factors that typically indicate an up move.

Trade Secrets

Server-held alerts are transferred from a trader's computer to the broker's host server, and can be set to go off or execute an action even if the trader isn't present or logged on. Such alerts can be handy for traders who can't constantly watch their screen.

Alert Actions

Just as interesting—and important—in setting alerts is defining the *action* to be taken when the condition is met. Basic alerts simply "beep" on your computer when the condition is reached. Alerts can also be set to play some stored sound or melody—handy when a number of alerts are set at once. And, unique to advanced trading platforms, alerts can be set to load or even fire off an order automatically.

Alert setup screen set to load an order to sell Starbucks when the bid price decreases to $50.50, a plausible stop-loss scenario.

© 2005 CyBerCorp Holdings, Inc. All rights reserved. Used with permission.

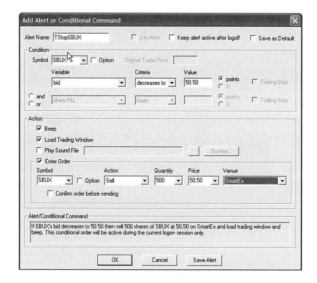

Screening Tools

Adding still more power to the trader's desktop is a series of screening tools designed to select baskets, or groups, of stocks exhibiting a defined condition. Naturally, these sets of stocks become a list of trading opportunities for a given trading day.

Screening tools can be used to create stock lists from a set of predefined conditions, usually related to strong price or volume movements. Such conditions can be simple, such as the top 25 gainers from yesterday's close. Or they can be more complex, such as measuring "gaps"—significant price moves at the open—or "lost gaps"—stocks that started with a big gain and lost it during the trading day. Screeners return a list with trader-defined data, usually real-time quotes and news-story links.

Trade Secrets

Many traders start their day with a stroll through several stock screens. For more on identifying trading opportunities, see Chapter 18.

The following illustration is an example of screened "gap up, stay up" stocks.

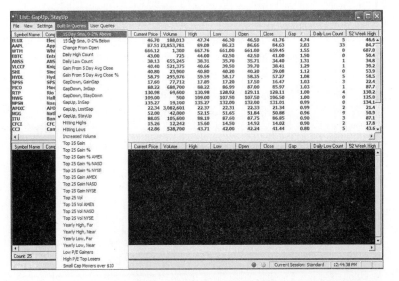

Stock screen for "gap up, stay up" stocks.

© 2005 CyBerCorp Holdings, Inc. All rights reserved. Used with permission.

Screening tools are available on advanced and hybrid platforms, although advanced platforms usually offer more complex and flexible conditions.

Tickers

Tickers track market trading activity throughout the day, bringing to light certain quote and trading patterns in the market. The trading screen, with Level II and Time and Sales windows, is the most basic type of ticker. More advanced tickers can be set up on several stocks at once. There are several kinds of tickers, which can be set up as desired through screen-driven menus. Tickers are generally only available on advanced platforms, not on hybrids.

A sampler:

- **Print** tickers are like the time and sales screen, but can be set up to watch multiple stocks at once, and to show only the "prints" that meet certain size or price move criteria.

Trading Terms

In trading terminology, a **hammer** is a very active market maker, usually in the market to buy or sell a large position for an institutional client. That market maker is at or near the inside most of the day, usually with large size. A hammer in one side of the market or the other will affect the balance of supply and demand, and hence the price.

- **Scan** tickers watch for a variety of quote and volume conditions, such as large block trades, preset price changes, or major quote changes.

- **ECN** tickers monitor activity through individual ECNs, providing a sort of time and sales screen for that ECN.

- **Market maker tickers** "lock on" to a particular market maker to watch quoting and trading activity. The dynamic ticker found in Schwab's CyberTrader Pro platform signals the direction of market maker activity, including quote changes and refreshes, in a handy graphic window covering selected stocks. The *hammer* ticker, from the same platform, shows strong and persistent market maker trades and quote refreshes.

Dynamic Ticker showing real-time change of selected S&P 500 stocks.

© 2005 CyBerCorp Holdings, Inc. All rights reserved. Used with permission.

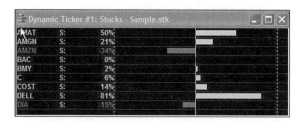

Trading Tools

Data converted to information, by itself, doesn't make money. Traders make money by converting information into knowledge and then into action. Advanced platforms do an excellent job of collecting and processing information, and they prepare the trader as much as possible to make a decision.

But they don't make the decision!

That part is up to the trader, who must implement the decision—that is, place a trade. Advanced platforms bring state-of-the-art tools and technology to the trading part of the process. Using high-performance military aircraft as an analogy, advanced platforms allow the trader to lock in on the target, then maneuver and fire with state-of-the-art precision.

Advanced platforms provide traders with direct access to the markets, a variety of flexible order types, and flexible order routing. Let's look at each of these features more closely.

Direct Access

Direct access means, simply, that the platform is hooked directly, via the broker's server, into the markets. That is, orders are launched directly into NASDAQ's SuperMontage, NYSE's SuperDot, and other market order–handling systems such as ECNs. Traders trade directly with market makers and other traders with no intermediaries.

Direct-access traders have instantaneous access to the markets, and can route orders as they choose. Combined with "smart" order routing (explained later in this chapter), direct-access traders gain the advantage in timing and routing to stay ahead of other investors and traders and get the best prices in the market.

Behind the Screen

Some traders describe traditional online broker platforms as "e-mail" trading. Orders travel from the platform to the broker in a manner not unlike an e-mail message, then onward to the market in the same manner. This system is inadequate for high-performance traders.

Order types

Advanced trading platforms can put all "standard" order types into play—market, limit, stop, stop limit—as described in Chapter 10. Beyond these, they introduce some "smart" order types, including the following:

◆ **Peg orders** automatically adjust as the bid or ask moves, allowing the trader to shadow a stock as it moves up or down. A dynamic trailing stop is a type of peg order.

◆ **Delta limit orders** automatically place a limit order at a predefined amount away from the current bid or ask.

Types of orders that can be placed in the CyberTrader Pro advanced platform.

© 2005 CyBerCorp Holdings, Inc. All rights reserved. Used with permission.

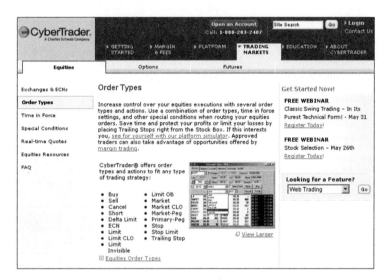

How these order types play into a trader's strategy is beyond the scope of this chapter, but traders will want to tackle them as they gain experience trading. Here, from CyberTrader, is a list of standard and advanced order types:

Order Routing

Advanced platforms, unlike online or even hybrid platforms, enable traders to preference individual market makers and ECNs. That is, a trader can use ECNs directly or trade with a specific market maker to get a preferred price or to test the resolve of that market player.

Advanced and hybrid platforms also offer *smart* order routing. That is, they can search across the markets and market players for the best price in the market.

Conditional Ordering

Conditional ordering, available on some platforms, is an exciting arena of platform development. Using conditional ordering, traders can specify a series of complex conditions, related to the security traded and to outside factors, to trigger an order. "Buy 500 shares of INTC when the Philadelphia Semiconductor Index hits an intraday loss of 2 percent while the NASDAQ 100 is down by less than 1 percent and AMD is down less than 25¢" might be an example of a conditional order.

Choosing a Platform

Selecting an advanced platform can take some time. There are a lot of choices, and each offers a somewhat different mix of features, cost, and additional "amenities" like training and support. Among the factors you should take into account when choosing a platform are …

- ◆ Market access.

- ◆ Information and decision support tools.

- ◆ Trading and execution tools.

- ◆ Account-management capability.

- ◆ Training and learning tools.

- ◆ Customer service and support.

- ◆ Cost of commissions, data feeds, and software.

- ◆ Initial qualifications and requirements.

Starting with the top of the list, the following sections explore each of these factors in more detail.

Market Access

Which markets does a platform access? Nearly all advanced platforms are set up to trade U.S. stocks and equity options. Some are set up to trade commodities, indexes, foreign exchange, and other specialized securities. Some platforms specialize in commodities or Forex (foreign exchange). Those wishing to enter these markets will need a capable platform.

Information and Decision Support

Many of the information and support features have already been described. Look for …

- Customizable news feeds.
- Advanced and multiple Level II quote capability.
- Advanced real-time charting and technical studies.
- Smart, easy-to-use alert capability.
- Specialized market tickers.
- Advanced stock-screening capability.
- Solid position and account-management tools.

Trading and Execution Support

Look for …

- Easy-to-use trading window design.
- Order type and condition choices.
- Direct-access trading (no intermediaries).
- Available ECNs.
- Routing and preferencing capability.
- Change and cancel capability (and cost).
- Conditional ordering.

Account Management

Account-management tools summarize account activity, positions open, gains and losses, and margin status. Look for …

- Total account size, buying power, and change.
- Positions open and profit and loss.

◆ Positions closed and profit/loss on positions over a period of time.

◆ Margin position and interest charged.

Training and Learning

Traders, especially new traders, need access to learning tools to develop and reinforce trading skills. Look for …

◆ Training courses, online and self-paced.

◆ An easy-to-use help facility.

◆ Simulators and hypothetical trading platforms.

◆ Knowledgeable telephone agents.

◆ An on-staff trading "guru."

Customer Service and Support

Service and support can be critical to resolving problems and understanding new features. Since software and connectivity offerings have become increasingly homogeneous among platforms, many providers today are using training and support together to differentiate their product. Look for friendly, helpful support available at all times.

Costs and Fees

Advanced platforms are expensive. The software is complex, and data feeds, particularly when exchange fees are thrown in, are costly to provide.

Platform providers recover software and data-feed costs through a combination of trading commissions, data service fees, and occasionally fixed prices for software products. Each provider has a different pricing formula, and there may be different pricing formulas available to traders with different levels of activity within a platform.

The following list should give you an idea of the kinds of services you'll have to pay for:

◆ **Data service.** Includes NASDAQ Level II quotes and feeds from ECNs and major option and commodity exchanges. Most firms offer a basic feed package costing anywhere from $150 to $300 per month. Many offer a break if paid in advance, and most waive the fee if a sufficient number of trades, maybe 40 per month, are made. Optional high-end feeds for NYSE Openbook or NASDAQ TotalView cost extra.

◆ **Trade commissions.** Today, per-ticket costs have dropped to around $10 for equities and options plus $1 or so per contract for the options. Small per-share or per-contract charges may be incurred for large trades exceeding 5,000 shares or 100 contracts. Some firms, vying for the very heavy trader, charge on a per-share basis instead of a per-ticket basis, offering preferred rates to the very active and large trader.

◆ **Other fees and costs.** Look at cancellation fees, exchange and ECN fees, costs of training tools, etc. And don't forget to factor in margin rates (see Chapter 11).

Adding it up: not including the cash you actually trade with, it can cost anywhere from $300 to $2,000 (or more!) a month to trade using a high-performance platform. Traders must look carefully at total costs and break points in trade volume and how they affect data-feed costs.

Trader Qualifications

Most platform providers require users to meet minimum financial qualifications. A typical requirement: $25,000 in the account (per SEC Rule 2520), $75,000 in liquid net worth, and $150,000 in total household net worth. Many platforms also require users to have some amount of trading experience and/or education.

List of Providers

The list of trading platforms, highly dynamic during the "gold rush" days of the late 1990s, has stabilized somewhat, at least in the equities (stock) space. Following are some of today's advanced direct-access platform providers, classified into two lists. The first list includes firms offering direct access trading and specializing in equities (stocks). Most of these firms also offer commodities and options trading. The second list includes firms specializing in commodities, futures, forex, and options trading.

Advanced trading platforms specializing in equities:

Bptrade Incorporated

CyberTrader Pro

DayTraderPro

DayTrading.net

DirectAccess Trader

e-brokerage, LLC

Edgetrade.com

Equity Trading Online

EquityStation

ETS Securities

GlobalTradz, Inc.

Great Eastern Securities

Interactive Brokers

Investors-Street, Inc.

Investscape, Inc.

JPR Capital

Lixit Capital, LLC

Lime Brokerage, LLC

MarketWise

MasterTrader

MB Trading

NDX Trading

Neovest

Nexa Securities

Pax Clearing Corporation

Preferred Trade

Princeton Daytrading LLC

ProTrader Securities LLC

R. J. Thompson, Securites, Inc.

RML Trading

SpeedTrader.com

SuccessTrade Securities

Terra Nova Trading LLC

Track Securities (MyTrack)

Trade Wall Street, Inc. (ECNDirect.com)

Traders Advantage

TradeStation Securities

TradePro

Trade Stream Global AG

Virtual Day Trader

Advanced trading platforms specializing in commodities, futures, forex, and options:

Active Futures, Inc.	GoFutures, Inc.
Alaron Trading Inc.	OptionsXpress
CMS Forex, Inc.	Refco Overseas Limited (Forex)
DT Futures	Summit Trading Group, Inc.
ExpressFutures (Orion Futures Group)	XPressTrade, Inc.

The Least You Need to Know

- ◆ Advanced trading platforms combine the best of information and trading engines into fully customizable desktops.

- ◆ Information tools on advanced platforms include news and data feeds and offer specialized features like alerts, screeners, and tickers to help the trader interpret information rapidly.

- ◆ Advanced trading platforms allow for flexible and conditional ordering.

- ◆ Advanced platforms are sophisticated tools and can cost anywhere from $300 to $2,000 a month.

Part 4

Reading Market Action

Part 4 examines the tools traders use to try to visualize what is happening and what is *going* to happen in the markets and with individual securities.

Chapter 14 looks at the "big picture": how to gauge the direction of the markets and individual market sectors. Market timing, seasonality, economic reports, and reading market "internals" are covered.

Chapter 15 changes gears to take a close look at one of the core tools of the trader: the NASDAQ Level II screen. This all-important screen shows, up to the split second, where the demand and supply is for a particular security.

Chapters 16 and 17 turn data into useful pictures through charting, technical analysis, and candlestick charts.

ENOUGH ABOUT *MY FUTURE*, WHAT'S GOING TO HAPPEN IN THE STOCK MARKET?

Chapter 14

Market Cycles and Behavior

In This Chapter

- ◆ Market timing and common market patterns
- ◆ External economic and business factors driving markets
- ◆ Internal indicators of market direction
- ◆ Market sectors and sector performance

This chapter is designed to give you an idea of the kinds of things that can affect market—and individual security—direction. Particular focus is given to some of the "macro" indicators of market direction.

Market direction is, of course, difficult to predict. But certain historical precedents and business and economic factors do—or at least seem to—influence it in a predictable way. In addition, traders can draw on some indicators of what those in the industry refer to as market "sentiment" and direction to get a sense of the day's activity and to select securities to trade.

After dealing with market behavior in the aggregate, the next three chapters examine behavior in specific securities through trading windows and technical analysis.

Market Timing

Much has been made over the years about whether anyone can—or should—try to "time" the market. Numerous studies have surfaced showing how long-term investors fare better holding their investments, avoiding the temptation to try to jump in and out at the bottoms and tops of market cycles. The jury is still out about whether market timing really can work for the typical long-term individual investor. But for traders, it may well be a different story.

In a nutshell, all traders try to turn a profit by timing market and individual security moves. It's still far from an exact science. The market is a hodgepodge of individual securities with external factors influencing their behavior such that no concrete, step-wise timing "guide" can possibly be accurate all of the time. Yet, certain aspects of the market are somewhat predictable. As a trader, you should at least be aware of these phenomena, though always keep in mind that, when it comes to trading, there are no guarantees.

Some timing patterns arise from the calendar itself and the underlying behavior of traders and the securities industry. Some arise from specific economic and business events, like the announcement of economic statistics, that can really influence near-term behavior.

The Market Almanac

Yale and Jeffrey Hirsch, a New Jersey father-son team from the investment industry, started examining historical market patterns years ago. Since 1950 they have published the definitive almanac on market behavior—38 editions in all—called the *Stock Trader's Almanac* (2005 edition, Wiley Inc.) The *Almanac* examines recurring market patterns and presents a day-by-day market calendar.

The *Almanac* points out a number of statistically significant repeatable market behaviors, as described in the following sections.

Yearly, Monthly, Weekly, Daily Cycles

Here is a smattering of the more interesting patterns for the active trader:

- ◆ The strongest bull markets occur during the middle of decades. No year ending in "5" has been a loser since 1885, and most "0" years (1990, 2000, etc.) have been down.

- The "January barometer" holds that a year's market direction can be predicted by January's direction with 91 percent accuracy. The year can be predicted by January's *first five days* with 85 percent accuracy.

- December and January are the strongest and most consistent "up" months, whereas September is the most consistently "down" month.

- Presidential elections can drive markets. Markets have gained 743 percent in aggregate in the second half of a presidential term versus 228 percent for the first half.

- Since 1990, Mondays are typically up days, whereas Fridays are typically down days. Before 1990, it was the opposite. Investors seem not to want to keep money on the table over weekends with today's unstable world.

- The first day of the month is strong. From 1997 to 2004 (83 months), the Dow Jones Industrial Average gained 3,559 points in aggregate on the first day of the month, while it lost 837 points during the rest of the month.

Seasonal Cycles

Beyond daily, weekly, and monthly cycles, there is a definite seasonal pattern to the markets. Since 1950, the months from November to April have been gaining seasons, whereas little to no gain takes place, on average, between May and October. Not only does market direction flatten out or decline in summer, but so does the volume. Many traders have advocated a strategy of trading actively during the late fall, winter, and spring, and "going to cash"—selling security positions—for the summer. Perhaps it's a useful "time off," but beware of the tax implications raised in Chapter 5.

> **Trade Secrets**
>
> Do markets fail to gain between May and October because Wall Street professionals are on vacation? Is the first day of the month a gainer because of new optimism? Because of IRA/401k deposits being invested? Understanding—or trying to understand—*why* these market moves take place makes them useful, and if nothing else, speculating on the subject is enjoyable.

Window Dressing

A number of market strategists follow end-of-month and especially end-of-quarter "window dressing" market moves. The moves are driven by the need for fund and other institutional managers to show solid performance to their shareholders and clients. Often stocks that are "popular" or have shown solid gains over a period tend to do well during the last few days of a calendar quarter (March, June, September, December) in part, at least, because fund managers, who may have been "left out" of such stocks, want to show these investments in their portfolio. Conversely, managers might weed out and sell poor performers. The behavior has little effect on the market as a whole but can influence sectors and individual stocks.

The Triple Witch and Her Friends

Markets may be driven in the short term by the expiration of options and stock index futures. Sophisticated market players "hedge" investments with options; that is, they buy or sell in directions opposite to their main position. An option expiration can mean large position closeouts (known as "unwinding") of baskets of stocks held against futures or options. What happens when options expire? Markets become more volatile, providing trading opportunities, though there is no definite pattern to the volatility.

The "triple witch" occurs four times a year when equity options, index options, and futures options all expire on the same day—the third Friday of March, June, September, and December. Other equity and index options expire monthly, but the triple witch expirations have the strongest effect on the market.

Investment Calendar

Public reports on business and economic performance shine new light on the condition of businesses and the economy. The types of reports are many and varied, and some have much stronger effects on the market than others. Successful traders follow these reports on a daily basis.

The Yahoo!Finance Economic Calendar, shown as part of the "Today's Highlights" page (see Chapter 9), is an example of a portal into such figures. Most key economic reports are announced and analyzed on NPR, CNBC, and other business news media sources.

The following indicators, selected from a much longer list, have the most profound influence on a day's action.

Pure Economic Indicators

"Pure" economic indicators reflect economic activity as a whole, and can be leading indicators of major market-driving factors like interest rates and inflation. Here are some key economic indicators:

- ◆ **Consumer confidence surveys** reflect consumer behavior, and, more importantly for markets, anticipated behavior. Look for monthly Conference Board surveys and the twice-monthly Michigan Consumer Sentiment Index.

- ◆ **Employment reports** show economic performance and tend to foretell inflation and interest rates. Look for weekly jobless claims and the monthly employment reports from the Bureau of Labor Statistics.

- ◆ Monthly **trade balance reports** summarize merchandise and total trade deficits and surpluses.

Inflation and Interest Rates

Inflation and interest rates can cast deep short- and long-term shadows over the markets. Inflation brings rising prices for raw material as well as higher interest rates, which in turn reduce the value of future investment returns.

Here are some key things to watch out for:

- ◆ **Inflation indexes** such as the Consumer Price Index (CPI) and Producer Price Index (PPI) show emerging signs of inflation or price stability.

- ◆ **Federal Reserve meetings** are the most significant interest rate events, where changes in short-term interest rate policy are announced and, perhaps more importantly to the market, statements of future sentiment are made.

Business Activity Measures

Business activity measures illuminate the level and direction of business in certain economic sectors. Such reports are interesting to traders in those sectors and may influence a day's market direction in total.

Here are just a few measures traders look to:

- ◆ **Sales of durable goods**—goods typically lasting more than three years—and auto/truck sales show strength or weakness in the manufacturing sector.

♦ **Retail sales** and **housing starts** reports are watched not only for the retail industry but as indicators for the economy as a whole. In fact, more than 75 percent of the U.S. economy is driven by consumer spending.

♦ **The National Association of Purchasing Managers** survey is a popular leading indicator of business, and especially manufacturing, activity.

Company Reports

It's hard to overestimate the influence of company-specific news on trading activities in that company's stocks. Earnings announcements and pre-announcements, major alliances or customer deals, or other news of fundamental shifts in business prospects can have a big impact on a stock price—and on markets in general.

Earnings reports tend to come in bunches, most at the end of calendar quarters. Markets can turn around—or accelerate in the direction already headed—depending on these announcements. Predictions for the future are important, too, especially from market leaders like Intel, Cisco, and General Electric.

> **Trade Secrets**
>
> Keep track of company announcement dates on stocks you trade frequently.

Many traders live for earnings announcements, going long or short on the typical "up" move prior to the announcement and capturing gains or new position entry on the ensuing "gaps," or large price moves, that often occur.

> **Behind the Screen**
>
> Does an individual stock or security behave in sync with the markets? Or does it behave on its own, driven by its own fundamentals and trading psychology? If it's the latter, it's said to be a secular performer, and its trends are known as secular trends.

Gauging Market Direction

Active traders need to gauge markets continuously through the day. Traders should always be aware of the "big picture" as they enter trades, even though their trades might not always correlate with what's going on in the market.

Some gauges track performance during the market session; others measure market sentiment or direction after hours.

Market Indexes

The purpose and construct of major stock indexes such as the S&P 500, S&P 100, Dow Jones Industrial Average, NASDAQ Composite, and NASDAQ 100 indices are well known. Other indexes track smaller or more specialized segments of the market (sector indexes and stock "baskets" are covered later in this chapter).

Stock Index Futures

Stock index futures are to stock indexes what oil futures are to oil. Traders, most of them professionals, use these financial futures to take a position in advance of a potential gain or decline in the major market indexes.

These futures trade around the clock, around the world, so traders (so inclined) can watch them through the night as leading indicators of opening market performance. The Bloomberg TV Network is a good "living room" way to watch these futures—but be careful not to bore the family!

Trade Secrets

If you watch CNBC or other financial broadcasts, you'll probably hear about something called the PREM indicator. PREM shows the premium—or discount—of the stock index futures contract vis-a-vis the cash index. A positive PREM can signal a time to buy. Some arbitrage strategies (see Chapter 18) actually kick in when these differences emerge, and you can trade the same way.

Market Internals

Analysts take "pulse measures" of the markets throughout the day to appraise so-called "market internals," or indicators of direction and strength lying below the surface of the major indexes.

The advance-decline line (also referred to as the "A-D line") is one of the more popular—it's simply the difference between the number of issues in positive and negative territory. Breadth is the term for the weight of the A-D line—that is, the excess of advancers or decliners, or vice versa. Some market watchers like to track a cumulative advance-decline line, totaling the number of daily advancers and decliners over a period of time. When the cumulative total gets too high, it is a sell signal; when too low, it is a buy signal. The so-called "TICK" is a very short-term measure of advances and declines, showing the number of stocks that have advanced or declined *since the last trade*.

ARMS is the name of a slightly fancier index weighing TICK by volume, to avoid distortions caused by a stocks trading only a handful of shares each day.

Other Overnight Indicators

Serious traders watch foreign market and after-hours activity to keep a finger on the pulse and to try to discern the direction of the next trading session. Asian and European markets may lead or lag the U.S. markets, most likely depending on recent events.

Observing after-hours trading is particularly useful for traders trading stocks in sectors typically active after hours—like technology stocks. After-hours activity is also an important indicator of how the market is absorbing earnings news, which is typically announced after market close.

Sentiment Indicators

The market indicators just discussed reflect the collective action of traders and investors worldwide. Another set of indicators, known as sentiment indicators, try to get closer to investor psychology and the psychology of the market. They, too, are based on real data, but the interpretation—which is often contrarian—is what's important.

Volatility Index, or "VIX"

The volatility index, or VIX, has become a closely followed measure of market behavior in recent years. Technically, the VIX measures the implied volatility, or anticipated frequency and magnitude of up and down fluctuations, of the S&P 100 Index, as estimated by its options prices. (See Chapter 4 for an explanation of how volatility influences option prices.) So it is an empirical, real-world measure of investor-anticipated volatility.

Trade Secrets

After the September 11, 2001, terrorist attacks, the VIX soared to a record 57.1. Did that turn out to be a buying opportunity? You bet.

So what does VIX indicate? Aside from higher option prices for all options (not just S&P), "sentimentalists" look at a high VIX as an indicator of investor anxiety and a low one as an indicator of investor complacency. The prevailing theory: anxiety occurs during market bottoms, and complacency appears at tops. So a low VIX, or implied volatility, of 18 to 20 percent indicates trouble, while 30 percent or greater suggests a buying opportunity.

Put/Call Ratio

Market watchers also study the aggregate behavior of investors trading options and draw conclusions based on their findings. Specifically, when investors buy lots of puts (options to sell stock), they are pessimistic; when they buy lots of calls, they are optimistic. The put/call ratio is simply the ratio of the two. The average is 0.60 over time—that is, for every 10 call options traded, there are typically six put options traded. When the ratio rises towards 1.0, investors are pessimistic and it is a buying opportunity; declines to 0.40 signal a sell.

Short Selling

Aggregate short interest is the total number of shares held in short-sale positions across all stocks. It is reported by the NYSE and NASDAQ monthly for stocks trading in these markets. Strong or rising aggregate short interest indicates pessimism. But like the preceding measures, it also indicates a buying opportunity, further fueled by the fact that such short positions must be covered by buying back shares.

CAUTION **Alert!**

Although the three sentiment indicators just presented are interesting market gauges, they aren't updated frequently enough to use for figuring out daily market direction. They can help traders figure out which way the winds are blowing more generally.

The Shape of the Day

For many traders, pictures are worth thousands of words. Visually oriented traders look at the shape of a day's trading charts measuring indexes, sectors, volume, and selected stocks. Those shapes are indicative of market behavior in themselves, and become more indicative when compared to the "shape" of previous trading days.

Trade Secrets

Many market followers believe that the most significant market activity occurs at the open and again at the close of the day. This is when traders and market makers are most active. So reading the first and last 30 minutes of the day is seen as especially important.

Patterns can be complex, and they may repeat better in some markets than others. Nonetheless, traders claim that such charts indicate "bullish" and "bearish" shapes.

Bullish Shapes

Positive market sentiment may look like a two-hump camel, with a strong open and close, or a valley at opening followed by a hill at the close.

The two-hump camel shows a buying surge at the beginning, a sell-off, usually on lower volume, through the day, and then a surge at the close. A larger hump at the end of the day, and particularly a close at the high of the day, indicates price strength for the next day.

The opening valley, closing hill pattern also indicates strength, and can indicate a failed profit-taking or even short-selling wave. Successive days showing this shape are very bullish, but the trader must watch for major deviations or reversals in the pattern.

Bearish Shapes

Logically, bearish shapes are the opposite of the bullish shapes just described. A valley at the open shows a selloff at the open. When there is also a sell-off (valley) at the close, it shows weakness in the security. When the open is positive but the price decays through the day into a weak close, it is even more pessimistic. The "smart money" is bailing at the end of the day. Like the bullish patterns, these patterns are more indicative when repeated over a series of trading days.

Sectors and Sector Performance

Markets are divided into sectors based on the types of industries or businesses they are in. Indexes have been created that track "baskets" of companies in each sector. More recently, sector, or index, funds have been created, making it possible for investors and traders to buy these "baskets" as a security.

Studying sector behavior can be a valuable tool for traders trading individual securities in a particular sector. For such securities, sector performance is more meaningful than the performance of the markets as a whole. But more importantly for many traders, sector performance signals "where the action is"—what's "in" and what's "out" during a given trading day. Such signals give the trader a map for where to dig deeper.

Sector Indices

Common sector indexes are provided by Standard & Poor's and also by Morgan Stanley. Standard & Poor's uses the Global Industry Classification Standard (GICS) to create their indexes. The indexes are presented in a hierarchy, starting with the industry and working down to a specific sector and subsector. Thus, a consumer electronics retailer like Best Buy, Inc. might be in the Consumer Discretionary industry, Household Durables sector, Consumer Electronics subsector. There is an index shown at each of these levels.

High-end and hybrid platforms offer sector windows to give the trader a quick view of current sector performance. The sector window offered by Schwab's CyberTrader Pro (also available in StreetSmart Pro) shows activity and price changes for sectors, and it is possible to "click through" the hierarchy to see the individual companies and securities that make up the sector.

Taking Sectors Apart

Each sector contains a group of companies (stocks) representing that industry or sector. As noted previously, sectors can be looked at in the aggregate or in parts. That is, a trader can look at the sector at a high level or industry, like Consumer Discretionary, Energy, or Financials—or break each sector down into industry and subindustry components.

Sector hierarchy shown with breakdown of Consumer Nondurables industry. Traders can open "+" or close "-" each level in the hierarchy down to individual stocks.

© 2005 CyBerCorp Holdings, Inc. All rights reserved. Used with permission.

Trade Secrets

In contrast to the Morgan Stanley/S&P sector definitions, ETFs provide a vehicle to actually trade the sectors, through buying and selling the ETF. Many traders use these vehicles to capitalize on short-term moves in the sector and to hedge other activity.

Exchange Traded Funds

Beyond the Morgan Stanley/S&P sector classification, traders can also follow the activity of Exchange Traded Funds (ETFs). These are baskets of stocks designed to follow a particular sector or segment of the market. Sectors can be based on traditional sector-industry classifications, or can represent certain cuts of the market like large-cap, small-cap, growth, income stocks, commodities, and so forth. Many international markets are represented by ETFs. There are about 180 ETFs in all, and the number is rapidly growing.

A preloaded ETF watchlist is available on CyberTrader Pro and StreetSmart Pro, or traders can create their own customized list. This illustration shows the preloaded version.

© 2005 CyBerCorp Holdings, Inc. All rights reserved. Used with permission.

Symbol	Company	Last	Open$	Close$	Close"
DIA	DIAMONDS Trust,Series1	107.30	107.33	107.81	-0.5
IYC	iShares DJ US Cons Svc Se	59.02	58.89	59.43	-0.4
IYH	iShares DJ US Hlth Sec In	58.87	58.80	59.00	-0.1
IYK	iShares DJ US Con Goods S	53.61	53.65	53.89	-0.2
IYR	iShares DJ US R/E Index T	116.66	118.70	118.50	-1.84
IYT	iShares DJ Transp Avg Ind	64.90	64.37	65.15	-0.2
MDY	SP MidCap Dep Receipts	120.72	120.64	121.04	-0.3
OIH	Oil Sv HOLDRs Tr Dep Rece	96.65	97.49	96.30	+0.3
PPH	Pharmac'l HOLDRs Tr Dep R	72.24	72.25	72.07	+0.1
QQQ	Symbol Changed to QQQQ			39.12	
RKH	Regional Bank HOLDRsTr	134.77	134.90	135.62	-0.8
RTH	Retail HOLDRs Tr Dep Rece	96.94	97.36	98.13	-1.1
SMH	Semiconductor HOLDRsTr	33.89	33.04	33.35	+0.5
SPY	SP Dep Receipts	120.00	119.90	120.39	-0.3
SWH	Software HOLDRs Tr Dep Re	34.98	34.84	35.05	-0.0
XLB	SP Sel Materials SPDR Fu	30.62	30.60	30.58	+0.0
XLE	SP Sel Energy SPDR Fund	42.64	42.50	42.05	+0.5
XLF	SP Sel Financial SPDR Fu	29.63	29.60	29.79	-0.1
XLI	SP Sel Industrial SPDR F	30.29	30.24	30.50	-0.2

The Least You Need to Know

◆ Studies have shown a number of consistent daily, weekly, monthly, and seasonal patterns. Although these patterns are statistically significant, they should be used with caution.

◆ External factors driving markets include pure economic data, inflation and interest rates, and business activity reports.

◆ Stock indexes, stock index futures, and a series of "sentiment" indicators can help predict market direction.

◆ Many sentiment indicators are actually contrarian—that is, the most pessimistic readings signal an upturn, and vice versa.

◆ Many traders examine sector performance more closely than overall market performance. Individual stock performance often ties closely to sector performance. Sector performance also reveals trading opportunities.

Using the Level II Screen

In This Chapter

- ◆ About the NASDAQ Level II screen
- ◆ Watching the market at work before your eyes
- ◆ Customizing Level II displays
- ◆ Reading Level II action: an example

The previous chapter examined some of the tools traders use to get a general, or "macro," feel for market action and direction. Here, we shift our focus to individual securities. The Level II screen, now coming to be known as the "Totalview" screen in NASDAQ parlance, is one of the most powerful trading tools. As much as any other tool available, Level II puts traders on an equal footing with the professionals, providing them with real-time information about the actions of other traders in the market.

This chapter expands on concepts introduced in Chapters 7 (NASDAQ) and 13 (advanced platforms) to examine some of Level II's more important features.

The Level II Concept: A Short Review

The NASDAQ Level II screen lays bare the forces behind the market. As a window to the NASDAQ electronic quote board, it shows *all* bid and ask prices—not just the "inside" or best bid and ask shown on a typical online brokerage quote screen—of all market participants, including market makers and ECNs.

At and Away from the Market

Using Level II, traders can see who's bidding what for how much, and who's offering what for how much, both *at* and *away* from the current market price. The full market, away from the inside, reveals patterns and the strength of supply and demand in the market as a whole. Traders refer to the visibility offered by Level II screens as *transparency*.

Time and Sales

The Level II screen itself is a quote board, and as such does not cover actual trades in the market. On most platforms, it is shown as part of a more complete *trading window*. In addition to showing Level II quotes, the trading window hosts the launch screen and the Time and Sales screen, providing the best very short-term information and trading tools all in one place. As noted in Chapter 13, the Time and Sales screen, usually shown alongside the bid and ask quotes, shows individual trades. It can also be customized to show quote changes.

In a sense, Level II captures market *status*, while Time and Sales captures market *action*. Stated differently, Level II tells where the market is going, while Time and Sales tells where the market has been.

An Action Movie

In all but the quietest stocks, Level II is a real action flick. Quotes move around with rapid-fire pace, so much so it's hard to keep track of them. This has become particularly true with the advent of decimal trading—quotes that change a penny at a time. All the action makes it a challenge to separate the "news" from the "noise." Fortunately, liberal use of color and a few other tools help.

In Living Color

It's unfortunate that this book is printed in black and white, because the NASDAQ Level II screen not only presents a lot of data, but presents it in vivid color. Each level away from the market is depicted in a different color, and different colors are used to show transactions. These colors help traders quickly discern patterns and strength.

By Way of Example

The following figure shows an example of a deep Level II screen for Restoration Hardware, Inc. (symbol "RSTO"). "Deep" means that the window has been expanded (by resizing it on the trading platform) to show a more complete list of quotes. Keep in mind that these quotes are always there; traders have a choice of how many they want to *see*.

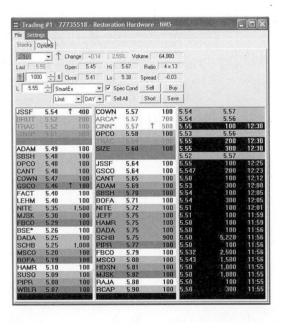

Expanded Trading Window/Level II Screen for Restoration Hardware, from CyberTrader Pro.

© 2005 CyBerCorp Holdings, Inc. All rights reserved. Used with permission.

A Nice Move Today

The top third of the trading window shows the day's activity in summary form and also contains the trading mechanisms to buy and sell the stock. The stock is experiencing a nice up move for the day, 14¢ from a price of $5.41 (a gain of 2.59 percent). The last trade occurred at $5.55.

The Inside Action

The current inside (best) bid of 5.54 is shown in the lower-left "bid" column. It was made by "JSSF"—the market maker JMP Securities, Inc. of San Francisco. The best offer, in the lower center, is from COWN—S. C. Cowan & Co.—at 5.57, leaving a 3¢ spread.

The next bids away from the market were made through the ECNs BRUT and TRAC at 5.52. (You can't see the color, but ECNs—ARCA [Archipelago], CINN [Inet], BRUT [Brut LLC], and TRAC [Track ECN] are shown in red to distinguish them from the other market markers.) Away from the inside offer, 700 shares are available through ARCA and 500 from CINN at 5.57, then the market maker OPCO (Oppenheimer & Co) posted 100 shares at 5.58. Note the asterisk next to CINN and ARCA ECNs; it means that quotes for these ECNs can be broken out into more detail.

Trading Terms

Traders talk a lot about **support** and **resistance**. Support is a price level where demand is sufficient to deter further decline; resistance is the opposite, where supply forces create price barriers to the upside.

Trade Secrets

There are about 2,400 different market players and symbols. No trader knows them all, but they learn the "big" ones and those active in stocks they trade. Appendix B has a list of the more active market makers, ECNs, and their symbols.

Away from the Market

The expanded-depth view shows a number of market makers playing in the market. Most are inactive and sit far away from the inside bid and ask. Still, it's worth watching their activity and movement.

Note the large size for "NITE" (Knight Trading Inc, a wholesaler) with 1,500 on the bid (left column) at 5.35. There are no big players on the offer. This quote has little bearing on immediate market action, but may start to exert influence if the price moves downward. The 5.35 level may become a "floor," or *support* level for the stock. The 5.48 level, with three active market maker quotes, might be another support level. Similarly, 5.75, with four active quotes, looks like a mild *resistance* level.

Time and Sales

The Time and Sales window, in the lower-right column, shows actual trades, or "print" activity, and also quote changes (this latter feature can be disabled).

Like the Level II window itself, Time and Sales makes ample use of color to depict whether trades are occurring at the bid, the offer, in between, or elsewhere. Though hard to see in the example, green is used for trades at the inside ask (a relatively bullish sign), red for trades at the inside bid (bearish), gray for in between (neutral), yellow for above the inside ask, and purple for below the inside bid.

Despite the day's healthy advance, RSTO is a fairly quiet stock and easy to follow. The Time and Sales shows a number of consecutive prints between 5.50 and 5.55 over a period of 35 minutes (from 11:55 A.M. to 12:30 P.M. EST). Because the quote change feature is enabled, we can see that there have been no quote changes during this interval; all supply and demand has been met in the marketplace. As 12:30 P.M. approached, the more rapid level of quote change activity signals a possible change in supply and demand.

Quote/Change Direction Arrow

The small "up" arrow next to the CINN ask quote (middle column) of 5.57 is one of the most important "quick-read" features of the screen. Simply, that arrow reflects the direction of a quote change. In this case, the lowest CINN offer moved down to $5.57 (and thus "up" in the offer quote stack). That foretells price movement downward, as this player is now willing to sell for a lower price. More active trading windows will have numerous arrows. On the bid side, market maker JSSF has moved their bid *up* to 5.54— indicating strength.

Trade Secrets

The relative lack of arrows on the RSTO screen reflects slow action. But on "faster" stocks, there are more arrows. A sizable number of up arrows on the offer means that players are reducing ask prices, bringing more shares to market at lower prices, a bearish sign. Down arrows on the offer mean the asking price is going up—a bullish sign.

Reviewing Market Maker Action

Let's now review the role of the market makers by translating their actions into what a trader might see on a Level II screen.

As you learned in Chapter 7, market maker quotes, or bids and offers, don't necessarily represent actual orders. They *may* represent orders, especially those of the firm's clients. Or the firm and its market maker may be trading for its own account. A trader doesn't know for sure, because market makers, especially with big orders to handle, might hide their intentions so as not to unduly influence price. This is understandable from any dealer's viewpoint. A dealer with a truckload of chickens to dispose of might only show a few at a time so as not to drive the price downward. So their quote might not reflect the true size of what they have available (or what they need), but it's likely that such a player will play close to the inside market.

For market makers, as for all other market participants, Level II shows …

- The *number* of bids and offers at a price.
- The *size* of those bids and offers.
- *Who's* bidding and offering.
- How they change bids and offers.
- How persistent they are through the day.

Predicting Market Direction

Watching Level II closely gives traders an advantage—though not absolute confidence—in predicting the direction of the stock. A large number of bids at or just off the inside market, with new market makers coming in to replace old stock sold to them, indicates demand. This is more strongly confirmed if the bid price increases. Similarly, a large number of offers at or just above the inside price, persistent replacement of these offers, and declining offer prices signal a down move. Again, these dynamics change with the beat of a jackhammer in an active stock, and watching it will keep a trader very busy, which is where color and tickers on advanced platforms come in handy.

> **Behind the Screen**
>
> Remember that all market makers for a particular stock must post a bid and an ask quote *somewhere* in the market. It may be deep—so deep that you can't see it. Traders should concern themselves mostly with action at or near the inside market. These are where the active market participants hang out.

Customizable Features

Like most advanced platform features, the trading and Level II windows are customizable. Most traders will find the "stock" Level II and Time and Sales screens useful as is, but some enhancements and controllable features are worth noting.

Window Size and Colors

The Level II example first presented in this chapter is an expanded version, created by increasing the size of the trading window box. Traders can place this window wherever they want on the desktop and can make it as large or small as they want. As noted previously, users can also change colors, font sizes, and other features to improve visibility.

Data View Controls

Most platforms allow users to customize windows through general and data view screens. The general screen mainly controls setup of the trading features, including default order size, type, and conditions. It also features a few simple tools for modifying the data display, for instance, whether or not to show Time and Sales, and whether Time and Sales shows quote changes. In addition, traders can decide whether size is shown in actual shares (100, 500, 1,200, etc.) or in hundreds (1, 5, 12, etc.).

In Schwab's CyberTrader Pro, the data view control (shown in the following figure) allows traders to expand the view of market maker and ECN quotes, see various details, and see aggregate quotes (discussed later in this chapter).

Data View control screen, used to manage format and data shown through the Level II trading window.

© 2005 CyBerCorp Holdings, Inc. All rights reserved. Used with permission.

Market Maker/ECN Depth

As a default setting, Level II only shows the best quote available for each market participant. For most routine trading, the highest bid and lowest ask is the clearest indication of a participant's intentions. However, in some situations it is interesting to look at all of a participant's positions in the market, and in the case of ECNs, all quotes inside that ECN. For ECNs, you can get quote detail by checking "Direct" access to the ECN (as in "Direct ARCA") on the data view screen (see the preceding illustration). To get complete market maker quotes, uncheck "MM/Exchange Best" on the data view screen. The following figure shows a trading screen with expanded views for the ARCA ECN.

Level II screen, showing multiple ARCA bids and offers at different price levels.

© 2005 CyBerCorp Holdings, Inc. All rights reserved. Used with permission.

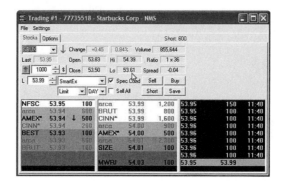

Aggregate Quotes

On busy stocks, several market makers and ECNs may camp at a certain level, a penny apart from another bunch of traders at the next level. Result? The weary-eyed trader must look through long lists of quotes just to see a little piece of the market. Aggregate quotes help the trader see a slightly bigger picture.

Aggregate quote view, showing all market bids and offers consolidated at the best three price levels.

© 2005 CyBerCorp Holdings, Inc. All rights reserved. Used with permission.

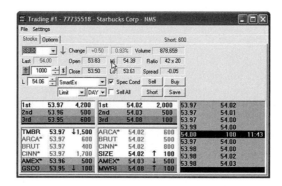

The aggregate view adds another subwindow to Level II, summarizing the inside quote level and the next two levels away from the inside.

In the accompanying illustration, you can see that all SBUX bid quotes combined total 4,200 shares at 53.97; the next level is 500 shares at 53.96, and the next level down is 600 at 53.95. The best combined offer is 2,000 shares total at 54.02, then 500 at 54.03, and then 100 at 54.08. (Note that the detailed breakdown is available just below the aggregate view.) Aggregate views are a far simpler way to look at the market, particularly when the action of individual market players is less important.

To display aggregate quotes, check "Display Aggregate Quotes" on the data view screen.

A "Live" Look at Level II

Level II activity is usually fast and furious. Like a fast-moving stream, there are factors above and below the surface affecting where the water goes and how fast it gets there. Overall market direction and actual and impending news about company performance all factor into the volatile mix. Beneath the water's surface, a number of undercurrents affect trading to the minute and second.

It's impossible to know or understand the intent and action of all market players. Traders can see *what* they do, but not always understand *why*. That said, it's still possible—and vitally important—for traders to understand how to detect minor changes in the underwater current. To that end, the following example should help you understand how to interpret market action using a Level II trading screen.

Trading Sequence No. 1: A Slight Push Upward

The stock is Starbucks (SBUX), and the overall market is having a choppy day brought on by higher oil prices and reduced consumer confidence. SBUX, however, opened strong, up 33¢ from the previous day's close at 53.83. Is it still strong? That is what the trader is looking to determine.

The last trade was at 54.16. The intraday high is 54.39, so some of the initial upward momentum has dissipated. After bouncing around midway between the opening and the high, here we find it on a slight updraft. There are four indicators on the following Level II screen indicating possible further upward moves:

♦ The last trade is positive, as indicated by the large arrow in the top left.

♦ Four market players, made up of ECNs BRUT and CINN, one outside exchange (AMEX), and one market maker (MWRI), have all raised their bid prices (see the quote/change direction arrow). On the other hand, GSCO (Goldman Sachs, a "biggie") has moved off, dropping its bid to 54.13. Two other players, both market makers, have also backed off, adding just a bit more negative flavor.

♦ The anonymous market maker "SIZE" has backed away on the offer, raising it to 54.20. This is positive. However, two other players have lowered their offer, but aren't that close to the inside market (PRUS at 54.27 and MADF at 54.38).

♦ Time and sales (right column) shows several quote changes, with the inside bid moving up a penny within the minute. A corresponding "up" move from 54.18 to 54.19 on the inside offer would confirm the move. By itself the strengthening bid sends only a weak signal, for market participants are holding firm on their offer price—the price at which they are willing to sell.

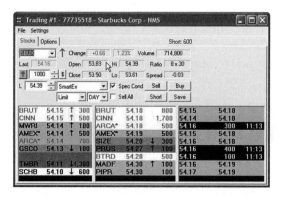

This is a slight updraft. Why? Because market player quote action isn't unanimous, and the inside size, as indicated by the ratio, is 8 × 30—that is, more shares are available on the inside offer than on the inside bid. A ratio strongly in favor of the offer shows weakness—that is, more shares are in supply at the offer than in demand at the bid, and the likely next price movement is down. The converse is true if the higher number is on the bid. The more lopsided the ratio, the stronger the signal it sends.

Trading Sequence No. 2: A Downdraft

In the Level II snapshot below, some eight minutes later (see Time and Sales screen; right column), the stock is reversing and giving ground. Level II gives no fewer than five signs of further price deterioration:

◆ The last trade was negative, meaning it was down from the previous trade, indicated by the large arrow in the top left.

◆ The ratio is a moderately negative 2 × 45—that is, there are 4,500 shares on the inside offer of 54.06 versus only 200 shares on the inside bid of 54.03.

◆ Two market players, AMEX and GSCO, have backed off on the bid. The downdraft would be further confirmed if players on the offer/ask side were coming up—that is, with up arrows—to the inside of the market.

◆ The presence of large size (1,800, 1,500, and 1,200 shares) from the top three players on the offer is a barrier to upward price movement.

◆ Time and sales shows a gradually deteriorating set of "prints," from 54.06 to 54.04 to 54.03. (Note that each event on Time and Sales, including at least eight prints—probably more on an expanded screen—and a quote change, has occurred within the current *minute*.)

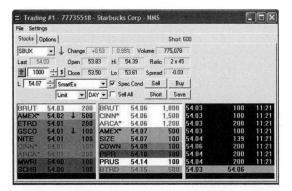

© 2005 CyBerCorp Holdings, Inc. All rights reserved. Used with permission.

Trading Sequence No. 3: Signs of a Turnaround

Some two minutes later, the action changes again. Some signs are bullish, but it's far from a clear signal:

◆ The last trade was at 54.07, and although the "prints" show no upward progress, the 54.07 level is on the offer, not the bid. So traders and market orders coming into the market are trading on the higher offer price—a minor sign of strength.

- Market makers and ECNs are getting stronger on the bid, as noted by six up arrows in the top seven bid quotes. This is the strongest bullish sign.

- The ratio, however, is still a weak 4 × 28.

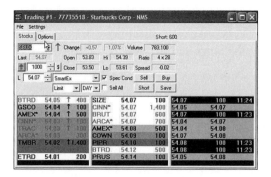

Will the stock continue to rise? Stay tuned ....

Trading Sequence No. 4: The Slight Up Move Continues

Nearly 40 minutes later, the action continues with an upward bias:

- The last trade is up at 54.09 (and the large direction arrow next to the stock symbol is up, too).

- Three market players have backed away—that is, raised—their offer.

- The ratio of 4 × 4, and the lack of increases on the bid side signal neutrality— any increase in the next few minutes is likely to be small.

- The spread is still 2¢, also indicating a relatively stable market. If the spread were larger, that might indicate a more dynamic and rapidly changing market with more change in store.

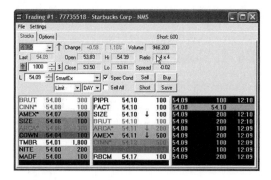

Will the stock continue to rise? Hard to say. Most traders would watch closely, and many would watch market maker TMBR (Timber Hill Trading LLC), an active player, to see what they do.

For the record, the stock did *not* hold its gains; a late-day market sell-off drove it down to a close of 53.68, which was still up 18¢ for the day.

> **Behind the Screen**
>
> It should be clear by now that the more market makers and the more size there is at a given price level, the more strength there is at that price and the less quickly the stock is to *break through* that price. Conversely, a lack of bids or offers at a price signal rapid movement through that price level.

Getting Used to Level II

Market activity is fast, jittery, and complex, and it takes a while to get used to watching the markets in real time. Most advanced trading platform providers are willing, even eager, to send self-paced training packages and demos to help traders get started with Level II. The investment—and the rewards—of Level II may not provide all the answers for traders, but most wouldn't trade without it.

The Least You Need to Know

◆ The NASDAQ Level II screen makes visible all bid and ask quotes of all market players, including market makers, ECNs, and exchanges.

◆ Market action is extremely dynamic for most stocks. Level II offers important features to help interpret this action, including the use of color and aggregate quote windows.

◆ The Level II window shows the status and future direction of the market, while the Time and Sales window shows past actual trades and quote changes.

◆ Traders look for multiple signs of upward or downward movement, including the size and direction of quote changes, recent Time and Sales activity, and the behavior of active market participants.

Chapter 16

Basic Technical Analysis Tools

In This Chapter

- ◆ The role of technical analysis in trading
- ◆ Trading range and pattern analysis
- ◆ Trend analysis and oscillators
- ◆ Support and resistance, breakouts, gaps, and reversals
- ◆ Combining investment "art" and "science"

If a picture is truly worth a thousand words, then this chapter and the next are what most readers have been waiting for.

By now it should be obvious that, no matter what their style or strategy, traders must contend with enormous amounts of data. Given the vast amount—and speed—of information, traders are constantly looking for ways to make sense of it all. This is where charting and technical analysis come into play.

Technical analysis has received a lot of attention from both the trading and academic communities. There are probably more books, articles, and charting and software packages devoted to the topic than any other aspect of trading.

A detailed treatment of technical analysis is beyond the scope of this book. This chapter gives an overview of four major types of charting and technical analysis. Chapter 17 explores a unique charting tool known as candlestick charts, which combine many types of charting and technical analysis into one widely used format.

What Is Technical Analysis?

Charts are pictures—often simple, sometimes complex—of data. Technical analysis goes one step further to identify what is really going on in the charts. Traders use charts and technical analysis to create usable, actionable pictures of trading data.

Analysts look for ranges, trends, and patterns inherent in a security's price movement. More sophisticated tools known as oscillators quantify price movement to give important indicators, or signals, to traders. The most sophisticated technical analysis combines ranges, trends, patterns, and signals into a trading system—a complex, software-driven approach to high-powered trading. At any level—simple or advanced—technical analysis gives a trader a sense of direction in the market.

Collective Behavior

At its most basic level, technical analysis zeros in on the collective behavior of all players in the market. A single trade, or even a handful of trades, is probably just noise to the observer. But a series of trades occurring in a pattern will mean something—if the trader knows what to make of that pattern. When enough data is assembled and analyzed, a collective behavior pattern emerges. That pattern may manifest itself in the form of an image on a chart, or be discerned by a more sophisticated mathematical analysis.

A Rear-View Mirror

The root problem with nearly all forms of technical analysis is that it is backward-looking. Charting and technical analysis show us where we've been, not necessarily where we're going. Just because something happened before doesn't mean it will happen again because there are too many forces—both external and internal—influencing market behavior. At the end of the day, the trick is to evaluate the strength of the pattern—and to figure out whether it is repeatable and thus dependable.

A Self-Fulfilling Prophecy?

Driving while looking at the rear-view mirror is dangerous, unless what the driver sees is repeated in front of the car. While counting on such repetition might be equally dangerous, at least one force comes into play that helps make the whole idea more plausible.

In any given market on any given day, there are hundreds, even thousands, of players. Many of these players are watching several things at once, and they depend on some of the same tools you might use to ferret out trading opportunities. So if a stock price crosses its moving average, signaling an uptrend, that same fact "rings up" on everybody's screens simultaneously. So the up move is sustained—not only by market strength but also by the fact that a commonly observed trading pattern has occurred. So to a degree, anyway, technical patterns are self-fulfilling.

Using Technical Analysis

Is technical analysis worth the time, effort, and cost? Will traders miss opportunities by focusing on a back-looking pattern while overlooking what is really going on in the market? Can technical patterns and indicators be truly predictive? These are questions all traders must grapple with.

What's It All For?

Like most trading tools, technical analysis helps traders make sense of what's going on in the markets. It also helps them understand what *other* traders are seeing and reacting to.

Most traders use technical analysis to select securities for trading—that is, identify stocks or other securities that meet certain criteria or conditions—and to time entry and exit from those securities—that is, figure out the entry and exit points most likely to generate profits based on the pattern. Traders also use technical analysis to judge the *significance* of a move—that is, to separate the numbers "news" from the numbers "noise."

Technical Analysis in Practice

Using technical tools for selection and timing requires both a long-term and short-term view of trading patterns. Some patterns are recognizable and significant over a long period of time, whereas others can be used to watch the minute-by-minute fluctuations of a security.

> **Trade Secrets** _____
>
> Technical analysis tools should not only fit the trader's style of trading but also the security being traded. Some securities behave more predictably than others—meaning that the collective behavior of market participants is more predictable.

Some traders, especially those using highly advanced trading systems, rely almost exclusively on technical analysis to select their trades and manage their timing. But such reliance requires expensive tools and a thorough understanding of how to use them—involving a long learning curve of education and experience. Most traders will never get this far. But the more they understand what the pros do in practice, the better.

Creating a Study

So how does one go about creating a chart or technical analysis study? Most trading information sources and platforms have a charting feature, and many come with basic and even more advanced technical analysis tools for interpreting the charts. Not surprisingly, advanced trading platforms offer more sophisticated analytical tools. That said, even free platforms like Yahoo!Finance offer technical tools with a surprising amount of depth and breadth.

Charts and studies are usually created using a simple platform menu. Users can combine several studies in a single analysis, and most platforms allow comparative analysis across multiple securities or with a market index or average. That is, the movements of one security or index can be compared with another to see if price and trading patterns are similar.

The following figure shows the control screen used to insert a study onto a chart in Schwab's CyberTrader Pro.

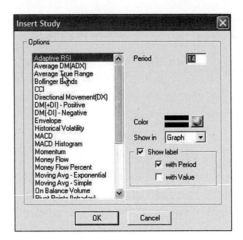

Types of Technical Analysis

Technicians classify their tools in many ways, and every book on the subject does it differently. Here, technical analysis is broken down into the following categories:

- **Channel analysis** is a favorite tool of the range trader. Really a simple form of pattern analysis (see next bullet), channel tools try to define support and resistance levels and a trading range between those levels. Trading ranges and Bollinger bands are examples.

- **Pattern analysis** looks at all types of patterns, not just channels or trading ranges. The idea is that trading occurs in distinct, repeatable patterns. Pennants and "head and shoulders" formations are examples.

- **Trend analysis** looks to discern trends and their strength. Moving averages are among the most popular trend analysis tools.

- **Oscillators** look for bias or direction in market behavior, and attempt to quantify data into signals helping traders find entry and exit points. Stochastics are an example.

Beyond the many tools available, traders can set different parameters on many of the technical studies. For instance, moving averages can be adjusted to weigh most recent data more heavily, or to look at longer or shorter periods. So it isn't just the tool itself, but how the tool is *used* that is important.

The following sections examine each of these types of analysis more closely.

Channel Analysis

Traders often use channel analysis to establish trading ranges for a security. When stocks reach the higher end of a trading range, they are said to hit resistance levels; when they hit the low end, they are said to hit support. Obviously, support becomes a potential entry point into a long position, while the resistance level becomes a candidate for a sale.

Why use trading ranges for timing entry and exit points? For one thing, other traders, including dealers and market makers, recognize trading ranges and are likely to buy and sell at support and resistance levels. When a stock hits resistance, more sell orders are likely to enter the market, adding to any limit orders already entered at these price points. Similarly, a stock reaching a support level gets support indeed, as limit and stop orders are activated and additional incoming buy orders flow into the market.

Support and Resistance

Support and resistance levels can be defined over a long or a very short period. Inside the market, more shares (contracts, etc.) are becoming available at the resistance level, while more demand shows up at the support level as traders look for bargains. Traders can add "flat" support and resistance lines on the chart electronically as a "study."

Intraday trading range, showing added support and resistance lines, for Cisco Systems.

© 2005 CyBerCorp Holdings, Inc. All rights reserved. Used with permission.

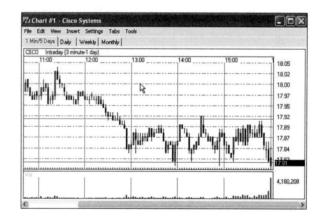

In this intraday chart, CSCO (Cisco Systems, Inc) has settled into a tight trading range between 17.80 and 17.90 after a more volatile opening. The stock has tried to get through 17.90 three times only to pull back, while also hitting and bouncing off of the 17.80 support level five times. Pure dealer–type traders might position themselves to buy at the support and sell at the resistance.

> **Behind the Screen**
>
> Technical analysis involves finding repeatable trading patterns. Traders benefit from observing a pattern and trying to apply it to future price movement. But traders should also understand the *why* behind the pattern observed.

Trending Ranges

The kind of intraday support/resistance levels described in the previous section are unlikely to hold up for a long period. So-called "range" traders look for more significant and longer-term ranges. (That said, many stocks will trade in a $2–$4 range for a long period of time, providing swing traders with a nice trading opportunity.)

Some range traders like to position support and resistance levels around a trend, instead of as flat lines. The following chart illustrates a trending trading range:

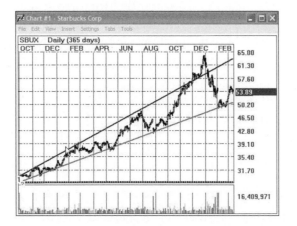

Starbucks, Inc. trading range established on an uptrend.

For SBUX (Starbucks, Inc.) the trend is definitely upward, with support and resistance levels along the way.

Breakouts

A breakout occurs when a stock moves sharply outside its trading range. On an upside breakout, the supply of stock available at the price finally dries up. Demand is still there, and players shadowing (watching) the trading range see this and get out of the way. The ensuing price move can be sharp. Of course, similar patterns can occur on the downside. Traders regularly look for breakouts in both directions.

Late-day trading range breakout, Starbucks, Inc.

© 2005 CyBerCorp Holdings, Inc. All rights reserved. Used with permission.

In the accompanying chart, you can see that SBUX (Starbucks, Inc.) traded quietly between 51.75 and 52.15 with a slight downward bias, only to experience a sharp breakout from the established trading range at the end of the day. Note the late pullback to 52.20 (resistance became support) and the ensuing resumption of the momentum and sustained breakthrough as demand finally took charge over supply.

Combining a few topics already discussed, the following figure shows a series of short trading ranges, followed by mild *retracements* and two *gap*-open breakouts, over a three-month period.

Trading Terms

A **gap** is a pattern or trading range breakout that occurs during the opening trading of a security. Often driven by news, rumors, or an event, the stock or security opens well above (or below) the previous closing price and usually outside the trading range. So-called "gap-open" securities are popular among traders.

A **retracement** is a movement in a direction opposite to a breakout. Traders watch "breakout" patterns closely to observe the size of the reaction to the breakout action. If the retracement (usually caused by profit taking) on an upward breakout stays above the top of the trading range, that is a sign of strength.

Carmax Inc. trading pattern, showing trading ranges formed over a 1–1½ month period, ending with upside breakouts.

Bollinger Bands

Bollinger bands are statistically determined trading range boundaries. The exact formula is beyond the scope of this book, but the volatility of the security, as measured by standard deviation, is factored into the support and resistance levels. The more volatile a stock is, the farther apart the resulting support and resistance levels will be.

The key to Bollinger bands is that they are dynamic; that is, the interval between support and resistance changes as the volatility changes through the measurement period. Their dynamic nature makes Bollinger bands effective support/resistance boundaries. The boundaries are established in the context of what's happened most recently. They also help a trader judge the importance of a move. A move to the top or bottom of a range is significant given the most recently established statistical pattern. A picture will help illustrate this concept:

Bollinger band chart for Microsoft, Inc. Note how the range contracts when the pattern is more consistent, then expands when it becomes more volatile.

The figure shows MSFT (Microsoft Corporation) in a moderate trading range at the opening, settling into a tighter trading range midday as indicated by the narrowing bands between noon and 1 P.M. (12:00 and 13:00 on the chart). During midday, the stock moved downward towards the bottom band and stayed there, moving steadily downward without much volatility. Three times in the afternoon, just before 2 P.M. (14:00 on the chart), and again just before 3 and 4 P.M., it tried to break above the resistance level as defined by the upper band. It failed, and all three times retraced back to the bottom of the band.

Trade Secrets

Many traders apply Bollinger bands to market indexes—not just individual securities—to visualize the significance of up and down moves.

Traders look at the top of a band as resistance, and may sell when the price hits that level, particularly if the price starts to fall away from the band. Likewise, stocks tracking near the bottom of the band are buying opportunities.

Pattern Analysis

While range analysts try to identify support and resistance levels, pattern analysts try to fit price behavior to commonly occurring pictures, or *patterns*. Patterns are based on underlying trading behavior—and to a degree, are influenced by other pattern analysts trying to trade off the pattern. There is usually an underlying rationale to the trading behavior supporting the pattern, and traders should try to understand what's going on behind any given pattern.

Among the most commonly seen (and used) patterns are pennants, multiple tops and bottoms, head-and-shoulders formations, and so-called "cup and handle" formations.

Pennants

Pennants are really variations of trading ranges. The idea is that without any underlying news or demand/supply imbalance, trading ranges gradually narrow and usually fade in the direction of the next large breakout. Why? Because, in the case of an impending advance, buying pressure gradually strengthens and fewer shares become available. Time-interval (daily, minute by minute, and so on) lows gradually rise. Supply gradually dries up. Finally, sellers who capped off the top of the trading range go away, and conditions are ripe for a breakout advance. Similarly, a pennant fading downward indicates strengthening selling pressure leading to a downward breakout when the buying support finally fails.

The following figures show an up-trending pennant, where daily low prices gradually fade upward against the resistance level, and a down-trending pennant.

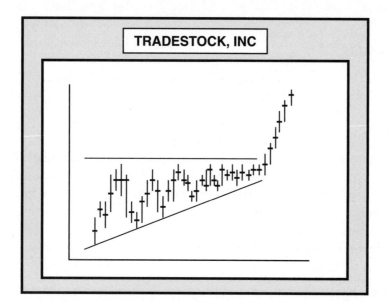

Up-trending pennant.

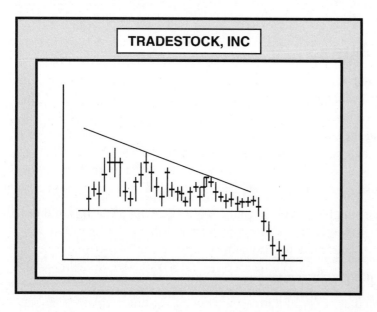

Down-trending pennant.

As a variation on pennants, traders look for periods where stocks make higher daily highs and higher daily lows (a sign of strength) or lower highs and lower lows (a sign of weakness).

Multiple Tops and Bottoms

Traders commonly look for reversal patterns in security charts. Reversal patterns indicate that a change in direction may be about to happen.

Traders look for double tops, triple tops, and even quadruple top (and bottom) patterns to signal reversals. A multiple top usually occurs after a long uptrend. It indicates steady resistance, or a cap, to the longer-term trading range. Each time the security makes the top, selling pressure arrives sending the security back down. Soon, buyers see the dip as a buying opportunity and push it back upward, only to have it bounce off again. Sometimes this happens three or four times over a trading sequence—which can occur over minutes, hours, or even days. Traders, seeing this activity, will suspect that eventually the buy-on-dip crowd will run out of steam and the security will reverse significantly downward.

In the same manner, a multiple bottom, after a long decline, signals a more substantial upward move.

Head-and-Shoulders Pattern

The so-called head-and-shoulders formation is a more pronounced variation of the triple top. Head-and-shoulders is a triple top, except that the center spike, or "head," is more pronounced. After the first peak, buy-side traders use the dip as a buying opportunity and send the security still higher. But after that peak, buying strength fades, and although there is a third peak, it is weaker and sellers take over. Many traders consider head-and-shoulders to be a stronger reversal pattern than the triple top, because without the head, a stock may have just settled into a new trading range.

Note that a head-and-shoulders pattern can be upside-down, indicating an upward reversal after a price decline.

The following figures show a conceptual head-and-shoulders diagram and a head-and-shoulders formation occurring for an actual stock.

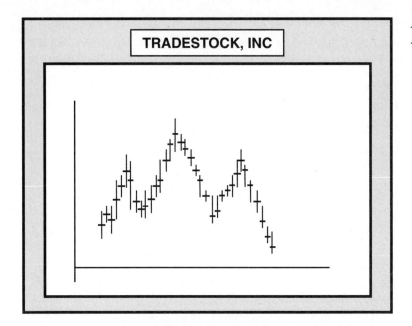

A conceptual head-and-shoulders diagram.

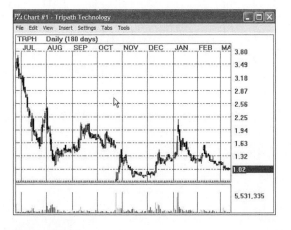

A real chart of Tripath Technology showing a head-and-shoulders pattern. The formation occurs at the right-hand half of the chart.

Cup-and-Handle Patterns

A cup-and-handle pattern looks like a long, protracted, gently curved "cup," followed by a sharp breakout to the upside.

Technicians generally consider rounded patterns as good indicators of a sharper move in the direction of the pattern. In a "cup" formation, selling pressure on the left side of the cup gradually gives way to buying pressure, first bringing equilibrium, then an upward price movement. Traders like to see the sustained change in the imbalance of supply and demand, and figure that bigger things are in store once the sellers run out of steam. The resulting breakout gives the "handle" to the cup-and-handle formation.

The same logic in reverse works for inverted cups; that is, sellers gradually take over and lead to a stronger down move. The following figures show a conceptual diagram and a cup-and-handle in practice.

A conceptual cup-and-handle pattern.

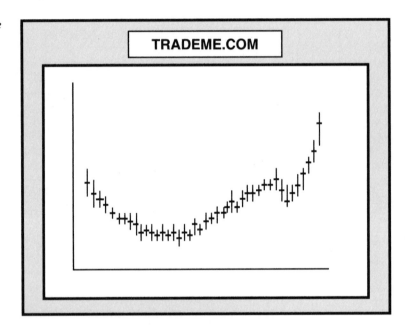

A cup-and-handle in practice (with a few failed retracements in the handle).

Trend Analysis

Trend analysts look for trends, and in particular, the *strength* of trends. Although there are sophisticated statistical tools for measuring trend strength, many traders stick to moving averages to assess trends and underlying trading strength and weakness.

Moving Averages

Moving averages are used to measure trend strength and also to suggest trend reversals—that is, changes in trends.

A moving average can be a simple or complex average of a specified number of periods of price data. In a simple moving average, or SMA, the closing price for the last x number of periods is added and arithmetically averaged. Each period has equal weight. Short-term SMAs might be calculated for 5, 10, or 20 days, while longer-term averages might cover 50, 100, or 200 days. The 10-day SMA will be influenced more by the most recent data, and will move sharply.

Exponential moving averages, or EMAs, weight the most recent data more heavily. That is, the most recently occurring closing prices have more impact on the average line than closing prices from earlier in the period. EMAs are thus more sensitive to recent trends.

Using Moving Averages

Traders use SMAs and EMAs to get a clearer picture of where a security is going, and how fast it is getting there. Many traders look at actual price behavior as compared to the moving average. They look for crossovers—that is, where the actual price crosses over the moving average, either in an upward or downward direction. In many trading sequences, crossovers are a sign of direction change, or reversal. Moving average crossovers, where short- and longer-term moving averages cross each other, are considered even stronger indicators of reversals.

Trade Secrets

Moving averages over shorter time periods are more reactive to changes in direction and can show short-term strength and weakness more quickly. But moving averages over longer periods, although less sensitive, indicate greater strength. A price crossing a 200-day moving average is more significant than a price crossing its 10-day counterpart. A short-term moving average—not just the price—crossing over a longer-term moving average may be the strongest signal of all.

The following figure shows a simple 20-day moving average as charted over about 6 months of elapsed time. Each point on the SMA line is a straight arithmetic average of closing prices over the previous 20 trading days. Note how the uptrend was confirmed for a while, even through the dip. But when the price crossed over the average line, it signaled a more significant drop. At the lower-right corner, traders will watch to see if the price can move sustainably above the average, confirming an uptrend. At this level, a bounce back downward is equally likely.

Avaya Inc. 20-day simple moving average. Note how the January priced "crossed over" the average to the downside, suggesting a longer downtrend.

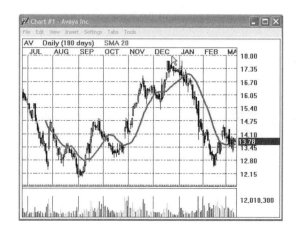

Oscillators

Oscillators are fairly complex statistical tools designed to analyze and interpret several series of data into specific trading signals. These signals are often based on biases found in the data. A bias occurs when data starts to fall one way or another around what would have ordinarily been a random pattern. Technicians look at signs of internal bias as signs of building or waning momentum, and thus buying or selling points for the security.

There are many types of oscillators. The Moving Average Convergence-Divergence indicator (MACD) and the stochastic indicator are among the more popular varieties.

MACD

The Moving Average Convergence Divergence (MACD) indicator examines the relationship between a short-range and longer-range moving average for the same security. The main idea is similar to that mentioned earlier: moving average crossovers signal changes in direction and momentum in that direction.

MACD is calculated as the difference between the 12-day and a 26-day exponential moving average (EMA) for the security. This difference is plotted against a 9-day EMA "signal" line. When the 9-day EMA crosses the MACD line, that is interpreted as a buy or sell signal. Specifically, when the MACD falls below its signal line, it is a sell signal, and when it crosses above, it is a buy signal. Additionally, when the short-term EMA pulls far above the longer term EMA, it is considered an "overbought" condition.

Complicated? Yes. But when this calculation is taken apart, it really separates sustained movements from shorter data "blips." Such is the characteristic of a good oscillator. Some analysts swear by this statistical method; others find that it doesn't fit their securities or trading style very well. Most find MACD indicators hard to understand, at least initially.

Behind the Screen

Many traders backtest old data to see if it really works. Backtesting is a means of testing the predictability of technical analysis models using historical data. Technicians run one of several models in a backtesting package against old data. They then compare the results of the test to what really happened. Advanced technical software or trading system tools—and a good data feed—are required to run effective backtests.

Stochastics

Stochastics attempt to quantify buying and selling pressure by observing bias in high, low, and closing prices. Specifically, the oscillator tracks the ratio of the difference between the most recent price and the lowest low divided by the difference between highest high and lowest low for a 14-day period. A second oscillator tracks a short-term moving average of these values. A tracking signal is generated by comparing these two values. Readings over 80 are considered overbought; readings under 20 indicate oversold conditions.

To make it a bit more complicated (as if that were needed!), there is a "fast" stochastic, which takes the first figure at face value, and a "slow" stochastic, which uses a moving average of the first figure. Slow stochastics give less frequent signals and don't give them as quickly, but traders consider them more reliable.

A Few Thoughts About Technical Analysis

The discussion of the MACD and stochastics probably raised more questions than it answered. It certainly didn't give you enough information to go out and start using them. The study and use of technical analysis is far deeper and more complex than could possibly be covered here, and more reading on the topic is strongly encouraged.

There are a few good books—and a lot of not-so-good books—on the topic. One of the good books is *Technical Analysis from A to Z*, 2nd edition, by Steven B. Achelis (McGraw-Hill, 2000). In addition, most trading platforms are amply equipped with technical analysis "help" tools, and there are good training courses out there as well.

Remember: Data Doesn't Replace Judgment

Trading is a combination of art and science. How much "science"? It's entirely up to the trader.

Although technical analysis is science, its application to trading is mainly an art. It's a little like weather forecasting. Pure science attempts to find predictable cause-and-effect relationships. Believe it or not, weather forecasting is based on cause-and-effect science. Temperature, humidity, and air pressure—all measurable causes of weather phenomena, each in turn having their own causes. Over time, study of these complex layers of causes helps forecasters predict effects on the weather. The "art" comes in deciding how well the combination of observed causes fits the pattern.

So why do the weather people blow it all the time? Because there are *so many* causes that change rapidly and work differently in different combinations. Taken together, no two days are exactly alike. So no mathematical model yet devised can figure them all out, and meteorologists are left to interpret the facts and judge how they fit together. Meteorologists are getting better at forecasting the weather, but a glance out the window still seems to work best.

Applying Science to Chaos

Scientists look for patterns, too, to try to predict the future. In using these patterns, the scientist might say, "There is certainly a pattern here. I can't find the exact cause underlying the effect, but it happens with such regularity that there must be one. Every time I see that pattern, the same underlying cause is likely to be present."

How do scientists find these patterns? They look at vast amounts of previous history—previous behavior—and use powerful models to discern a pattern. In theory, the more data crunched and the stronger the pattern, the more predictive it is. The art comes in deciding whether a pattern is there, and whether or not it is important.

Just as scientists use a little "art" to determine whether a pattern exists and what it means, so do traders. Remember—finding a pattern, by itself, doesn't make money. The pattern supports a judgment, which the trader must make by incorporating a wide variety of observed phenomena; it is this judgment that really drives the trade.

The Least You Need to Know

- Data never replaces judgment. Your computer can't make trading decisions for you.

- Technical tools measure collective behavior, which may or may not repeat itself. Traders try to understand what is happening in the market "behind" a technical pattern.

- Trading range analysis looks for support and resistance levels using flat lines or trend lines.

- Pattern analysis looks for certain repeatable patterns often found in trading behavior.

- Moving averages are used to detect trends, momentum, and reversal points. Like most technical tools, there are many ways these averages can be set up.

- Oscillators and more sophisticated backtested statistical models should be clearly understood before being used to trade.

Candlestick Charting

In This Chapter

- ◆ Candlestick charting as an alternative to basic technical analysis
- ◆ Interpreting individual candles
- ◆ Interpreting double and multiple combinations of candles
- ◆ Finding candlestick patterns in a real chart

Candlestick charts were invented in the seventeenth century by Japanese rice traders as a means of interpreting the behavior of local rice markets. Today traders use them to visualize market activity.

Candlestick charts help traders read between the lines of ordinary charts to pick up nuances and small patterns in security price behavior. These charts and the patterns contained within them capture the essence of several technical analysis tools in a single picture.

Candlestick charts are a type of chart available in most charting tools and trading platforms. They can be used to interpret both long-term price direction and short-term market action. They have become many traders' favorite way of getting a quick read on price behavior. If there is a chart on a trader's desktop today, it is probably a candlestick chart.

This chapter explains candlestick charts and explores some of the more common candlestick patterns and their interpretations.

What Are Candlestick Charts?

Candlestick charts are like ordinary charts or graphs, except that each data point on the graph is further developed into a symbol called a "candle." The candle represents the price activity *within* the interval of time represented by the data point—which can be anything from a minute to a month.

A candlestick chart with each candle representing a one-minute interval of time early in the trading day for Avaya, Inc (AV).

Parts of a Candle

Each candle shows the opening, closing, and highest and lowest prices within the time interval. Because the "candle" concept is easier to show by picture than to explain in words, a series of charts are shown throughout the chapter to help you learn how to interpret candle charts.

Each charting candle has a wick and a body. The wick is the thin part, and represents the highest and lowest prices reached by the security during the time interval between the open and the close. The body of the candle represents the difference between the opening and closing prices of the interval.

The color or shading of the body represents the direction. In this chapter, a black shaded body signals a down interval—that is the close was lower than the open. An unshaded (white) body signals an up interval—the close was higher than the open. Note that trading platforms can be customized to change the color of the candles; many traders prefer green for up candles and red for down candles.

Reading Individual Candles

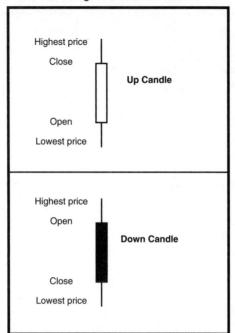

Basic up and down candles.

How to Use Candlestick Charts

Like other forms of technical analysis, traders use candlestick charts to get a better understanding of market action and the driving forces behind it. Candlestick charts, in a single view, can show ranges, trends, momentum, and reversal signals. Single candles tell a lot about the "size and shape" of the market behavior for a given time interval. Candlestick patterns—sequences of two or more candlesticks—reveal still more about trends and reversals and their strength.

Candles and candle patterns are usually classified as bullish, neutral, and bearish. Some indicate a continuation of trends, others signal reversals, while still others only signal a change in direction to be clarified by the next intervals. Candles show the "shape" of the trading interval—whether the bias was downward, upward, or neutral.

It's About Size, Shape, and Position

Candlestick devotees learn to look for the size and shape of the candles and their position relative to one another. The size of both the body and the wick matter a lot.

Larger size signals larger movements. Large bodies indicate that directional movement held up during the interval, and long wicks indicate direction movement that did not hold up. The relative position of opening and closing prices in successive intervals also matters. A candle showing an opening or a closing outside a previous close conveys a different message from a candle contained entirely within the range of the previous candle. These relationships will become clearer with the following examples.

Single Candle Patterns

Single candles are the easiest to read. They convey a surprising amount of information, and of course, are the building blocks for more complex patterns. The rest of this chapter shows groups of related candles and candle patterns, and explains the usual interpretation of each one.

Basic Candles

The following candles are most often seen and used as building blocks for patterns.

Basic single candle patterns.

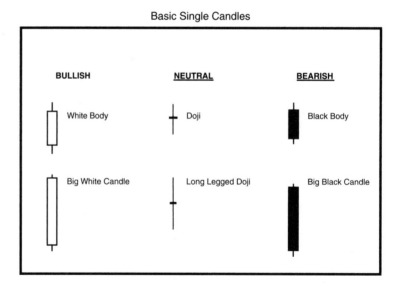

Basic Single Candles

BULLISH   NEUTRAL   BEARISH

White Body   Doji   Black Body

Big White Candle   Long Legged Doji   Big Black Candle

One at a time:

♦ **White Body.** The close is higher than the open, and the security traded both below the open price and above the close price (as shown by the wick). White bodies indicate normal in upward trends.

♦ **Big White Candle.** Like a White Body, but the range between the open and close is much larger and stands out on a chart. This is a stronger bullish signal.

♦ **Doji.** A doji occurs when the open and close prices end up the same but with interval activity measurably higher and lower then the open/close. Dojis signal indecision and a narrowing trading range, and signal the trader to watch the next bars closely.

♦ **Long-Legged Doji.** Long-legged dojis are like regular dojis except that the interval high and low are much farther apart. This candle suggests a stronger "struggle" between demand and supply and a likely stronger move in one direction or another.

♦ **Black Body.** Black Body candles are analogous to White Bodies, except that the indication is bearish. The close is lower than the open, with a normal range of action through the day. Strong opens and weak closes are clearly bearish.

♦ **Big Black Candle.** Big Black Candles are like Black Bodies but with a larger range. Prices open near the day's high and close near the day's low. The bearish indication is stronger.

Sharper Images in Single Candles

The following single candles occur less frequently and give more pronounced signals. The signal might vary according to whether the security is already in an up, down, or neutral trend.

Continuing:

♦ **Hammer.** After a struggle through the interval, where the low price is well below the open, the security works its way back to the open—and even a little higher. This is a strongly bullish reversal signal when preceded by a downtrend, and indicates end-of-day strength, a positive in most scenarios. During an uptrend, the hammer signals a sell-off that failed, and the price is likely to rise. If the top of the hammer is black (the closing price was below the opening price), the indication is weaker.

Single candles with more specialized shapes.

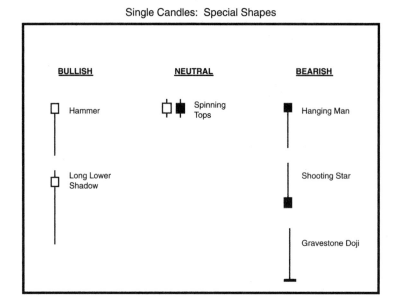

Single Candles: Special Shapes

- **Long Lower Shadow.** This pattern is distinguished by a long lower wick, indicating a stronger mid-interval reversal and a signaling a stronger uptrend. The length of the upper wick is much shorter. The same works in reverse in a Long Upper Shadow, which exhibits a small black bar near the bottom of a large wick.

- **Spinning Tops.** Spinning Tops signal indecision, and if the wicks are short, a narrowing trading range, usually implying a breakout one way or another soon.

- **Hanging Man.** The Hanging Man is similar to the Hammer, except that the body may be larger. Particularly when followed by an identical formation with a black body, it is a bearish signal during an uptrend—buying strength is waning.

- **Shooting Star.** This aptly-named candle shows a strong upward push during the interval—that failed to hold up. Look out below.

- **Gravestone Doji.** Also well named and like the Shooting Star except that opening and closing price match exactly, this pattern shows price failure during the interval.

Double Candle Patterns

Double candle patterns pair up single candles to create more meaning and stronger signals.

Tweezers and Engulfing Lines

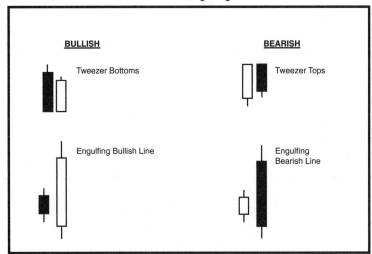

Double candle patterns: tweezers and engulfing lines.

Continuing:

 ◆ **Tweezer Bottoms.** When two or more candles have the same bottom, especially in a downward pattern, it is a sign of support—and a reversal to the upside. The color of the bodies doesn't matter.

 ◆ **Engulfing Bullish Line.** A small black body followed by a much larger "engulfing" white one is a strong bullish signal, especially if it appears at the end of a downtrend.

 ◆ **Tweezer Tops.** Like the Tweezer Bottom, the security is opening or closing at the day high, but can't get through that level. It may be a reversal if on an uptrend.

 ◆ **Engulfing Bearish Line.** This is a strong bearish signal, especially if it appears at the top of an uptrend. The security failed to move higher and closed weakly, a sign of profit taking.

Stars and Doji Stars

Double candles: star patterns.

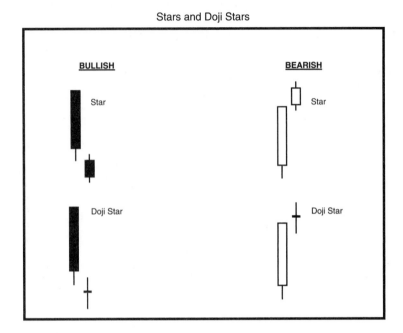

Stars and Doji Stars

Star patterns signal weakening momentum in a direction and a possible reversal, depending on what happens in the next few intervals. Contracting candles signal reversal, while a return to the larger bodied candles of the same color show a continuation pattern.

Here's the rundown:

- ◆ **Bullish Star.** This pattern occurs when a strong downward black body candle is followed by a candle with a shorter body and wick. It indicates a slowdown in downward momentum, to be confirmed (or not) by the next candle.

- ◆ **Bullish Doji Star.** Similar to the Bullish Star, except that the bottom is signified by a doji. A stronger reversal signal, as bottom "action" is truly undecided and the downward momentum has stopped.

- ◆ **Bearish Star.** In contrast to the Bullish Star, upward momentum has slowed and the trader must watch closely for what is next.

- ◆ **Bearish Doji Star.** Upward momentum has given way to indecision.

Haramis

In a *harami*, the second candle in the pattern is wholly contained within the first one.

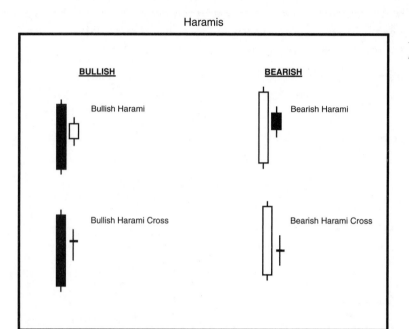

Haramis

Double candle patterns: haramis.

◆ **Bullish Harami.** A large black body is followed by a smaller white one contained within the first body. This signals reversal to the upside after a downtrend and possible continuation if on an uptrend.

◆ **Bullish Harami Cross.** This pattern is similar to the Bullish Harami, except that the follow-on pattern is a doji. Like the Bullish Harami, it signals downtrend reversal but with greater indecision.

Trading Terms

In Japanese, the word **harami** means "pregnant." The "wholly contained" nature of the second candle makes the description apt.

◆ **Bearish Harami.** A large white body is followed by an entirely contained black body. The signal is bearish when preceded by an uptrend.

◆ **Bearish Harami Cross.** Like the Bearish Harami but ending in a doji. More indecisive.

Other Double Patterns

Here is a selection of other common double candlestick patterns:

- ◆ **Piercing Lines.** A long black candle is followed by a long white candle, and the white candle's open is lower than the black candle's previous close. This pattern indicates a strong reversal signal to the upside.

- ◆ **Bullish Separating Lines.** This pattern is similar to the Bullish Harami, except that the follow-on pattern is above the original black candle. This is a strong upside pattern.

- ◆ **Dark Cloud Cover.** A large white body is followed by a large black body. The signal is bearish when preceded by an uptrend.

- ◆ **Bearish Separating Lines.** Like the Bearish Harami, but the black second bar is mainly below the first. Strong bearish pattern.

More common double candle patterns.

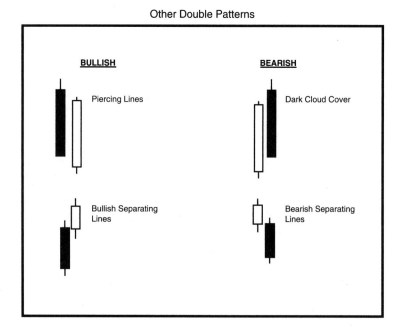

Other Double Patterns

Multiple Candle Patterns

If double patterns are like a word made up of letters, than patterns of three or more candles become more like a sentence. The amount of information conveyed grows rapidly. Naturally, the list of possible combinations is long. The next two sections show some of the more popular multiple patterns, but there are many others, including some patterns that apply uniquely to individual securities.

Soldiers, Crows, and Threes

By now you've probably noticed the creative naming conventions of candles and their sequences; this next set is no exception.

Soldiers, Crows, and Threes

Multiple candle patterns: soldiers, crows, and threes.

- ◆ **Three White Soldiers.** These "Soldiers" are three consecutive white candlesticks with consecutively higher closes near their highs. This pattern signifies a strong uptrend, or reversal if near a bottom of a downtrend.

- ◆ **Bullish Three.** This pattern, actually five candles in all, signals a failed sell-off attempt. The strong uptrend should resume. Key to this pattern is the fact that the three black bodies were entirely contained within the first white candle. The position of the second long white body, entirely above the three black bodies, is also important.

- ◆ **Three Black Crows.** The "crows" are the opposite of the "White Soldiers," with three black bodies closing near their low of the day. The pattern is decisively negative.

- ◆ **Bearish Three.** Mirroring the Bullish Three, the Bearish Three signal the resumption of a downtrend after a failed recovery.

Morning and Evening Stars

Again colorfully named, and frequently used by candlestick enthusiasts, are the Morning and Evening Star formations.

Multiple candle patterns: Morning and Evening Stars.

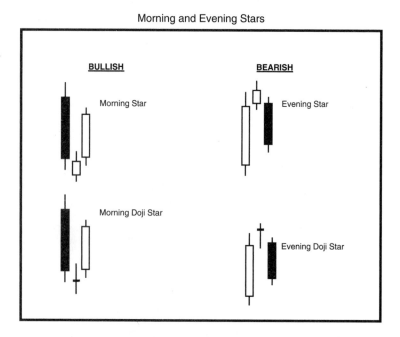

Morning and Evening Stars

- ◆ **Morning Star.** A large black body is followed by a small white body, opening with a "gap" lower than the previous close. The middle body is small but positive, and is followed by a larger white body closing more than 50 percent into the first black body. This pattern signals a bottom.

◆ **Morning Doji Star.** Like a Morning Star, but the middle candle is a Doji. The interpretation is similar.

◆ **Evening Star.** A large white body is followed by small white body with a "gap" opening above the white candle. But the trend doesn't hold, as the following black body closes more than 50 percent downward into the first white body. This signals a market top.

◆ **Evening Doji Star.** The pattern is similar to the Evening Star except the center candle is a doji. Since the second bar didn't even show a close higher than the open, the signal is a more definite reversal and more bearish.

Looking at a Real Chart

Now that you know what to look for, it's time to consider some common candlestick patterns as they apply to real stocks.

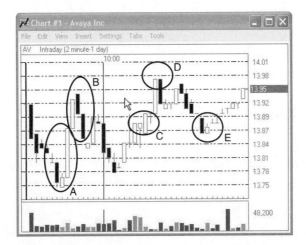

A real candlestick chart example, showing a combination of candle patterns.

© 2005 CyBerCorp Holdings, Inc. All rights reserved. Used with permission.

This chart is an intraday chart for Avaya, Inc. Each interval represents two minutes of trading, and the chart shows some noticeable reversals and trends, albeit over a moderate price range (13.75 to 14.00).

◆ **Morning Star.** Group A is a fairly typical Morning Star, except that the third bar shows an even stronger uptrend than usual. The reversal continued for a short time, until …

- **Evening Star.** Group B shows the same pattern in reverse. This particular Evening Star is a little more bearish, because the middle candle gave way to a lower close, signifying that the reversal started even before the end of this interval.

- **Uptrend Hammer.** Group C shows a hammer occurring during an uptrend. An attempted sell-off, creating the long bottom wick, didn't hold up, and the price pushed higher.

- **Tweezer Top.** Group D shows a classic Tweezer Top, although the downtrend didn't fully materialize until a few intervals later.

- **Tweezer Bottom.** Group "E" shows a tweezer bottom. Although the amplitude (size of bars) is less than the previous Tweezer Top, it actually signaled a more definite following uptrend. Note the indecisiveness along the way shown by the small dojis. Incidentally, the stock reached 14.18 and closed at 13.97, slightly above the top of this uptrend, so indeed it was not a decisive advance at day's end.

> **Behind the Screen**
>
> It is interesting how many "book" candle patterns emerge when looking at a chart. Some match the book picture exactly; others are slightly different. A candle may have more "amplitude" or size than in the book. But the pattern is still the same and is likely still valid.

The Least You Need to Know

- Candlestick charting has been around for 400 years, and is a well-practiced means to read price movement.

- Candlesticks work as an alternative to technical analysis and can be applied quickly and effectively during the trading day.

- Individual candle "specifics," like the size of the body and wick, are important.

- In candle patterns, the position of candles with respect to others in body and wick size and open and close price are important.

- Candlestick patterns may not exactly match "book" patterns, but so long as a trader understands the underlying activity, they work.

Part 5

Developing Your Own Trading Style

Tools and technique, by themselves, won't do it. A good airplane doesn't make someone a pilot, and a good guitar doesn't make someone a musician. Likewise, traders need to add in their own mix of style, character, and habits to make the tools work. Part 5 shows how to develop a successful trading style, what pitfalls to avoid, and how to get started.

Chapter 18 examines three primary trading styles—pure dealing, momentum trading, and range trading—and what works and what doesn't in each style. Chapter 19 expands into good and bad trading habits and the all-important topic of risk and money management. With everything in place, Chapter 20 gives ideas for how to get started, how to develop as a trader, and where trading is headed as a practice.

I LIKE ZEE STYLE OF ZEE *FRENCH.*

Chapter **18**

The Day Trader's Playbook

In This Chapter

- ◆ Three "core" trading styles
- ◆ How to decide *what* to trade
- ◆ The how and why of pure dealer trading
- ◆ The how and why of momentum trading
- ◆ The how and why of range trading
- ◆ Short selling as a strategy and trading tactic

Just knowing how things work doesn't make anybody a successful day trader. No more than knowing how an airplane works makes one a pilot, or how a piano works makes one a musician. Knowing how things work is a necessary first step. But that's only a start. From there, traders need to develop the knowledge, skills, and character to turn metal and mechanical energy into flight and to turn notes and keys into music.

This chapter looks more closely at the three styles introduced in Chapter 3—"pure" dealing, momentum trading, and range trading—and how each style makes use of the tools you've learned about in this book.

Deciding What to Trade

Before digging into *how* to trade, you need to decide *what* to trade. Without a good approach to selecting stocks and other securities, traders might waste the day searching for opportunities or, worse yet, pick the wrong ones.

Most traders develop a set of habits, sort of a morning routine, in their search for trading opportunities. Obviously, every trader's approach varies somewhat, but there are common themes.

Traders may choose to "specialize" in a certain narrow group of securities, or to take a more generalized, opportunistic approach. The specialist focuses on a few securities, perhaps just a single stock, while the opportunist scans the radar to see what's "hot" on a daily basis.

> **CAUTION**
>
> **Alert!** _____
>
> Sounds simple—just learn three quick trading styles and march to the bank, right? Wrong. These styles are *general*, and by nature will apply differently in different situations. They involve a mix of strategies and tactics unique to the trading situation—the security traded, the market, the tools available, and skills of the trader.

The Specialist Expert

Like the market makers they emulate, specialists become experts on the securities they follow and trade. They watch the trading patterns closely. After a while, they pick up on the patterns of market makers and other players in the stock, price behavior, sensitivity to news, and even corporate and industry events playing into the behavior of the stock. Eventually, they "get good" at trading the stock, and keep coming "back to the well" to trade it on a daily basis.

Specialists develop their expertise over time through careful study and experience. They may focus on a single security or a chosen few, but seldom more than 5 or 10.

The specialist approach is most closely aligned to the "pure dealer" trading style, although it is compatible with other styles as well.

Searching the Radar: The Opportunist

Unlike specialists, opportunists enter the trading day with little to no preconceived notion of what to trade. They use the trading tools and newswires to figure out "what's hot," dig in further to identify trading opportunities, and start trading.

Opportunists may start their selection routines the evening before the trading day, combing technical analysis tools, news, and event calendars for signs of opportunities the next day. Before the market opens, opportunists continue to watch the radar closely, and at market open, the search intensifies. Opportunists look for "gap" opens, breakouts, unusual volume—any sign of new price movement.

The opportunist approach is most aligned to the momentum trading style, but works with all styles.

By the News

Naturally, opportunists keep a close eye on the newswires for breaking news stories. Brokerage or analyst recommendations, company news, and even general economic news can drive opportunities.

Traders also stay attuned to commentary, news reports, and analysis. These reports focus on news and events and may bring technical trading conditions to light. Many of these reports come through the newswires, and more can be accessed through websites and subscriptions.

By the Numbers

The "Top 10" screen on their trading platform is one of the opportunist's favorite tools. From the opening bell, traders can track the top 10 stocks by volume and price movement, with customized color codes highlighting new entrants to the list. These traders also watch the screening windows closely for gap openings and other significant price or volume movements.

By the Sector

Many traders start the day by keeping tabs on sector activity. They hope to get a big-picture sense of what's happening for the day, then use that information to trade individual securities tied to the sector. If the energy sector is hot, individual energy stocks and commodities are likely to be also. Traders will then seek to trade the leaders—or laggards—of the group.

Trade Secrets

Should a trader go with or against the "madding crowd"? There is no pat answer—it depends on what works for the trader. Some find opportunity using a contrarian approach—that is, betting against the crowd—on a given day. The idea is that if the crowd is wrong, being one of the few on the "right" side will be more profitable. Sometimes, of course, going with the crowd is the right approach.

Trading Styles Reviewed

The remainder of this chapter examines the three major trading styles first introduced in Chapter 3, showing you how various traders employ the tools and techniques covered in Parts 3 and 4 of this book. Before moving on, let's review the three styles:

◆ **Pure dealers** work in and out of the market to capture spreads and small price movements, in much the same manner as a market maker. This style of trading is sometimes called "scalping." Pure dealer trading requires constant close focus and (usually) expertise on the security being traded.

◆ **Momentum traders** identify the big movers, up or down, and play them for what they're worth. A momentum play can span a few minutes to a few hours. Momentum traders look for price breakouts and gaps—significant price moves that can be followed through the day. They watch market maker activity closely for signs of large players, and watch constantly for signs of increasing or decreasing momentum.

◆ **Range traders** trade off of support (upper) and resistance (lower) ranges of security price behavior. They work back and forth, buying low and selling high, for as long as the range holds up. Some range traders use the range for pure day trading; others might take a longer-term "swing" approach.

In the interest of brevity, what follows centers on stocks, particularly NASDAQ stocks. A few tips and pointers will be given on using these styles with "listed" stock (NYSE) where it makes sense.

The Pure Dealer

The pure dealer's objective is to capture the spread between bid and offer as often as possible, turning a profit just like a market maker. He watches the market pulse and uses limit orders to trade back and forth. He may make anywhere from a handful to hundreds of trades per day, depending on spreads and intraday trading patterns. Pure dealing is far and away the most intense of trading styles.

Pure dealers stay focused on the spread and the behavior of individual dealers in the market. They have no regard for the performance of the company or any other factor extrinsic to the market for the security for that day.

> **Trade Secrets**
>
> Pure dealers make their money by repetition. When making hundreds of trades even a few dollars count, and many prefer the newer "per-share" commissions offered by advanced platforms (see Chapter 13).

How and Why

Pure dealers usually take the "expert" approach to learning the intimacies of a stock and the players in that stock. They watch it like a hawk, looking for signs of market maker strength and weakness. They often rely on market maker tickers and other advanced tools to help expand their powers of observation.

When pure dealers trade, they use limit orders exclusively—otherwise they'd forfeit the spread, the primary trading objective in the first place.

Stock Selection

Pure dealers trade stocks they can understand with market players they can understand. The pure dealer may choose a less-active stock because there is less competition—fewer other dealers and traders in the market. When there are fewer traders, the patterns can be more predictable and spreads can be larger. With fewer dealers, there is more opportunity to *front run* the competition.

Trading Terms

When a trader places a limit order in an attempt to get to the top of the order or quote queue it is known as **front running**. Here's an example: if a less-active stock is quoted at a bid of 25.45 and an offer of 25.50, a front runner might place a limit order to sell at 25.49, thus capturing 4 of the 5 cents available on the spread. Front running is a common strategy for trading NYSE stocks because specialists are required by exchange rules to post customer limit orders ahead of their own, even at the same price.

Signs of Strength, Signs of Weakness

Pure dealers are constantly looking for signs of strength or weakness in the stocks they trade. Bid and offer size and depth are extremely important. Depth refers to the number of market players bidding or offering at the inside market. The pure dealer looks for new market participants, increasing or decreasing size, quote refreshes, and greater volatility in the stocks they trade. Essentially, they are looking for signs of pressure, in one direction or another.

Level II quotes and Time and Sales (see Chapter 15) are essential to pure dealer trading. The pure dealer watches the progression of bids, offers, and prints like a hawk, and also pays close attention to the "direction" arrows showing which market participants are moving towards or away from the inside.

Additionally, pure dealers monitor intraday charts, most likely one-minute interval candlestick charts (though because the time periods are so short, candlestick patterns may have less meaning), looking for signs of increased volatility or upward/downward pressure. Pure dealers may set alerts and will use market maker tickers to track behavior.

Knowing the Market Makers

Pure dealer trading requires understanding the motives and techniques of (other) market makers. Turning a profit as a pure dealer used to be a lot easier—market makers simply posted their quotes for whatever size they had to buy and sell and traded accordingly. Pure dealers could swoop in and capture the spread by buying shares coming up for sale on the bid and reselling them on the offer. But because of the increase in trading activity and the entrance of many more pure dealers into the marketplace, market makers have become better at disguising their activities and intentions. It should also be noted that pure dealer trading has become more difficult with penny spreads, as opposed to the one-sixteenth/one-eighth/one-quarter spreads common in the market before the year 2000.

Today's market makers (and NYSE specialists) often post quotes higher or lower than the real market. NASDAQ dealers will post a lot of quotes with 100-share size to avoid showing a bigger hand and avoid large SOES transactions.

Head Fakes

Market makers will also post feint, or "head fake" bids or offers to try to drive other buyers and sellers from the market. If a stock is trading with size quotes in the hundreds of shares, and suddenly a market maker posts an offer quote for 50,000 shares (indicating that many shares for sale), buyers will run for cover. Bid quotes will drop anticipating this new large seller in the marketplace. Often the market maker or specialist really intends to buy (or has a large buy order) and is simply trying to drive the price lower before doing so.

Savvy traders see these market maker quotes for what they are. If a market maker is consistently back in the market on one side with large size, those quotes are probably real. But if they flash by in an instant—particularly with no corresponding Time and Sales print, it's a game. Such are the tactics—and there are many others—that a pure dealer watches for.

Discipline

Discipline is required in all forms of trading, but the discipline required of the pure dealer may exceed that of other types.

The pure dealer's discipline involves getting out of a trade quickly if it goes the wrong way. If the spread collapses, and the purchase price becomes the offer price while others back away on the bid, that is an immediate bad sign. Pure dealers try to hit their profit objective almost immediately, and if they don't, they move on.

Trade Secrets _____

Arbitrage is an offshoot of the pure dealer style. An arbiter tries to pick up on differences in price movement among several different securities. If the energy sector—and big oil stocks—are showing a nice 2 percent gain, why is Stock A, which is in the energy sector, showing only a 1 percent gain? Some pure dealers specialize in two related stocks and trade off of the differences in their movements—that is, they buy the stock seemingly left out of part of the move. This is called "pair trading." Doing this well takes careful study over a long period of time.

Momentum Trading

While scalping, or pure dealing, is an almost rote, repetitive, mechanical trading style, momentum trading is an exciting sensory experience requiring extreme skill and vision. A momentum trader's objective is to jump on something that's moving and jump clear when the time is right.

Momentum traders comb the news and charts to see what is "in play" on a particular day. They look for a favorable entry point, watch closely for certain patterns through the trading day, and "bail" when the momentum slows or looks like it will reverse. While pure dealers look for pennies and nickels, momentum traders look for larger gains—50¢, a dollar, or more.

How and Why

A breakout is a significant change in direction, usually from a relatively stable price pattern, and is usually accompanied by high volume. Momentum traders look at "breakout" stocks as trading opportunities. Most momentum traders are generalists, and follow what is moving on a given day rather than becoming experts on a select few stocks.

Trade Secrets _____

Momentum players usually don't try to time the market perfectly to catch the exact top or bottom. If they get 80 percent of the play, that's fine. Large opportunities can be lost fighting for small pennies.

Once they've identified a breakout, momentum players must decide if it will continue. If they decide to jump on, they must watch closely for an exit point. Most momentum players set a price target and watch closely for signs of slowdown or reversal. They are ready to pull the plug if conditions change or objectives are met. Many momentum traders—especially if they are trading multiple stocks or otherwise occupied—use alerts to signal changes or reached targets.

Finding Breakouts

Momentum traders scan the news and premarket activity prior to market open in the hopes of identifying potential breakouts. Newswires are quite active in the early part of the day. They bring stories from many wire services, including Dow Jones, Business Wire, Reuters, and AP. These services feed so-called "Hot Stories," "most active," "biggest gainers," and "biggest losers" lists.

The first half-hour is probably the busiest time of the momentum trader's trading day. The momentum trader uses screeners (see Chapter 13) to find stocks with large up or down moves, either in point or percentage terms, and "gap" openings. Momentum traders keep a close watch on the Top 10 list, which is very dynamic and tells a lot during the first part of the day.

Trading Breakouts

Some apparent breakouts come from rumors or from market makers or specialists playing games to get better prices on market orders. Patient traders watch trading activity, including Level II activity and charts, for a while before making a move. When they decide it's time to get in, they may use market orders to get in as fast as possible and to avoid being left behind (remember, a limit order guarantees price but not execution or size).

Once in, the trader will probably set an alert, and may use trailing stops to protect the position (in case the breakout was an illusion).

Momentum traders watch closely for signs of congestion or saturation in the market at price points along the way. Saturation occurs when a number of market makers pile in with offers at a price level. When a stock gets saturated, the momentum slows, and if the supply exceeds demand, it will reverse. These patterns can usually be seen on Level II and intraday candlestick charts. As might be expected, momentum

> **CAUTION**
>
> **Alert!** _____
>
> In the "old days," before decimal trading, it used to be easier to see saturation in advance. A dozen market makers piled up with size at 22½ was easy to see when the stock advanced to 20⅛. Now, between ⅛ and ½ (12¢ and 50¢), there are 37 "penny" levels for market makers to spread across, so today it's a little harder to see saturation coming.

trading on NYSE stocks is harder, because a trader can't see ahead to supply and demand (orders) away from the inside market.

Note that momentum trading works equally well—and sometimes better—for down market moves. This is where short selling comes in, and there's more about this form of trading later in this chapter.

> **CAUTION**
>
> **Alert!** _____
>
> Many traders advise against using market orders in *any* situation, claiming that it cedes too much control to market makers and specialists and entails paying the spread. However, when trying to board a momentum move, market orders are the fastest way to enter a position, and a few pennies shouldn't matter in the context of a dollar trade. Using market orders is safer when there are a lot of market participants.

If It Doesn't Work, Bail

Seasoned momentum traders learn to bail if the momentum reverses or fails to materialize. Whereas pure dealers consider winning on 15 trades while losing on 10 a success, momentum traders are trying to score some big winners while suffering only minor losses.

Trading Gaps

Gap trading is a special type of momentum trading. Gaps occur when a stock opens at a price significantly different from the previous close, either up or down. Gaps can be driven by news, brokerage recommendations, or pure emotion. Often the trading at the end of the previous day can give clues to the reasons. If the stock closed on a sharp upswing, professional traders close to company events were probably at work entering or exiting positions, and there may have been a short "squeeze" happening as well.

Suppose a stock closes the previous day at 56 and opens the next day at 61—a "gap-up" opening. What happened? Obviously a lot of demand piled up at the opening, from the public, from market makers, or both. Market makers and specialists providing the liquidity had to get the shares from somewhere, usually by short-selling them out of their own inventory with the hope of buying them back cheap later in the day. But if the public buying persists, they're likely to lose; but if it subsides for any reason, look out! Market makers and specialists do what they can to come out ahead, and they'll drive the price down if they can.

So they try to "test" the market. If they are able to reverse the market to buy their sold shares back cheap, they break through the other way. As a result, traders will see a sharp downward move after the gap opening. If this move fails, strength is confirmed, and the stock will chase the opening price upward and move beyond.

The Day Trader's Play

Let's take a look at a gap from the day trader's perspective. The first thing they see is the gap-up open. Then, often, a short burst of continued buying as other investors move in to the market. Then, shortly after the open, usually less than an hour, the price will weaken. If the stock crosses back below the opening price, it's probably headed even lower. If it doesn't, the advance starts forward again. This is a sign of strength. The day trader uses this point of decision to place a momentum trade, either up or down.

Finding Gap Stocks

Traders can find gap stocks using the stock screener on their trading platform. The screener allows the trader to screen for "gap up, stay up," "gap up, lost gap," "gap down, stay down," and "gap down, lost gap." In a "gap-up, lost-gap" scenario, the stock opened with a "gap up," then lost the gain and likely is trading lower than the opening price. "Gap down, lost gap" means the stock opened "gap" lower—significantly below its previous close—then gradually recovered to a level above the original opening price. So the gap "down" was "lost" to an upside recovery.

Big Players: The Hammer and the Ax

A hammer, also called an ax, is a market maker, often one of the big investment houses—Merrill Lynch, Morgan Stanley, Goldman Sachs, etc.—bringing large institutional orders to the market as buy or sell orders. Large orders naturally create a lot of demand or supply in the market at a given price level or sequence of price levels. A hammer can bring a strong resistance or support point to a trading day, or can add momentum to an already shaping move.

The hammer is a seasoned professional trader, and is usually making a market for his or her firm while also trying to fill the order. The hammer will play persistently in the market until the order is filled. Traders watching closely can often see the hammer, either with large size or consistent positioning and quote refresh at a given price level.

> ### Behind the Screen
>
> Hammers are much easier to see with NASDAQ Level II transparency. At the NYSE, a hammer or ax can hide away from the market in the specialist's book (or by physically standing at their post). Sudden 10x or 100x increases in inside bid/ask size may indicate the presence of a hammer. If the specialist seems to be "nudging" prices higher and lower by showing large size, a hammer might be present. It should also be noted that ECNs provide an alternate outlet for dispersing large size, so very large "hammer" positions appear less frequently in today's markets.

The Day Trader's Play

A trader can profit by "shadowing" the hammer, essentially following their lead and trading in the wake of their presence. A large hammer on the offer—indicating a large sale into the market—will drive the price lower. Traders can pick up shares at the lower price on the assumption that the hammer order (or quote) will eventually fill and disappear, allowing the price to rise back into the vacuum created by their departure. The market may actually track strongly higher as the resistance point is lifted. The danger is that the hammer may stay in the market or drive the offer lower if it's anxious to unload the position or to further drive down the price of the stock.

Fake Swings

With the increased number of savvy traders out there, hammers are increasingly likely to disguise their intentions. They might remove the bid or offer intermittently and spread it across price levels. They may even post large bids or offers on the opposite side of the market to drive the price to where they want it.

Momentum Trading Pitfalls

Greed is the number-one enemy of the momentum trader. Once a stock moves in a trader's direction, it is extremely tempting to try to ride it into the sunset. All too often traders mistake reversals for short retracements and they wait too long to sell. Like gamblers, unseasoned momentum traders are likely to give their "winnings" back to the house.

Similarly, momentum traders often get caught in a pattern of thinking that compels them to try to capture *all* of a move. They try to buy too low and miss out entirely, and try to sell too high, missing out on the gain. Successful momentum traders are satisfied with 60, 70, or 80 percent of a price move. They capture as much of the trend as possible, but know it's foolhardy to try to capture it all.

Momentum traders must also learn to bail if the trade "goes bad." Following momentum in the opposite direction, "hoping" for a reversal, is a common mistake. While it's hard for pure dealers to pull the plug on trades, it is even harder for the momentum trader, for things "looked so good to start with."

It should be noted that momentum trading works equally well for downside moves. Short selling is examined in greater depth at the end of this chapter.

Range Trading

Range trading is all about identifying trading ranges and support and resistance points throughout the trading day. It is about finding the "natural" selling and buying pressure at given price points.

How and Why

Range traders pick securities that trade steadily within observable trading ranges. More supply becomes available at the high end of the range, creating resistance, while more demand comes in at the support low. Stocks can trade within trading ranges during a trading day or over a longer period of time. Many traders specialize in finding slow, steady stocks that may trade in a 50¢ trading range day in and day out.

Traders find ranges using charting and technical analysis, often drawing support and resistance lines manually on a chart. Consistent reversals occur at support and resistance points, as more demand or supply enter the market. Support and resistance can also be observed on the Level II screen, where it's possible to observe the "congestion" of market players at certain price points. This latter method, however, is less dependable, as some of these players will adjust their quotes as the price nears the end of the range.

Range traders watch such stocks actively, or in many cases, simply place limit orders at or near support and resistance points. The latter strategy can expose range traders to breakouts and minor changes in the trading pattern, so traders must always be on guard for these events.

Signs of Change

Obviously, if securities traded in predictable patterns all the time, range traders would make all the money at the expense of everyone else. Ranges do change, and to be successful, the focused trader must see the signs coming in advance. The range trader watches for signs of change in the numbers and in market psychology. Sooner or later, all trading ranges end with a breakout—that is, a larger price move out of the previously established range.

Breakout Patterns

A breakout can be brought on by any number of factors internal or external to the trading pattern. Large market moves or news items percolate down into individual security demand. An ax or hammer may fulfill needs and go away. Specific company or industry news can change trading psychology. Some stocks just seem to get tired of trading in a certain range and seek new ground (meaning, market players have run out of orders or shares at current price levels). Whatever the triggering event, breakouts can be sharp.

Higher Highs, Lower Lows

Securities might—or might not—exhibit clear signs of breakout in advance. One of the more frequent observations is a gradual strengthening of interval highs and lows prior to an upward breakout, or a deterioration of interval highs and lows prior to a downward breakout (sometimes referred to as a "break*down*.") Higher highs and lows mean that selling pressure is gradually drying up and fewer shares are being made available at the low end of the range. The "pennant" chart pattern (see Chapter 16) shows this phenomenon as a picture.

Narrowing Ranges

Range trading has become more popular and more available to more players. Trading tools make it easy to see tops and bottoms in real time, and more players try to "buy low and sell high" in unison. The predictable result: in the absence of other market influences, trading ranges narrow. More sellers (including market markers) try to catch the highs and more buyers try to catch the lows. Eventually, they try to "front run" each other, and the range contracts, meaning that supply and demand have reached equilibrium.

Finally, volatility almost disappears. Market players lose interest and start to back away. Then, some external influence—a news item, analysis, market change—comes along and, suddenly, everyone tries to get back onboard again. It would be almost impossible to expect this renewed interest to emerge with perfect supply-and-demand equilibrium, so the price moves sharply as players pile on, often in one direction or another.

Trade Secrets _____

What does the range trader do during a breakout? Narrowing ranges are a sign of breakout and that the "range" game is over, at least temporarily. The range player either backs away to the sidelines or becomes a momentum player during the transition.

When Resistance Becomes Support

Seasoned range traders recognize that range patterns often repeat—at different price levels. Why? The same players are in the market doing the same things—but in a different place. Stocks will tend to set new trading ranges after a move, although there is no guarantee that the range will last as long or be the same size.

Frequently, a pattern emerges in which the previous resistance level becomes the new support level. Why? Because many traders—whether right or wrong before—have entered or exited positions at the previous resistance level. Moreover, that level might be a *number*—a round dollar or cent amount psychologically important to the market.

Trading Terms _____

In trading lingo, a **number** is a round figure, usually an integer, without a fraction. So "14.80," "20.50," "30.00," or "75.00" are referred to as the number, while 52.06 is *away* from the number. What's the significance? Most people think in round numbers. Limit orders are placed at 52, not 52.06. On the way up, 52.00 may have been the resistance—but after the breakout, it may become support. In today's trading, 51.95 may well become the support, because many traders place their trailing stops slightly below the number. Daily lows ending in ".95" are common. Lessons: be aware of the "number" and place orders in odd-cents amounts to stay away from the crowd.

The Day Trader's Play

Most range traders do their homework offline (before or after market sessions) to identify stocks trading in predictable ranges. Range traders tend to become "specialists" in a few securities with predictable (to them, anyway) ranges.

Many range traders try to identify ranges holding up for periods of a few days to a few weeks. This type of trading lends itself to less active traders or traders with something else to do. These traders can place limit orders at the ends of the range, and move on to other things.

Very active, intraday range traders watch the open, which is usually more volatile, as news is digested and large orders placed overnight are cleared. About half an hour into the day, trading range patterns start to emerge, and the trader enters a position, or places limit orders at either end of the range.

Whether playing intraday or longer ranges, range traders make ample use of limit orders and alerts. They may watch Level II action closely. On the charting side, they use candlestick charts, Bollinger bands, and moving averages in addition to pattern charts. All range traders watch closely for signs of change.

Range Trading Pitfalls

The pitfalls of range trading are fairly obvious:

- Seeing ranges that aren't really there. Stocks may settle into a true trading range, or they may pause somewhere along a major up or down move.

- Range traders can get so comfortable with their ranges that they fail to see, or acknowledge, a breakout. Range traders must be willing to accept change; not doing so can be costly.

- Traders often feel compelled to do *something*, lest they be left out. It is easy to force a trade on a range that isn't really there.

Short Selling

Throughout the book, most discussion of strategy and technique has centered on the idea of buying low and selling high. But clearly any trader must not overlook the opportunity to "go the other way"—that is, to sell high and buy low, or sell short, in trading vernacular.

Most investors—and still the majority of traders—think first in terms of capturing price advances. Short sellers think about, and profit from, price declines.

It's probably safe to say that short sellers are fewer in number and stronger in skill than the average trader. Because risks and costs are higher, short sellers really must know what they are doing. That said, savvy traders are always looking for ways to be among the "right" few instead of the "wrong" masses. Such a position is eminently more profitable.

How and Why

Boiling it down, short sellers are looking for securities that are overbought. Short-selling investors look for stocks overvalued related to their fundamentals, while short traders look for stocks in or near a reversal or showing downward momentum.

When too many buyers pile onto an "up" move, the subsequent absence in demand and abundance of supply is aggravated by the presence of so-called "shorts," who essentially "borrow" supply to add fuel to the fire. In many cases, when a security starts down, it heads downward faster than it ever went up, as less experienced buyers get scared off and short sellers pile on.

Smart traders see overbought situations before they turn the corner.

CAUTION **Alert!**

Remember that short-selling rules prohibit shorting on a downtick—that is, a transaction at a price lower than the previous.

Short-Selling Situations

Short selling works best when a security finishes a long run upward or when bad news hits the market. Savvy traders look at charts, technical conditions, market maker activity, and specific events as shorting opportunities.

Charts give clues to shorting situations by showing stocks advanced above trading ranges or in a clear reversal pattern after an up move. Gap openings, as described earlier, create shorting opportunities when the price moves fail to follow through. When the number and size of market maker quotes on the offer start to increase, that is a sign to short—though traders must watch for head fakes designed to stimulate temporary small price drops.

Events, and especially earnings announcements, create shorting opportunities. Pending announcements frequently drive a stock price upward anticipating possible good news. When the news is bad—or even not good enough—the stock tends to fall, if only for a brief period of time.

The Day Trader's Play

Short traders must walk a fine tightrope between shorting too soon—that is, before a reversal or downward momentum—and shorting too late, when the absence of an uptick makes it hard to initiate the trade. Short sellers must be quick traders. They must decide quickly, act quickly, and be ready to pull the iron out of the fire if it doesn't go their way. Short sellers usually use limit orders to sell, and many place "buy stop" orders to guard against runaway upward moves.

Why do short sellers have to act quickly? Traders need to remember the extra risks inherent in short selling. While the loss of a "long" player is limited to the price of the security, the potential loss of a short is infinite. Further, a "short squeeze"—when too many shorts play in only to have to get out at once—can cause sharp upward price moves. Market makers are just as eager to shake out the shorts as the longs—and the shakeout process can be swifter and more painful for the more-exposed short. The relatively few shorts, if wrong, can be crushed by the stampede of onrushing longs.

Trade Secrets

In April 2005 the SEC announced a one-year hiatus on the uptick rule as part of a pilot program. This temporary suspension may have important effects on short selling in practice.

Short traders should remember that not only do they face greater risk, but costs are also higher. Shorting means selling stock borrowed on margin, so a short player pays margin interest. Further, if the stock pays dividends, the short is liable for those dividends, which must be rightfully paid to the lending owner.

Trade Secrets

When short sellers want to hedge, or guard, against runaway upward moves, many buy insurance in the form of out-of-the-money call options. For a small premium, the trader is protected from a short squeeze.

Even though it's a bit riskier, traders should learn short selling and be prepared to use it occasionally. It increases versatility, making it more likely to make money in all kinds of market conditions. That said, short selling should be approached with respect, a degree of caution, and a healthy appetite for learning by experience.

The Least You Need to Know

◆ "Specialists" become trading experts on specific securities while "opportunists" look across markets for trading opportunities each day.

◆ Pure dealers look for small profits, usually the spread or a few more cents, captured several times during a trading day.

◆ Momentum traders seek stocks in play or making sharp moves based on news, rumors, or strong players in the market. They look for gap plays and try to capture larger price moves, staying ever sensitive to reversals.

◆ Range traders look for support and resistance levels and trade between them. Securities that break through support or resistance can become momentum plays or can set new trading ranges.

◆ Short selling entails a little more risk and expertise, but it is a very important trading tool in today's markets.

Chapter 19

Developing Good Trading Habits

In This Chapter

- ◆ Trading as a business and profession
- ◆ Four core trading habits
- ◆ Good tactical habits for daily trading
- ◆ Risk management, money management, and the difference between the two
- ◆ Bad habits traders should avoid

The first 18 chapters of this book concentrated on the tools and techniques of trading. No doubt technique is important, but few traders can survive on technique alone. It takes a businesslike approach and a set of well-developed habits and character traits to put technique into practice successfully and consistently.

Like a business, good trading is a managed activity. In the absence of good trading habits, success is more a matter of luck than anything else.

In Chapter 1 I pointed out that trading is only gambling if you're a gambler. But with the right habits and hard work, trading turns into something much more substantial than gambling.

Trading Is a Business

The first step towards developing a good trading practice is to view trading as a business—really, as a profession. A profession requires sustained learning, hard work, and close tracking of results.

Traders as Professionals

Too many traders simply dive in, assuming they will be able to figure things out as they go. Does it work out? Only if they're lucky. Consider the example of a lawyer. A lawyer must not only learn the core principles of law, but also the nuances of what it takes to win. That doesn't happen overnight, and the patient law student spends hours looking and listening to what works for others and on the courtroom stage.

The Professional Ethic

Successful professionals put in the work and hours necessary to stay on top of their game and its latest developments. They plan their work and work their plan. They constantly track their results and use them to build their next plan.

Professionals maintain a steady demeanor. They do not get caught up in the emotions of their work. They accept failure as part of the learning process and accept victory without excess pomp. They see both as part of the game, part of the process. They don't let success or failure move them too far from their original plans or practice.

The Trading Business

Just like anyone running a business, good traders watch revenues and costs, cash flow, and return on investment. They look for opportunities to improve their operation without taking undue risk.

Like any business person, traders directly manage what they can control—stock selection, trading tools, platforms, research, time, money, and the like. For those things they can't control—market performance, news events, lack of information, actions of competitors—they put a risk management plan in place to minimize losses. They make assumptions, test assumptions, and avoid risking too much on unknowns.

Core Habits

Taking the perspective of a business professional into a trading practice is a good place to start. In addition, there are some common threads of character that all traders share. Traders who have trouble with any one of the following basics will have trouble trading over the long haul, even though they may have a few short-term successes.

Discipline

For traders, discipline involves sticking to a set of principles and a trading plan. It means acting consistently (though not necessarily exactly the same) in similar situations. It means not getting carried away with hope or false expectations. It means doing the required hard work and staying within yourself during the trading day.

Detached Emotions

The trader who gets too emotionally involved in trades or trying to "beat the market" will get sucked into bad decisions again and again. Most traders are, by nature, very competitive and anxious to show positive results. Traders must park their egos at the door and make rational decisions through the day. Those who can't do this will fall into the trap of trying to "win"—and tend to lose more. Traders must understand their own risk profile—their willingness to accept and tolerate risk—and modify their trading styles accordingly. Traders must not get angry under any circumstances. They must take what the market gives them, and move on.

Positive Attitude

Traders must be confident in their abilities and must stay positive. Anger and negativity cloud trading decisions. Negative traders tend to be tentative and tend to dwell on the last trade—not the next one.

Willingness to Learn

Successful traders know they must invest the time to learn their tools. They learn from their mistakes *and* successes. They look at trading charts and news every night. They track their results and try to learn as much from every experience as possible.

Tactical and Practical Considerations

The preceding "big four" trading habits are essential for becoming a successful trader, but they do little to shape the real action of the day. The next few habits help traders to make better decisions.

Select Stocks Consistently

Successful traders employ a consistent approach to selecting stocks or other securities to trade. Without consistency, traders tend to flounder in the first few critical minutes of the trading day. They waste time digging into the characteristics of the new securities or, worse yet, they make bad decisions. This isn't to say that traders can't employ more than one approach on a given day or even different approaches for different days—this is common. It just means that the approaches should already be part of the trader's system.

Trade Only When There's an Opportunity

When the opening bell sounds, traders often feel compelled to do something—anything—lest they get left out. This often leads to bad decisions or bad timing. Traders must keep in mind that it's okay to do nothing, if in fact there's nothing to do or if indications aren't clear enough.

Don't Wait for the Perfect Trade

But trading only when there's an opportunity doesn't mean you should sit around waiting for a perfect trade. No such trade will ever show up, and meanwhile, several "good" trading opportunities will have elapsed. So although traders shouldn't jump at anything that moves, they should be willing to venture in even if the trade setup isn't perfect.

Don't Wait for the Perfect Fill

The overly cautious or "perfectionist" trader tries too hard to get the best "fill"—meaning the lowest buy or the highest sell price. Many a profitable position has been blown by a trader trying to stretch that extra penny out of the position. Traders should be content with 80 to 90 percent—or even less—of a trade. Particularly in today's world of decimal trading, that extra tick isn't worth much.

Don't Forget About Gravity

This mantra, borrowed straight from the world of ordinary investing, means that traders shouldn't get so caught up in a momentum move that they forget basic physics. Every action (usually) has a corresponding reaction, and no matter how good things look for the moment, traders must always anticipate the reversal.

Don't Fight the Tape

This one's closely related to the "detached emotions" principle. Traders get into the psychology of thinking that they are right and the market must be wrong. The stock marches steadily upward—or downward—and everyone else must be all wrong, right? Well, gravity usually does take over, but it may not be within the trader's time horizon. Although trading is often a contrarian activity, a single trader can't push an entire market. If a stock is moving, and the forces behind the move all look legitimate, go with the flow, not against it.

Get Out at the Right Time

Most new traders are better at entering a position than exiting one. If a stock goes with them, they tend to hold on for more. If it goes against them, they hold on hoping for recovery. If it does nothing at all, they hold out for action. Traders need to watch closely for exit points and act on them when they appear.

Alert!

Traditional investing tells us that time is an ally, and that the more time for investments to grow, the better. But for traders, time can actually be a bad thing. Why? Given more time, more things can go wrong.

Be Willing to Move On

Traders who dwell on old trades—good or bad—are asking for trouble. The tendency to dwell comes out of an instinctive desire to make things right with a bad trade or bask in the success of a good one. "Making things right" leads to the destructive behavior of revenge. There is no way to "get revenge" on the market. Let go. Traders should file the old trade away into the tax file and move on. Exception: it's worth thinking about it for a while *after* market close to learn whatever lessons there may be.

Pick Targets—And Stick to Them

Successful traders choose price targets and stick to them. If a trade is entered with the goal of capturing 50¢ on an upward move, the successful trader takes this payoff and moves on. Conversely, if the trader is willing to lose 10¢ and 10¢ only, he or she closes the position when that level is reached. Such actions require a lot of discipline. Traders who keep in mind that success is based on the number of successful trades, not the success of each trade, have an easier time sticking to their targets.

Avoid Greed

This bit of advice was inevitable, and is closely connected to all the rest. Greed is the leading cause of trouble for most traders. It feels good when something works, so why not ride it higher? Likewise, it feels bad when something fails, so why not wait it out to see if it will come back. If conditions *truly* point to a reversal or a per-petuation of a momentum move, it may be okay to stay onboard. But traders must not let greed make decisions for them.

Stay with What's Comfortable

Too many traders, especially those with a few successes under their belts, think they're invincible. They think anything will work, so why not try it? Traders strug-gling with a few losses might also decide to try something different—and head into a quagmire. It's true that successful traders must adapt to change, keep learning, and expand their skills. But entering unfamiliar terrain as an arrogant reaction to success or a desperate response to failure can only spell trouble.

Common Sense

With all the fancy tools and the rush of numbers, it's easy to get caught up in overly complex trading strategies and patterns. Keep in mind that common sense is important, and that successful trading depends on instinct, too.

Managing Your Money

Many traders say that trading success is 90 percent money management. It makes sense, then, that every trader needs to develop a good set of *money-management* and *risk-management* practices. Without such habits, even the best trading strategies and choices may not produce acceptable results.

Risk management is *part* of money management. How much risk to take on an individual trade—and how to control that risk—is all part of making sure you turn a profit at the end of the trading day.

Money management is making sure the ending trade balance for the day, week, month, and year is positive. It is about making sure that positive trades turn into positive cash flow *after* expenses. It involves looking at trades as building blocks in an overall portfolio. It is the "business management" part of the trading business.

> **Trading Terms**
>
> **Risk management** involves managing the risk on an individual trade—carefully calculating how much capital to commit and how to control the downside risk of the trade.
>
> **Money management** is managing *all* trading activity to make sure the net balance of all trades produces a positive cash flow after expenses.

Risk Management

Risk management means managing the amount of capital "at risk" in a trade, and making sure the potential loss amount isn't excessive and doesn't exceed a predefined limit. The more specific the risk parameters, the better, for they force traders to stay within bounds. The downfall of most risk-management practices is that traders let them float—that is to say, they lose the predefined amount, but decide to hold on anyway, hoping to recover it.

Risk vs. Reward

The first step in managing risk in any trade is to assess the risk-reward profile of the trade. Most traders do this intuitively as they select the trade, but it's a good idea to anticipate what could go wrong with the trade and by how much. If there are more factors pointing to a loss than a gain, traders should reevaluate the trade. Bad chart patterns, heavy bids or offers on the wrong side, support, resistance, market direction, and news are among the downside risks a trader must consider.

> **⚠ CAUTION**
>
> **Alert!** _____
>
> Thinking positive doesn't mean overlooking the downside risks. Traders should appraise all risks, up and down, and be prepared to exit a trade if the downside risks prevail.

It is surprising how many traders enter a trade overweighing the upside potential and underweighing the downside.

At-Risk Amount

Before you decide how much you are willing to lose on any individual trade, you should first determine a maximum loss amount—that is, what percentage of your overall trading capital you are willing to part with. Based on this amount, you can work backward to determine how much of your overall trading capital you could lose. Or you can work "forward" to determine the downside exit point based on a loss amount you don't want to exceed.

Suppose you decide that the maximum amount you want to lose in any trade is 1 percent of your overall trading capital. If you have $50,000 in trading capital, that means you would need to back out of the trade as soon as you lose $500 (1 percent of $50,000 is $500).

Many traders use a 2 percent threshold—that is, they limit the loss on any trade to 2 percent of their invested capital.

> **💡 Trade Secrets** _____
>
> Should you think in *dollar* or *percentage* terms when examining a trade? Dollar terms are specific and help traders think in terms of specific results and risk-reward profiles (is it really worth the effort and risk to produce a $130 return?). Percentage terms give a more accurate indication of the return on an investment, and avoid clouding the issue with share price differences (is 10¢ on 2,000 shares better than 50¢ on 200 shares?). Experienced traders tend to work in percentage terms.

When to Hold, When to Fold

The ability to cut losses is obviously a central part of risk management. Traders learn to employ all available techniques to alert and "stop out" loss positions. Alerts are important—not only at the target loss amount, but along the way. Such alerts can be set by share price but also by percentage or total dollar amounts. Trailing stops—orders that fire when certain downside price points are met—are equally important risk management tools.

Alert!

Why are individual trade loss limits so important? One main reason: what a trader has to gain to recover the lost money can be a far higher percentage. To recover a 5 percent loss, a trader has to produce a 5.2 percent gain. To recover a 50 percent loss, a trader has to produce a 100 percent gain.

Hedging

Good traders are skilled at hedging their bets using opposing trades or derivative securities such as options. Shorting a stock and buying a cheap, out-of-the-money call option to protect the position can work, as can going long on a trade and on a put option. Each hedging strategy must be judged on a risk and cash flow basis—a 50¢ gain objective disappears pretty quickly with a 40¢ option premium paid as a hedge. As traders get more experience they figure out other ways to protect trading positions.

Trade Secrets

Remember that true day traders reduce risk by not taking positions home overnight.

Money Management

Money management is about managing the combined risk and reward of individual trades to preserve capital and make money in the long run. It is about keeping tabs on the total cash flow, meaning the positive trades less negative trades and expenses.

Keeping Score

Central to the task of money management is keeping tabs on financial results and updating them regularly. Traders should watch daily account balances and changes in those balances. The phrase "what is measured can be understood, what can be understood can be altered" captures the essence of tracking financial results. Plus, you'll thank yourself for keeping good records at tax time.

Selling Rules

Good money management involves creating a set of sound selling rules. Selling rules go further than downside protections to include selling *gaining* positions.

Half Selling

Most traders set rules to sell after a targeted gain is reached in a trade. Such discipline locks in the gain and avoids the trader's worst nightmare—watching a gain turn into a loss.

Many traders also have *half-selling* rules—where they sell half or some portion of a winning position to lock in the gain, while leaving some chips on the table to capture further gains. If the stock reverses, the resulting loss is smaller and offset by the gain already captured. Furthermore, capital is freed up for other trades.

Doubling Down

Some traders will also use a *doubling down* approach on losing trades. The idea: enter the trade with half the capital that might be committed, then double the original investment if the trade falters temporarily. This provides a hedge against taking a larger loss on a downside move and provides some protection if wrong about a trade at the outset. But many traders consider this "throwing good money after bad" and avoid the technique. The down move by itself points to the fact that the trade may have been wrong in the first place and should be reevaluated. Doubling down must be approached very carefully.

Trade Secrets _____

At the heart of money management, the trader strives to avoid …

- ◆ Turning small losses into large losses.
- ◆ Turning gains into losses.
- ◆ Turning large gains into small gains.

Never Overextend

Good money management means never overextending or overstepping boundaries in terms of money or technique. Traders get the impulse to "swing for the fences" in order to recover after bad trades or to "make a killing" after good ones. Overextension violates the steady discipline required of a trader and makes a trader's actions look more like gambling than trading.

> **CAUTION**
>
> **Alert!** _____
>
> This is as good a place as any to remind you that day trading should *not* be done with household finances, retirement savings, college savings, or business capital. Including these items in the day-trading nest egg makes for more emotional and less rational trading. It isn't a good place to go.

If You Prefer: Bad Habits to Avoid

Some people prefer to learn what *not* to do. So here is a list of things to avoid in creating a set of effective trading habits:

- Don't get emotionally involved; stay detached. Emotions work against your game plan.

- Don't think that "the market is stupid." The market is always right.

- Don't *hope*.

- Don't form opinions. You don't have time, and they let emotions enter the picture.

- Don't get angry.

- Don't wish for revenge. Revenge doesn't happen.

- Don't be afraid of losing. Scared money never wins.

- Don't blame losses on others. Accept responsibility and move on. Nobody else "did it to you."

- Don't swing for the fences. Hit singles and doubles—lots of them.

- Don't try to hit tops and bottoms.

- Don't try to win on *every* trade. It's the total dollar *amount* gained that counts, not the *number* of wins.

◆ Don't be lazy or gloss over important factors. Remember—it's real money and requires real work.

◆ Don't think of trading as a game or as gambling.

◆ Don't let a bad start ruin your day. Recover from a loss, put it behind you, and move on.

◆ Never stop keeping score. Stay on top of the business results of trading. Analyze and learn from results.

◆ Don't expect to be an expert right away. As in all other professions, expect to pay your dues.

◆ Don't expect to come out ahead, especially in your first three to six months. Be patient.

◆ Don't try to focus on everything. You can't. Do what you're good at.

◆ Don't expect trading to be easy. It's hard work. Profits are *earned*. Maybe not the "old-fashioned" way, but they *are* earned.

◆ Don't feel compelled to trade. Trade only when there is a trading opportunity.

◆ Don't act too soon, and don't let indecision delay actions.

◆ Don't see things that aren't there just to support a trade position.

◆ Don't forget the big picture. Stocks and commodities are part of a larger business landscape.

◆ Don't forget to press winners and cut losers. Surprisingly, many traders do the opposite.

◆ Don't ignore risk management. Use escape routes.

The Least You Need to Know

◆ Successful traders treat their trading as a business and take a professional approach to it.

◆ Traders must have good "core" trading habits, including strong discipline, emotional detachment, a positive attitude, and a willingness to learn. Absence of any one of these traits can quickly lead to failure.

◆ Tactical trading habits help traders make good decisions at the right time without becoming greedy or emotional.

◆ Risk-management tools help traders prevent excessive losses on individual trades, while good money-management habits help traders make money overall.

20

Trading at the Speed of Thought

In This Chapter

- ◆ Preparing to be a trader
- ◆ Balancing technique, psychology, and money management
- ◆ Getting started—learning, shopping, setting up, practicing
- ◆ Training your brain by *doing*
- ◆ On the future of trading

Day trading is a high-performance, information-intensive, real-time, do-it-yourself, technology-based way to play the securities markets. It is dynamic, exhilarating, engrossing, and intense. Trading is investing in a broad sense, as capital is invested to produce a return. But beyond that, it bears little resemblance to the kinds of "investing" our parents did.

The first 19 chapters examined the trading landscape—the markets, the tools, the strategies, the personal traits and habits needed to make it work. This concluding chapter steps back a little and take a broader look at trading and *you* as a developing trader.

A Bigger Picture

Early on I described the elements that make day trading possible: rule changes, improvements in personal technology, and real-time access to information and trading. I explained that volatile, medium to high volume, liquid securities and markets are favorable places to trade. I talked about major trading strategies and tools, and offered up a long list of trading tactics and personal habits that lead to trading success. I told you about Level II screens, market makers, ECNs, limit orders, momentum trading, and what a "hammer" is.

Are You Prepared to Trade?

But are you now prepared to be a trader? Yes, in a broad way. You could probably put this book down and start trading with a reasonable understanding of the basics. You at least have a reasonable knowledge base and are prepared to read more and take more training on the subject. But there's still more learning ahead; in fact, there will *always* be more learning ahead.

No book can teach the techniques and tactics of trading from A to Z. True trading, especially high-performance day trading, becomes more a matter of mental reflex and fast response to a number of simultaneous stimuli. It's really a form of mental athleticism requiring incredible concentration, stamina, conditioned reflexes, and hand-eye and brain-eye coordination.

Practice Makes Perfect

Like most athletic endeavors, you'll only get good by doing it, gaining experience, learning from failure, and trying again. No sport was learned from a book. So this book is only a part of a learning process. As a trader, you'll have to do more reading, more research, and get plenty of practice.

Strengths and Weaknesses

Along the way, you will figure out what makes you tick as a person and how much of the trading "character" you already possess. You will make use of the character traits and habits you have, and will develop new ones. You will capitalize on strengths and fix or learn to live with your weaknesses.

The Trader's Trifecta

Common trading wisdom boils down successful trading into three key elements:

◆ Technique

◆ Psychology

◆ Money management

Technique refers to understanding markets, information, trading, and analysis tools to make fast, rational, well-informed, ahead-of-the-pack decisions. Psychology refers to the personal tactics and habits necessary to keep your eye on the ball. Detachment, discipline, ability to act, ability to move on, and knowing your strengths and weaknesses are all part of psychology. Although psychology helps you stay focused and able to make rational decisions, it is really money management that keeps you in the game and that makes it profitable.

All three—technique, psychology, and money management—must be present in a balanced way to trade successfully. The best technicians in the world won't succeed if they can't overcome fear or handle money. The most cold-blooded, steely-eyed mental "toughs" won't win without understanding the tools and the market. And the former accountant who keeps track of every penny won't succeed either without … you get the point.

Every day trader should work relentlessly to develop technique, character, and effective money management *simultaneously*. The best in the business all have good rhythm and balance between these important factors.

About Risk

Trading is inherently a risky exercise, particularly in the beginning as you acquire vast amounts of knowledge and skills and find your "niche" in the market. Before trading, traders should take a close look at their own risk behavior and tolerance.

Traders need to accept some risk—and more risk per transaction than most investors. Markets move fast, and despite the tools now available, you can't possibly know everything

Trade Secrets _____

It may seem counterintuitive, but traders starting out may want to try the "pure dealer" trading style. Sure, this trading style is faster, harder work, and more intense than others, but *if managed correctly*, losses are smaller. Remember, the more time a trade is on the table, the better the chance of losing, and losing more.

and won't always know what can be known fast enough. In other words, you can lose a lot of capital in a very short period time.

Traders learn to accept the risk on the capital deployed and use the tools introduced in the last few chapters to minimize exposure. Still, as Warren Buffett points out, albeit regarding a far different style of investing, "the biggest risk comes from not knowing what you're doing."

Start at the Right Pace

Throwing yourself headfirst into the swimming pool to learn how to swim is usually not a good idea. The same goes for diving into the trading "pool." Novice traders tend to lose money—a lot of it. New traders easily become overwhelmed and lose confidence, which will have a negative impact on their trading performance over a much longer period of time. That said, it is important to get some real experience somewhere along the way. Taking the opening analogy further, traders should wade into the trading pool at their own pace. Those who stay on the beach will never learn to swim.

Traders must prepare to accept some risk and can expect to make some mistakes as part of the learning process. Capital deployed must be risk capital—that is, capital that can be affordably lost (and hopefully replaced).

Expect to Lose at First

Statistics vary on this topic, but most experts suggest that somewhere around 70 percent of all traders lose, and 90 percent of all traders lose *in the beginning*.

Alert!

Traders will lose at first. It's part of the learning process, and they should be ready for it. It can be compared to having a second-best hand at a poker table—it almost worked, but not quite. Continuing with the analogy, good traders may fold more often, but they don't leave the table.

Expect to Be Overwhelmed

It's worth repeating: trading is very hard work. The constant stream of news and numbers and tiny fluctuations will set most people on edge. You will get headaches, eye strain, fatigue, and have sleepless nights, at least for a while. It takes a while to get used to the rigor and intensity.

It also takes a while to learn how to separate the news from the noise—like in any new job or profession.

Turning Experience into Learning

Any investor or trader, no matter how big or small, long-term or short-term, should track results. It doesn't have to be anything fancy—a daily scoresheet kept in Excel or even on a KFC napkin is okay, if that's what works for you.

You should keep a daily trade log and cumulative position tracker (many advanced platforms provide this). You want to know how far ahead or behind you are, up to the second if possible. This helps guide your next move, and helps you decide how much risk you want to (or can afford to) take on the next trade. More than that, it gives clues as to whether a given trading strategy or security is successful.

Alert!

It's not enough just to keep a trading diary—you must look at it once in a while. Looking back over a week's worth of trades—good and bad—can help you spot moments of indecision or hasty decisions. Take time each week, perhaps each day, to review each trade. By identifying behavior patterns, you'll be better able to react when the same situation arises.

Learn to Diversify

Many traders like to diversify their trading activities. Why? To avoid becoming overly dependent on a single style or security.

You can diversify among trading styles, among securities, or among different kinds of securities. To be sure, becoming an expert in a single security has its merits. But when something changes, or there's no action in a security, it's nice to have somewhere else to go. Without such an outlet, you might force bad decisions and stick with that one thing long beyond its useful and profitable life. Diversifying also means that you'll be learning new and different things, always good for a trader. There are innumerable ways to "mix it up," with options, commodities, or new families of stocks.

Alert!

There will be days when it's better to turn off the computer and walk away. If you can't walk away from time to time, that's a sure sign of trouble.

Getting Started

In any new endeavor, getting started is sometimes the hardest part. The choices are overwhelming. What books to read? Which trading platform to use? What stocks to buy? What part of the house to work in?

Making a Good Plan

The first step is to plan your approach. What is the best way to learn? Do you have time to read books? Take online training courses offered by platform providers? Do you have a mentor or guide? Or will you try it a step at a time on a trading platform? Everyone learns differently and has different resources at their disposal, and no single approach works for everyone.

Deciding on Your Level of Commitment

New traders should enter the game with a well-thought-out plan for how active they want to be. If you want to be a full-time trader, it's important to make a full-time commitment to learning the tools and the market. Like any profession, if you skimp on up-front investments in time, training, and tools, you'll be less likely to succeed.

If you simply want to "dabble" in trading with a small portion of your investment portfolio when time and other conditions permit, you can develop your skills more slowly. Dabblers will get the experience they need, but producing sustained earnings from the venture is less likely.

Learning by Doing

As with sports, driving a car, or playing poker, you can *start* by watching, but sooner or later you have to *do* it. And the sooner the better, so you can get the feel as quickly as possible, learn from your mistakes, and develop a successful style. That said, it's okay to take five cards and fold away your ante for a while—so long as you're getting the experience you need by watching cards (and maybe, by watching others). By starting out trading very small amounts, you'll limit your losses while gaining experience.

Shopping Carefully

I've already discussed the myriad trading tools at some length, so I won't repeat it all here. Suffice it to say you should shop carefully before choosing trading platforms, especially expensive ones with long-term contracts. Spend your money—*invest it*—as you would for any other tool or piece of capital equipment vital to a business. Where possible, test drive using simulators and free trial periods.

It's important that you have what you need to support your trading style. Maybe a little *more* than what you need—in the interest of getting exposure to more advanced styles and tools. But avoid overkill. A high-end platform with four Level II windows simply isn't necessary for swing-trading NYSE stocks from your desk at work. It will cost a lot of money, confuse you, and compromise your concentration on both your trading and your job.

Setting Space Aside

Traders soon encounter the very practical matter of *where* to trade. "Where" in this case doesn't mean NASDAQ, NYSE, or CBOT. It means what room or what corner of what room in your house to work in. It means balancing between this corner and other places you might find yourself in, like in a cubicle, on the road, or at a coffee shop.

You need room for a computer, a decent monitor, and a printer (to print charts, trade logs, etc.). Many traders have a second Internet connection as a backup, should their primary connection fail.

The physical layout of the trading space isn't that important—it is a "whatever works" thing, although you should consider the need to concentrate when you plan your space.

Paper Trading

Between initial learning and actual trading, many traders take the step known as "paper trading," where they trade just like real traders, but don't commit real money to trades. It's like the hypothetical investing high school economics students do. Buy, sell, buy, sell, log the rationale and results, and evaluate at the end. And along the way, learn how the trading tools work.

Behind the Screen
If you're the kind of person who works more intensely and effectively under live fire, simulated or "paper" trading might not be the best way for you to learn. If you hit better shots on the golf course than you do on the driving range, you might want to consider getting real trading experience earlier on.

Many day trading platforms and trading firms allow users to do simulated, or paper, trading. Generally, these services are free.

Some traders may sail through paper trading only to "crash and burn" with real money. Most likely, their behavior changed when they migrated to the real thing. If that happens to you, go back to paper trading and try to figure out what changed when you went live.

Training Your Brain

I've taken a pretty deliberate approach to preparing you as a day trader. Rules, markets, information tools, trading tools, strategies, tactics, and styles. But like hitting a fastball or a golf ball, there are so many little elements and mechanics that can't be taught—and that you can't stop to think about during your swing.

As your day trading technique, psychology, and money-management skills all mature, trading will become less cognitive and more of a reflex or "action" skill. When this happens, you're starting to arrive.

Brain-Eye Coordination

You could say that skilled trading requires "brain-eye" coordination. As your eyes and ears scan the screenscape and listen to CNBC drone on in the background, your brain picks up things and makes instant semiconscious decisions. "Haven't I seen Dell do this before?" you'll wonder, or, "Looks like upward pressure is building on the S&P 500." You find yourself visualizing the future in very small, fast increments. You'll be able to pick up the rotation of the ball before you swing.

Learning How Your Brain Works

This sounds like it might entail long sessions with a therapist, but it really is about something else. Everybody has different reflex actions and ways of interpreting stimuli. Some things can be learned, others take a long time or never come at all. Otherwise, traders could make millions hitting curve balls and golf balls instead of by trading.

As you move from *thinking* day trading to *feeling* day trading, you'll start to get an idea of what your brain does well and what it doesn't. If you simply can't see things in charts, don't use charts. If news feeds do nothing for you, don't use news feeds. If you can't react quickly enough to market maker tickers, don't use them. Learn how your own brain works, and trade accordingly.

Getting the feel is part of developing your skills, character, and habits. You begin to sense what's going to happen based on an assortment of stimuli. Then you make a conditioned response.

What do you need to "get the feel?" Practice and more practice. Try new things. Talk to others. Watch closely and keep track of what you've done and what it's done for you. And above all else, keep learning and conditioning your brain.

The Future of Day Trading

The evolution of trading has been fascinating to watch, and it stands to reason that it will continue to be.

Markets and trading tools continue to become more "democratized"—that is, accessible and practical for the masses. Competition among brokers—and recognition of the importance of the active/day trader segment—will continue to lead to more and better products over time.

Many new traders have arrived on the scene, and many have left it as well. The 2001–02 shakeout was scary but necessary. Competition, decimalization, and unpredictable markets have made trading a more difficult endeavor. Today's traders must be sharper and more diverse than ever before; they can no longer simply sit out there and collect sixteenths and eighths scalping Intel.

Markets continue to evolve. The specialist system at the NYSE is intact for now, but who knows for how long? Will NASDAQ-like transparency become available for NYSE stocks? Will Archipelago (ArcaEx) succeed in its merger with the NYSE and unleash a whole new set of securities trading practices into the nation's oldest trading institution? Will individuals at all levels become their own market makers—trading on eBay-like securities venues—as the dealer/market maker/specialist system fades away? Will commodities and other noncorporate assets become securitized in such a way that 100 barrels of oil can be traded as easily as 100 shares of Exxon-Mobil?

And will trading become a 24-hour-a-day activity? Futures and foreign exchange markets already allow traders to trade around the clock. The expansion of ECNs and after-hours trading suggests that, sooner or later, traders might be able to trade any time they want. The growth of international traders will only help drive this process.

Finally, technology has done so much to make trading more inclusive. The personal computer and the Internet have made it possible for people to trade at home, a concept hardly thought possible 30 years ago. People can already trade from work, from coffee shops, and even from airports. An entire advanced trading platform adapted to a Blackberry and augmented by voice activation and artificial intelligence software doesn't seem that far off.

What it all comes down to is this: trading is here to stay, and its possibilities will only continue to grow.

The Least You Need to Know

- Successful day traders employ a healthy balance of technique, character, and money management skills. They know their strengths and weaknesses and work continuously to develop or correct them.

- Trading is a mental reflex activity, much like sports or flying. Through practice you will learn how the tools work and develop your reflex actions.

- Almost every trader loses in the beginning. Count on it. In addition, be prepared for hard work, headaches, and sleepless nights.

- Trading is here to stay, and the future looks promising.

Appendix A

Trading Terms

arbitrage   The simultaneous purchase and sale of substantially identical assets in order to profit from small price differences between the two assets.

ask   The price at which a market maker or specialist will sell a stock. Also known as the *offer*. If you place a market order to buy a stock you will buy it at the ask price.

at the market   A price quote equal to the highest bid or the lowest offer currently available.

away from the market   A bid lower than the highest bid currently available, or an offer higher than the lowest offer currently available.

ax   *See* hammer.

backwardization   Occurs when a near-term futures contract is priced higher than a longer-term contract. Anticipates greater supply in the future and may indicate a short-term overbought condition.

balanced market   One in which there is an equal number of buyers and sellers evenly distributed at all prices, both at and away from the inside market.

bid   The price at which a market maker or specialist is willing to buy a stock. If you place a market order to sell a stock, you will sell it at the bid price.

Bollinger bands   A charting technique showing support and resistance points, or a trading range, defined by the standard deviation, or volatility, of a stock's price.

breakthrough   A stock that has been hovering for a long time just under a milestone price is said to have broken through when it closes significantly and consistently above that price. Also known as a *breakout*.

buying power   The total of free equity funds plus funds that can be borrowed within margin rules, which in turn represents the total dollar amount of stock you can control.

call option   A traded contract that gives the owner the right, but not the obligation, to purchase a specific quantity of a security at a specific price by a specific future date.

close a position   To sell out a position bought earlier, or to buy "to cover" a position sold short earlier.

coverage   When a stock is tracked and analyzed by a brokerage house it is said to be "covered." When a brokerage house announces that it will be initiating coverage on a stock for the first time, it is taken as an endorsement of that stock by the professional community.

day trading   Buying and selling stocks or other securities during the course of a single trading day.

delayed quotes   Price quotes that are behind the current market prices—20 minutes for NYSE, 15 minutes for NASDAQ.

direct connection   A computer connection direct to a host computer (broker or clearing house), bypassing the Internet. Also called *direct access*.

downtick   Refers to any sale price that is lower than the previous price. The stock is said to be in a downtick.

ECNs   Electronic communications networks, alternate trading paths allowing NASDAQ and listed stock traders to trade directly with each other or to place orders directly into the market.

figure   Trading slang for the nearest whole-dollar price.

front running   Placing a limit order for a share size and price ahead of the current best market bid or offer. If the offer on a stock is 25.30, a front runner places a limit order at 25.29 (NASDAQ) or 25.30 (NYSE). NYSE rules require specialists to post customer orders in front of their own.

hammer   A market maker acting as a driving force at a point in time—minutes, hours, days, or longer—holding his bid or offer position or even improving it after every execution. The hammer probably has a large order from the firm it is representing and is aggressively trying to acquire or dispose of stock to meet the order. Also known as an *ax*.

hedge fund   A lightly regulated investment fund with a few select participants. Most originate a lot of day trading activity.

hitting the bid   Trading slang for selling a stock at the bid price.

index   Statistical aggregate measure of a market, market sector, or group of markets based on representative securities in that market. Examples include the S&P 500, Dow Jones Industrials, Russell 2000, NASDAQ 100, or Philadelphia Semiconductor Index.

initial margin   The amount of equity a trader must have when entering a transaction. The Federal Reserve specifies that stock traders must have at least a 50 percent equity position at the time of purchase. Individual brokers may require more. Commodities exchanges require much less, and it varies by commodity and trader experience.

inside bid and offer   The highest bid and lowest offer currently available in the market. Sometimes referred to as the *inside market*. A market maker bidding or offering at the inside bid or offer is said to be bidding *at the market*.

intraday   Events that occur within one trading day.

join the bid   When a market maker enters a bid at the current inside, or high-bid level.

join the offer   When a market maker enters an offer at the current inside, or low-offer level.

leave the bid   When a market maker removes its bid from the inside, or high-bid level.

leave the offer   When a market maker removes its offer from the inside, or low-offer level.

Level I   Basic-level NASDAQ quote, showing inside bid and ask quotes, last trade, volume, tick direction, open, high, and low for the day.

Level II   More advanced NASDAQ quote, showing market maker bids and offers at and away from the current inside bid and ask. Available only on high-performance trading platforms or from certain brokers, usually at a charge.

Level III   Most advanced NASDAQ screen, showing Level II information and allowing market makers to post or adjust bids and offers. Only available to market makers.

leverage   The use of borrowed funds to maximize an investing position otherwise available with a given amount of cash. Increases your percentage return on an up move, but increases your percentage loss on a down move.

lifting the offer   Trading slang for buying a stock at the offered price.

limit order   A fixed price order. A "buy limit" order is to buy a stock at or below a specified purchase, or "limit," price. A "sell limit" order is an order to sell at or above a specified price.

liquidity   Refers to the availability of enough buyers and sellers to quickly and easily execute transactions in a market.

listed stocks   Stocks listed and traded on the New York Stock Exchange, American Stock Exchange, or on regional stock exchanges (not NASDAQ).

long position   Your trading position when you initially buy a security.

maintenance requirement   The minimum equity percentage that must be maintained at all times in your account, according to broker or clearinghouse rules.

margin account   An account allowing a trader to borrow funds from a broker or clearinghouse to buy stocks and other securities on credit.

margin call   A requirement to deposit funds into your account or sell securities to increase the equity percentage above the minimum maintenance requirement.

marginable securities   Securities that your broker and the SEC deem appropriate for purchase with margin funds. Many speculative and "penny" stocks and recent IPOs may not be purchased with margin funds.

market makers   Firms licensed to buy and sell a particular security or securities on NASDAQ. These firms are usually brokers or investment banks and can be large or small. The term also refers to individual employees acting in the market on the firm's behalf. A partial list of market makers appears in Appendix B.

market order   An order to buy or sell a security "at the market," that is, with no specified fixed price.

momentum trader   Day traders who watch for stocks that are suddenly actively traded as a result of breaking news or other factors.

moving average   An average of a security's prices, calculated over a specified number of past periods, with a specified weighting of each period's price.

NASD   The National Association of Securities Dealers.

NASDAQ   Original acronym for the National Association of Securities Dealers Automated Quotations system, now a trade name for the NASDAQ stock market.

opening delay   A stock not trading at the market open due to news events or an extreme imbalance of orders. The specialist has 15 minutes from the opening bell to indicate a price range at which the stock will begin trading. (Listed stocks only; doesn't happen on NASDAQ.)

options   A contract to buy or sell a stock, commodity, or futures contract at a particular price by a particular date.

order imbalance   An excess of buy or sell orders that makes it impossible to match orders up evenly. For listed stocks, it may cause trading to be temporarily suspended.

oscillators   Oscillators compare the current price of a stock to its trading range over a defined period of time.

paid for order flow   Paid for order flow occurs when retail brokers sell your order to another firm for execution.

paper trading   Simulated stock trading by identifying and recording hypothetical trades and keeping track of all trades and daily profit and loss. Can be done by recording trades literally on paper, or with special software simulators.

position traders   Investors who take a position in a stock based on the performance or expected performance of the company.

put option   A traded contract to sell a specific quantity of a security at a specific price by a specific future date.

range trader   Trader intending to capitalize on security fluctuations within a trading range, buying at support and selling at resistance levels.

real-time quotes   A price quote which shows the price at which a stock is selling at that exact moment in time.

refresh the bid   When a market maker reestablishes the bid after being hit by an SOES execution. Refreshing the offer is a similar reestablishment of the offer.

Regulation T   Specifies an initial margin requirement—that is, a minimum equity requirement for a trader to enter a position—and a maximum that can be extended by the broker in the form of margin. Currently the initial margin requirement is 50 percent.

resistance level   A price at which a stock receives considerable selling pressure.

Rule 405   The "know your customer" rule that full-service brokerage firms must comply with. Stockbrokers must be well-acquainted with their customers' financial situation and long-term goals, and may only make recommendations appropriate to those goals.

scalpers   Day traders who try to make money by trading to capture very short-term spreads, usually a penny or two. Many trades last only a minute or two. Before decimal trading, it was much more profitable.

short selling   Selling stock borrowed from a broker anticipating a downward price move.

short squeeze   A short squeeze occurs when a sizable number of short traders get pushed to the exits all at once (have to buy the stock to cover their positions). This creates momentum and the price rises further, faster.

size   The volume of shares in a trade or available in a limit order or market maker quote.

size ask   On NYSE, total shares available to be bought from limit order sellers (or from the specialist) at the quoted ask or offer price. Also called *size offer*.

size bid   On NYSE, total shares being sought by limit order buyers (or by the specialist) at the quoted bid price.

slippage   The movement of the actual trade price away from the price at the time the order is placed.

SOES (Small Order Execution System)   A system implemented by NASDAQ to provide automatic electronic execution for small orders from the public without the market maker's intervention. All market makers are required to participate in SOES. Specific trading rules apply.

specialist's book   An electronic record of all fixed-price orders (stop, limit) and market and short-sale orders that a specialist has received, and the specialist's inventory. Used to execute orders on the NYSE or AMEX.

spread   The small price difference between the bid price and the ask price, normally representing a profit margin for a market maker or specialist.

stochastics   A way to measure the position of a stock's closing price relative to its price range over a specified number of periods and relative to its overall trend.

stock ahead   Situation preventing a limit order from being filled even when the limit price is reached; there are other "stock ahead" orders chronologically ahead that may consume the available demand and supply at that price.

stop order   A fixed-activation price order. An order becomes an active market order when the price reaches your specified "stop" price. A "buy stop" becomes an active market buy order when the stock rises to the stop price; a "sell stop" becomes an active market order when the stock declines to the stop price.

SuperDot (Super Designated Order Turnaround system)   An automated electronic system used to route orders on the NYSE floor to the appropriate specialist. Also used to route confirmations back to the source.

SuperMontage   NASDAQ's quote and order-routing system.

support level   A price at which a stock receives considerable buying pressure.

swing trader   A stock trader who holds onto a position for more than a day, usually a few days at a time.

teenies   Stock-market slang for a sixteenth of a point. The cash value of a teenie is 6.25 cents per share. The term is virtually obsolete with today's decimal trading.

trading range   A consistent price pattern characterized by definable resistance and support levels. The stock appears to bounce back and forth between these levels for a period of time.

trendline   A straight line, or two parallel straight lines bracketing highs and lows, indicating the direction in which a stock has been moving and can be predicted to move.

unlisted stocks   Stocks that don't trade on the NYSE, but rather on the NASDAQ or OTC markets.

uptick   The opposite of a downtick, a move upwards in the price between sales. A short sale can only be opened when the market is on an uptick.

zero-plus tick   A minor exception to the uptick rule: a zero-plus tick occurs when the last trade was made at the same price as the previous one, but the previous one was higher than two trades ago.

Market Maker and ECN Symbols

Following are some of the major market makers and players with their four-letter symbols as seen on the Level II screen. A complete list is available at www.nasdaqtrader.com.

ABLE	Arnhold and S. Bleichroeder, Inc.
ABNA	ABN Amro Incorporated
ABWD	A. B. Watley Direct, Inc.
AFGI	Access Financial Group
AGED	A. G. Edwards
AGIS	Aegis Capital Corp.
AJAY	A. J. Pace and Co.
ALGR	Fred Alger & Co.
AMEX	American Stock Exchange, Inc.
ARCA	Archipelago Trading Services, Inc. (ECN)
AXCS	Access Securities, Inc.
BAMM	Brokerage America, Inc.
BARC	Barclay Investments
BARD	Robert L. Baird, Inc.
BEST	Bear Stearns & Co.
BOFA	Banc of America Securities
BRUT	Brut, LLC (ECN)

BTAB	BT Alex Brown, Inc.
BTRD	B-Trade Services LLC (ECN)
BUCK	The Buckingham Research Group Inc.
CAIN	Carnegie Investor Services Inc.
CANT	Cantor Fitzgerald & Co.
CIBC	CIBC Oppenheimer
CJDB	CJLawrence/Deutsche
CLYN	Carlin Equities Corp.
COAS	Coastal Equities, Inc.
COBR	Coburn & Meridith, Inc.
COHI	High Point Capital Inc.
COWN	S. G. Cowan & Co
CRWN	Crown Financial Group, Inc.
CWCO	Crowell, Weedon & Co.
DADA	D. A. Davisdon, Inc.
DAIN	RBC Dain Rauscher, Inc.
DBAB	Deutsche Bank Securities, Inc.
DEAN	Morgan Stanley Dean Witter, Inc.
DEMP	Dempsey & Company, LLC
DKWP	Dresdner Kleinwort Wasserstein Securities, Inc.
DLJD	HarrisDirect LLD
DOMS	Domestic Securities
DOTC	Dougherty & Company LLC
EDJO	Edward Jones
EQTS	Equity Securities Investments, Inc.
ETGP	Electronic Trading Group, LLC
FACT	First Albany Corp.
FBCO	Credit Suisse First Boston LLC
FBRC	Friedman, Billings, Ramsey & Co.
FLCM	Fulcrum Global Partners LLC
FLTT	Fleet Trading
FMSC	First Montauk Securities Corp.
FNET	Wachovia Securities Financial Network, LLC
FORD	Fordham Financial Management
FPKI	Fox-Pitt, Kelton, Inc.
FRAN	Wm. V. Frankel & Co.
FWSI	First Western Securities, Inc.
GFIG	GFI Securities LLC

GROW	Pacific Growth Equities, Inc.
GRST	Garden State Securities, Inc.
GSCO	Goldman Sachs & Co.
GVRC	GVR Company, LLC.
HAMR	W. R. Hambrecht & Co. LLC
HDSN	Hudson Securities, Inc.
HILL	Hill Thompson Magid and Co., Inc.
HLIX	Helix Trading LLC
HOWE	Howe Barnes Investments, Inc.
HRNB	Harris Nesbitt Corp.
INET	Inet ATS, Inc. (ECN)
JANY	Janney Montgomery Scott LLC
JBAR	Julius Baer Securities, Inc.
JEFF	Jeffries Co., Inc.
JOLE	Johnston, Lemon & Co
JPMS	JP Morgan Securities
JSLP	Joseph Stevens & Company
JSSF	JMP Securities LLC
KENS	Kensington Capital Corp.
KING	C. L. King and Associates
LABS	LaBranche Financial Services, Inc.
LASS	LaSalle St. Securities, Inc.
LAZA	Lazard Freres & Co.
LEGG	Legg Mason Wood Walker, Inc.
LEHM	Lehman Brothers
LYON	Calyon Securities (USA) Inc.
MADF	Bernard Madoff
MCBT	Moors & Cabot, Inc.
MHMY	MH Meyerson & Co.
MDLD	McDonald & Company Securities, Inc.
MJSC	Miller Johnson Steichen Kinnard, Inc.
MLCO	Merrill Lynch Pierce Fenner & Smith Inc.
MOKE	Morgan, Keegan & Company
MONR	Monroe Securities, Inc.
MSCO	Morgan Stanley & Co, Inc.
MWRE	FTN Midwest Securities, Inc.
MWRI	McAdams Wright Ragen, Inc.
NATL	National Securities Corporation

NEED	Needham & Co.
NELS	Nelson Securities, Inc.
NFSC	National Financial Services LLC
NITE	Knight Equity Markets, L.P.
NMRA	Nomura Securities Intl.
NOYS	David A. Noyes & Company
NTMG	Nutmeg Securities, Ltd.
NTRC	Northern Trust Securities, Inc.
NTSI	Nesbitt Thompson Securities
NWST	Nevwest Securities Corporation
OGRU	Oscar, Gruss & Son
OHIO	Fifth Third Securities
OLDE	H&R Block Financial Advisors, Inc.
OPCO	Oppenheimer & Co, Inc.
PACS	Pacific Crest Securities, Inc.
PAUL	Paulson Investment Company, Inc.
PBLC	Public Securities, Inc.
PERS	Pershing LLC
PERT	Pershing Trading Company LLC
PFSI	Penson Financial Services Inc.
PIPR	U.S. Bancorp Piper Jaffray, Inc.
PMCS	Prime Capital Services, Inc.
PRUS	Prudential Equity Group, Inc.
PTNM	Putnam Investments
PUGS	Puglisi & Co.
PWJC	UBS Financial Services
RAJA	Raymond James & Associates
RAND	Barnard Jacobs Mellet
RBCD	RBC Capital Markets Corporation
RBCF	Dominion Securities, Inc.
RBCM	RBC Capital Markets Corporation
RDWD	Redwood Securities Corp.
RHCO	SunTrust Capital Markets Inc.
RHIC	R H Investment Corporation, Inc.
RHIL	Round Hill Securities, Inc.
RMRK	Richmark Capital Corporation
RODM	Rodman & Renshaw, Inc.
RSEC	Rothschild Lieberman Ltd.

RSSF	BancBoston Robertson Stephens & Co.
RTJC	R.T. Jones Capital Equities, Inc.
RYAN	Ryan, Beck & Co. LLC
SBSH	Citigroup Global Markets Inc.
SCHB	UBS Capital Markets L.P.
SEAB	Seaboard Securities, Inc.
SHWG	Schonfeld Securities LLC
SIMM	Simmons & Company International
SIZE	Anonymous Interest (NASDAQ)
SKYC	Sky Capital LLC
SMHI	Sanders Morris Harris Inc.
SNDS	Sands Brothers & Co.
SNDV	Soundview Technology Corporation
SPIN	Spencer Edwards, Inc.
SSIC	Scottrade, Inc.
STFL	Stifel, Nicolaus & Company
STGI	Secure Trading Group, Inc.
SUSQ	Susquehanna Capital Group
SUTR	Sutro & Co, Inc.
SWST	Southwest Securities, Inc.
TACO	Traders Advantage
TDCM	TD Waterhouse Capital Markets Inc.
TGUL	Tucker Anthony Cleary Gull, Inc.
THNK	ThinkEquity Partners LLC
THRC	Thor Capital LLC
TJAS	Tejas Securities Group, Inc.
TMBR	Timber Hill LLC
TNIS	Terra Nova Trading, LLC
TORY	Torrey Pines Securities, Inc.
TRAC	Track ECN (ECN)
TRIM	Trimark Securities
TSRV	Trading Services Group, Inc.
VFIN	VFinance Investments, Inc.
VIEW	Viewtrade Securities, Inc.
VOLM	Neovest Trading
VOLP	Volpe Welty
WACH	Wachovia Brokerage Services
WATH	TD Waterhouse Investor Services, Inc.

WBLR	William Blair & Co.
WCHV	Wachovia Capital Markets LLC
WDCO	Wilson-Davis & Co
WEAT	Wheat First Securities, Inc.
WEDB	Wedbush Morgan Securities, Inc.
WEED	Weeden & Co. L.P.
WELS	Wells Fargo Securities, LLC
WJCO	Walton Johnson & Company
WMIN	Westminster Securities Corporation
WOOD	Wood, Arthur W. Company Inc.
WSFG	Wall Street Financial Group, Inc.
WSPD	Wachovia Securities, LLC
WVBD	Wave Securities, Inc.

Index